Speculative Pragmatism

Speculative Pragmatism

Sandra B. Rosenthal

Open ❈ Court

La Salle, Illinois

First printing of the paperback edition 1990

Copyright © 1986 by The University of Massachusetts Press
All rights reserved
Reprinted by permission of The University of
Massachusetts Press

Printed and bound in the United States of America

Library of Congress Cataloging-in-Publication Data
Rosenthal, Sandra B.
  Speculative pragmatism / Sandra B. Rosenthal.
  p.   cm.
  Reprint. Originally published: Amherst: University of
  Massachusetts Press, 1986.
  Includes bibliographical references.
  ISBN 0-8126-9109-1
  1. Pragmatism.   2. Philosophy, American–20th century.
I. Title.
[B944.P72R67   1990]
144'.3'0973 – dc20   89-77293
                            CIP

For Stan,

A ceaseless source of wonder;

And for the three generations

Who dearly enrich us both

Contents

Acknowledgments

There are many friends to whom thanks are due.

First and foremost, I wish to acknowledge a tremendous gratitude to Peter Hare and John McDermott. Each in his own way has helped make this book a reality—through encouragement stemming from a belief that it could and should be written, through suggestions that helped determine its scope, through comments based on readings of the manuscript, and through a general and generous giving of time and energies in ways uniquely his to provide.

Additionally, John Lachs read the manuscript in its entirety, and his observations helped bring into final focus my own perception of its nature. The work has benefited also from suggestions made by Darnell Rucker and Charlene Seigfried during various stages of its development.

At Loyola University there are two people whom I especially want to thank. Rev. Alvin J. Holloway, S.J., chairman of the philosophy department as long as I have been there, has continually worked to provide the time and the atmosphere conducive to scholarly activity. The running philosophic dialogue that I have maintained with my colleague Patrick Bourgeois since my first days at Loyola has provided a valuable and vigorous context for the development of ideas.

I wish to express my appreciation, also, to Mrs. Gertrude Burguieres, my sole typist since graduate-school days, for her willingness to see me through another manuscript and for her usual perfection in doing so.

Last, but far from least, I send along a special thanks to Santa Claus for being the special kind of person he is.

Speculative Pragmatism

Introduction

CLASSICAL American pragmatism represents a historical period in American philosophy, spanning a particular time frame and including the particular doctrines of its five major contributors—Charles Peirce, William James, John Dewey, C. I. Lewis, and G. H. Mead. It also represents a philosophic spirit, a philosophic pulse, enlivening an incipient cosmic vision that, though brought to life in a particular period through diverse specific doctrines, is yet not confined within the limits of that particular period or those specific doctrines. Speculative pragmatism hopes to capture, systematize, and develop this elusive spirit, not as a study in the history of philosophy, but as an ongoing philosophic enterprise, as a philosophy still in the making. Such a spirit can best be brought to light, not through the doctrines of any one of the pragmatists, but through the collective corpus of their writings. The ensuing work draws its inspiration from this collective corpus.

Though what emerges in the following pages is not intended as a historical analysis of the doctrines of the classical American pragmatists, much of it is a speculative synthesis of what is to be found there. At times, however, the specific doctrines of speculative pragmatism cannot be seen as a synthesis and development of the doctrines that lie in the collective corpus, for they are not to be found there, though they are inspired by what is there. Chapter 6 perhaps best represents this aspect. The alteration of the metaphysical categories and the resultant metaphysical doctrines developed in that chapter may be seen as an alternative to, rather than an expansion or a synthesis of, the specific doctrines of any or all of the classical American pragmatists. They are not, however, an alternative to classical American pragmatism, for they are developed to capture and further its spirit, and in so doing provide a framework for interpreting the significance of the various pronouncements to be found in its collective corpus. Indeed, speculative pragmatism may be said to go beyond the writings of the pragmatists by the very fact that it is put forth as a systematic framework. Thus, the concluding chapter concerning the nature of speculative pragmatism as philosophic system can in a sense be said to lie beyond the specific concerns of the several pragmatists, though it is animated naturally by the spirit of classical American pragmatism.

Within the context of speculative pragmatism, the types of general contrasts that are most commonly made among the pragmatists will be seen to represent differences of emphasis within a common vision, rather than conflicting or competing claims which fragment philosophic kinship. The alternatives in terms of which such differences are expressed, like so many of the alternatives emerging from traditional philosophy, dissolve within the structure of speculative pragmatism. Among these frequently held contrasts are, for example, the supposed tensions between the "staunch individualism" of James and the emphasis on the social by Mead, Peirce, and Dewey; between Peirce's view of truth as "finding," Dewey's view of truth as founded on a "transforming," and James's view of truth as a "making"; between the approaches of Lewis and Peirce from the direction of logic, the approach of James from the direction of psychology, and the approaches of Dewey and Mead from the direction of biological activity; between the practical emphasis of James and Dewey, and the theoretical emphasis of Peirce; between James's concern with the limitations of the scientific mind and the blatant focus on science by Dewey, Mead, and Peirce. These supposed tensions will all be seen as various ways of focusing on a common philosophical vision which guides the manner in which the different interests of the pragmatists forge various pathways of entrance into it, and the nature of what is found through a particular focus will be seen to implicate what is highlighted by the interests of one or several of the other pragmatists.

The following pages, then, will evince little interest for the many factors that are held to divide and often to place at odds the various doctrines of the pragmatists. Rather, they will focus on a creative synthesis of a common core that transcends their individual differences, and lies deeply embedded in their particular philosophic claims. The present work will, at various times, incorporate, unchanged, doctrines of one or several of the pragmatists, modify certain claims, develop what lies incipient in their thought, creatively synthesize and extend the partial claims of several or all of them, and develop doctrines which are inspired by, but not to be found in, the collective corpus of their work. At no time, however, will it depart from what this author sees as the spirit or intent of their thinking. It will use the writings of the pragmatists to elucidate an elusive common spirit, a common philosophic pulse, permeating an incipient cosmic vision, and will in turn use this commonness to shape a contemporary systematic position in a way that, it is hoped, will intensify the spirit, quicken the pulse, sharpen the vision, and cast them in a light perhaps not possible at the time of their inception.

Thus, it may be said that "speculative pragmatism" is speculative in three senses. First, it is a pragmatic position which incorporates a full-blown speculative philosophical stance; second, it is a speculative synthesis of what is to be found in the writings of the classical American pragmatists; third, it is a speculative development of unique doctrines inspired by, and incorporating the spirit of, classical American pragmatism. These three senses will be intertwined throughout the following pages.

One

Scientific Method and the Structure of

Speculative Pragmatism

CLASSICAL American thought, as pragmatic, is usually identified as a theory of meaning and belief rooted in biological habits of response, and as a theory of truth understood in terms of workability and reflecting the dynamics of scientific experimentalism. Such pragmatic doctrines reject foundationalism and the related problematics of epistemology narrowly conceived. Yet the study of pragmatism is considered to be fundamentally a study of knowledge problems, now understood as relative to the sociohistorical conditions in which the human biological organism happens to be situated. In addition to these distinctively pragmatic elements, within the writings of the classical American pragmatists there are to be found their uniquely perceptive descriptions of the richness of experience that philosophers within the American tradition often hold to rival, if not overshadow, their pragmatic tenets, and that existential phenomenologists frequently extract as providing, contrary to pragmatic doctrines, the insightful aspects of their thought. Further, there are to be found metaphysical insights of a speculative nature to which more visionary minds turn for interests far beyond the bounds of pragmatism.

Though an understanding of a particular philosophic method is perhaps the key to understanding any philosophic position, this is more than usually crucial to understanding the position of classical American pragmatism, and hence of the present speculative pragmatism. The linkage of pragmatism with the method of science has been a key source of its limitation to a theory of meaning and of truth, and of antispeculative interpretations of its central claims. If pragmatic doctrines are given a more extended range, this is usually accomplished by rejecting, ignoring, or at best implicitly separating these doctrines from issues of scientific method.

The present chapter proposes to focus on the model of scientific or experimental method to clarify its meaning within the context of pragmatic thought and to reveal the beginning outlines of this method as the key to understanding pragmatism, not as a related set of doctrines about meaning and truth, but as a speculative world vision pervaded by the methodology to which it is linked.

Before turning to a positive analysis of the pragmatic understanding of scientific method, it will be useful to clarify to some extent what this method does not imply, since past interpretations of pragmatism have been largely influenced, at least implicitly, by the understandings of the relation between pragmatism and science.

First, scientific method does not imply any particular type of content. Pragmatism arose in part as a reaction against the modern world view Cartesian understanding of the nature of science and of the scientific object. This understanding resulted from the general fact that the method of gaining knowledge that was the backbone of the emergence of modern science was confounded with the content of the first "lasting" modern scientific view—the Newtonian mechanistic universe. Such a confusion, based largely on the presuppositions of a spectator theory of knowledge, led to a naively realistic philosophic interpretation of scientific content. This resulted in a quantitatively characterized universe and in either dualistic causal accounts of knowledge in terms of correlations between mental contents and material objects, or reductionist causal accounts in terms of stimulus-response.

In rejecting the spectator theory of knowledge, and the illicit reifications to which it gave rise, pragmatism rejects the philosophic abstractions of Cartesian dualism. The human being, for the pragmatist, is within nature, not outside of nature and causally linked to it. This human being does not perceive mental contents somehow caused by physical particles; does not, through introspection, arrive at something "inside" which has been caused by something "outside." In brief, not only Cartesian dualism, but also the entire philosophical baggage with which it became linked is rejected by pragmatism. Such a rejection, however, when interpreted in the light of the modern world view Newtonian understanding of nature, can be glibly read as a type of reductionism. If the organism is a part of nature, then it is reducible to nature. The model for understanding this relation to nature, since it is not that of mental contents causally linked to physical particles, must be the behavioristic model of stimulus-response in one of its several versions, or at best some more general causal-genetic account of the origin of knowledge.

Though the reductionistic interpretation of pragmatic doctrines has happily and rapidly begun to wane, yet the focus on one of the several forms of causal analysis as the keystone of naturalism and of scientific method has not. Thus, phenomenologists, because of their own rejection of causal accounts of knowledge, generally tend to attack or at best ignore those aspects of pragmatic thought which touch upon scientific method. Attempts to link the scientific method of pragmatic thought with phenomenology tend to view it as providing a causal-genetic account of knowledge to complement the phenomenological approach to the understanding of knowledge in terms of an intentionally grounded linkage of man and world.

Recent claims that epistemology should be naturalized go hand in hand with a causal theory of justification in terms of causal processes that produce psychological belief-states that are true. Further, this type of analysis is held to be patterned after scientific inquiry and theory construction. Epistemology thereby becomes dependent on scientific inquiry, and scientific inquiry, like naturalism, centers around doctrines of causal analysis.

The above understandings of scientific method, however, have still not rid themselves of that confusion of scientific method with scientific content to which pragmatic naturalism so strongly objects. While claiming to be patterned after the method of scientific inquiry, they are in fact using the contents of particular sciences as the materials for attempting either to understand or to build an epistemological theory. Indeed, causal connections are always expressed as relations among particular types of objects or events, and the nature of the events or objects being connected enters into the very understanding of the nature of the causal relationship sustained. This focus on scientific method still not purified of content represents a lingering influence of modern world view thought, is contrary to the pragmatic focus, and provides the basis for misinterpretations of the pragmatic concern with scientific method as at least implicitly reductionistic.

A focus on the pragmatic interest in scientific method from the direction of contemporary philosophy of science leads, in various ways, to the loss of some of the key pragmatic tenets emerging from its focus on scientific method. This approach to pragmatism reflects an understanding of scientific method in terms of a formalized deductive model of scientific explanation that allows for verification by operations of testing, but cannot grasp or deal with any process by which ideas are generated. A lack of focus on the nature of the generation of ideas leads also to the frequently made connections between the pragmatic maxim of meaning in terms of conceivable consequences and Bridgman's operational definition which reduces meaning to verifying operations. Further, the pragmatic focus on method is viewed as a focus on pure method in the sense that it neither entails nor emanates from broad metaphysical and epistemological issues. Nonetheless, though the pragmatic focus is on pure method as opposed to content, yet the method itself will be seen to have far-ranging philosophical implications.

The focus on the pragmatic understanding of scientific method from a second and more recent direction within contemporary philosophy of science, that of concern with the structure of scientific revolutions, finds pragmatism falling short in its understanding of scientific method as the method of attaining truth. But what is held to be lacking in this negative evaluation is precisely what is lacking in the assimilation of scientific method within pragmatism to the formalized deductive model —that is, a full appreciation of the significance of the creative dimensions involved in the pragmatic understanding of scientific method.

Recent discussions of pragmatism, which, conversely, view it in isolation from its concern with scientific method as the model for gaining knowledge, lose its constructive phase as a restructuring of traditional philosophic problems and alternative solutions, and view it only in its role as critic of philosophical attempts to solve problems by providing wrong answers to wrong alternatives. Finally, even those most immersed in the spirit of American pragmatism often tend to view it as limited, by its linkage to the nature of scientific inquiry, to a theory of meaning and of truth.

The following pages, by contrast, will examine the pragmatic focus on scientific method to indicate the nature of the pathway this carves toward a full-blown speculative philosophic vision. What, then, does classical American pragmatism find when it examines scientific methodology by focusing on the lived experience of scientists rather than on the objectivities they put forth as their findings, or the type of content which tends to occupy their interest; on the history of modern science rather than its assertions; and on the formation of scientific meanings rather than on a formalized deductive model?[1] The beginning phase of

---

1 / This stress on pure method is not intended to deny that pragmatism is influenced in its philosophical claims by the findings of various sciences. Indeed, it pays careful attention

scientific method exemplifies noetic creativity. The creation of scientific meanings requires a noetic creativity that goes beyond what is directly observed. Without such meaning structures there is no scientific world and there are no scientific objects. A focus on such creativity will reveal several essential features of scientific method that permeate the structure of a distinctively pragmatic world vision.

First, such scientific creativity arises out of the matrix of ordinary experience, and in turn refers back to this everyday ordinary "lived" experience. The objects of systematic scientific creativity gain their fullness of meaning from, and fuse their own meaning into, the matrix of ordinary experience. Though the contents of an abstract scientific theory may be far removed from the qualitative aspects of primary experience, such contents are not the found structures of some "ultimate reality" but rather abstractions, the very possibility of which requires and is founded upon the lived qualitative experience of the scientist. As Mead observes, "Controlled sensuous experience is the essential basis of all our science." Further, "The ultimate touchstone of reality is a piece of experience found in an unanalyzed world. . . . We can never retreat behind immediate experience to analyzed elements that constitute the ultimate reality of all immediate experience, for whatever breath of reality these elements possess has been breathed into them by some unanalyzed experience."[2] In Dewey's terms, the refined products of scientific inquiry "inherit their full content of meaning" within the context of actual experience.[3]

However, the return to the context of everyday or "lived" experience is never a brute return, for, as Dewey continues, "we cannot achieve recovery of primitive naivete. But there is attainable a cultivated naivete of eye, ear, and thought, one that can be acquired only through the discipline of severe thought."[4] Such a return to everyday primary experience is approached through the systematic categories of scientific thought by which the richness of experience is fused with new meaning. Thus, the

---

to these findings. The model of scientific method, as pure method, to which pragmatic philosophy is inextricably linked, is, however, one thing. Its attention to various findings of various sciences achieved by the general method is something quite different. These two issues should not be conflated.

2 / G. H. Mead, "The Definition of the Psychical," *Mead: Selected Writings*, ed. A. J. Reck (New York: Bobbs-Merrill Co., 1964), p. 34; G. H. Mead, *The Philosophy of the Act* (Chicago: University of Chicago Press, 1938), p. 32.

3 / John Dewey, *Experience and Nature*, vol. 1 (1981) in *The Later Works*, ed. Jo Ann Boydston (Carbondale and Edwardsville: Southern Illinois University Press, 1981–), p. 37.

4 / Ibid., p. 40.

technical knowing of second-level reflective experience and the "having" of perceptual experience each gain in meaning through the other.

Further, such creativity implies a rejection of the "passive-spectator" view of knowledge and an introduction of the active, creative agent, who, through meanings, helps structure the objects of knowledge, and who thus cannot be separated from the world known. Both the scientific perception and the meaningful backdrop within which it occurs are shot through with the interactional unity between knower and known. As James well notes of scientific method, there is a big difference between verification, as the cause of the preservation of scientific conceptions, and creativity, as the cause of their production.[5] Dewey summarizes this noetic creativity in discussing the significance of Heisenberg's principle of indeterminacy: "What is known is seen to be a product in which the act of observation plays a necessary role. Knowing is seen to be a participant in what is finally known."[6] Further, either the position or the velocity of the electron may be fixed,[7] depending upon the context of meaning structures in terms of which the interactions of what exists are grasped. Thus, both perception and the meaningful backdrop within which it occurs are shot through with the intentional unity between knower and known. Using this characteristic of the model of scientific methodology in understanding everyday experience, Dewey can observe, "What, then, is awareness found to be? The following answer . . . *represents a general trend of scientific inquiry. . . . Awareness*, even in its most perplexed and confused state, that of maximum doubt and precariousness of subject-matter, means things entering, via the particular thing known as organism, into a peculiar condition of differential—or additive—change."[8] As Peirce emphasizes the same point, the creative abductions of scientific endeavors "shade into perceptual judgments without any sharp line of demarcation between them."[9] Or, in Mead's

5 / William James, *The Principles of Psychology*, 2 vols. (1981), *The Works of William James*, ed. Frederick Burkhardt (Cambridge: Harvard University Press, 1975–), 2, pp. 1232–1234.

6 / John Dewey, *The Quest for Certainty*, vol. 4 (1984) in *The Later Works*, p. 163.

7 / Ibid., p. 165.

8 / John Dewey, "Does Reality Possess Practical Character?" in vol. 4 (1977) of *The Middle Works*, ed. Jo Ann Boydston (Carbondale and Edwardsville: Southern Illinois University Press, 1976–1983), pp. 137–138 (italics added).

9 / Charles Peirce, *Collected Papers*, vols. 1–6, ed. Charles Hartshorne and Paul Weiss (Cambridge: Belknap Press of Harvard University, 1931–1935); vols. 7 and 8, ed. Arthur Burks (Cambridge: Harvard University Press, 1958), 5.181 (hereafter cited using only two part conventional notation). The difference, however, is that the latter are beyond criticism.

terms, experimental method is embedded in the simplest process of perception of an object.[10]

In brief, for the objects of everyday perceptual experience, as for the objects of science, the role of the knower enters into the object known; there is, on both levels, an intentional unity between knower and known. And, true to the reciprocal relation between the objects of secondary and primary experience, the dynamics of everyday perceptual experience disclosed with the help of the model of scientific method in turn help make more meaningful the model itself. Thus, Lewis clarifies the noetic creativity ingredient in scientific objects by turning to common-sense objects to understand the nature of "thinghood" common to both levels,[11] while Dewey, in his discussion of the dynamics of everyday perceptual awareness, asserts, in clarifying the model, that the scientific object "marks an extension of the same sort of operation."[12]

Such dynamics, however, lead to a second general characteristic of the model of scientific method. There is directed or purposive activity that is guided by the possibilities of experience contained within the meaning structures that have been created. It can be seen that such a creative structuring of experience brings objects into an organizational focus from the backdrop of an indeterminate situation, and, as constitutive of modes of response, yields directed, teleological, or goal-oriented activity. The system of meanings both sets the context for the activity and limits the directions which such activity takes, for such meaning structures are constituted by possibilities of acting toward a situation. Thus, James remarks that conceptions are "teleological weapons of the mind,"[13] while Peirce claims that a concept is the mark of a habit of response or general purpose.[14]

The objects of everyday experience, like the objects of second-level reflection, are the results of meaning organizations used to turn a potentially problematic or indeterminate situation into a resolved or meaningfully experienced one. If, at the level of science, "the object" is an abstraction or meaningful focus marked off within the larger context of the richness of concrete experience, then such a situation can be anticipated at the level of perceptual experience as well. At neither level can

10 / Mead, *Philosophy of the Act*, p. 25.

11 / C. I. Lewis, *Mind and the World Order* (New York: Dover Publications, 1929), Appendix A, esp. pp. 395–397.

12 / Dewey, *Quest for Certainty*, p. 190.

13 / James, *Principles of Psychology*, 2, p. 961.

14 / Peirce, 7.498.

"the object" be hypostatized as absolute independently of the meaning structures through which it emerges in experience. Nor can such meaning structures be understood apart from modes of response to a potentially problematic situation. As Dewey elucidates this point, relating it to James as well, "*The* table is precisely the constancy among the serial 'thises' of whatever serves as an instrument for a single end. . . . In the degree in which reactions are inchoate and unformed, 'this' tends to be the buzzing, blooming confusion of which James wrote. . . . *The* object is an abstraction, but unless it is hypostatized it is not a vicious abstraction."[15] Further, just as the second-level object gives added significance to the level of everyday experience, so the object of everyday experience can be expected to give added significance to the more concrete immediacies of experience. Thus, meaningfully constituted objects at all levels emerge from the indeterminately rich backdrop of experience and cannot be hypostatized as absolute independently of the meaning structures through which they emerge. Dewey's comments are again concisely instructive when he notes that "the abstracted object has a consequence *in* the individualized experiences, one that is immediate and not merely instrumental to them. It marks an ordering and organizing of responses in a single focused way in virtue of which the original blur is definitized and rendered significant."[16]

As a third general characteristic, the adequacy of such meaning structures in grasping what is there, or in allowing what is there to reveal itself in a significant way, must be tested by consequences in experience. Only if the experiences anticipated by the possibilities of experience contained within the meaning structures are progressively fulfilled— though of course never completely and finally fulfilled—can truth be claimed for the assertions made. Initial feeling of assurance, initial insights, initial common assent, or any other origins of an hypothesis do not determine its truth. Rather, to be counted as true, a claim must stand the test of consequences in experience. In brief, scientific method, as representing a self-corrective rather than a building-block model of knowledge, is the only way of determining the truth of a belief. Thus Peirce stresses that scientific method is the only method of fixing belief, for it is the only method by which beliefs must be tested and corrected by what experience presents.[17] Such meaning organizations are judged by their ability to turn a potentially problematic or indeterminate situation into a resolved or meaningfully experienced one.

15 / Dewey, *Quest for Certainty*, pp. 189–190.
16 / Ibid., p. 190.
17 / Peirce, 5.384.

At this point one may object that after all, scientific knowledge is theoretical knowledge and thus can surely not provide the model for understanding lived experience. Is not the present analysis once again, though in a different manner, confusing the world of science with the world of lived experience? The above discussion has already spoken of a concept as a teleological instrument or as an instrument for an end. Is all experience to be understood in terms of manipulation and control, and all objects as theoretical constructs for such manipulation? Have we in fact replaced dualistic or reductionistic man with "technological man"? The answer here is a decisive "no." The use of the model is in no way an attempt to assert that perceptual experience is really a highly intellectual affair. Rather, the opposite is more the case. Scientific objects are highly sophisticated and intellectualized tools for dealing with experience at a second level, but they are not the product of any isolated intellect. Rather, the total biological organism in its behavioral response to the world in ways to be discussed is involved in the very ordering of any level of awareness, and scientific knowledge partakes of the character of even the most rudimentary aspects of organism-environment interaction. Further, the scientific purpose of manipulation of the environment, and its use of scientific concepts as an instrument of such manipulative control, are not technological maneuvers into which human activity is to be absorbed. Rather, again, the opposite is more the case. All human activity, even at its most rudimentary level, will be seen to be activity guided by direction and noetically transformative of its environment. As such it is instrumental, and the abstractly manipulative and instrumental purposes attributed to science have their roots at the foundation of the very possibility of human experience in general.

All experience is experimental, not in the sense that it is guided by sophisticated levels of thought, but that the very structure of human behavior, both as a way of knowing and as a way of being, embodies the features revealed in the examination of scientific method. It is not that human experience, in any of its facets, is a lower or inferior form of scientific endeavor, but rather that scientific endeavor, as experimental inquiry, is a more explicit embodiment of the dynamics operative at all levels of experience, and hence the ingredients are more easy to distinguish. The pursuit of scientific knowledge is an endeavor throughout which are writ large the essential characters of any knowing, and it partakes of the character of even the most rudimentary ways in which human activity involves habits of anticipations of a next experience to come.

Pragmatism, in focusing on scientific methodology, is providing a phenomenologically or experientially based description of the lived-through activity of scientists that yields the emergence of their objects. In so doing, it is focusing on the explicit enlarged version of the conditions by which any object of awareness can emerge within experience, from the most rudimentary contents of awareness within lived experience to the most sophisticated objects of scientific knowledge. In providing a description of the lived experience within which the objects of science emerge, pragmatism is uncovering the essential aspects of the emergence of any objects of awareness.

In brief, an examination of scientific method provides the features for understanding the very possibility of its existence as emerging from rudimentary experience. If this interplay is not understood, then there results the paradoxical criticisms that are hurled repeatedly against Dewey: on the one hand, that he is too "intellectualist" because all experience is experimental; and on the other hand, that he is too "subjectivistic" because of his emphasis on the rudimentary, "felt" aspect of experience. These, then, are the features that are found from an examination of scientific methodology as fundamental to pragmatic thought. What philosophical directions are to be found inextricably intertwined with such a focus on scientific methodology as the method of gaining knowledge?

As has been shown, a proper understanding of the lessons of scientific method reveals that the nature into which the human organism is placed contains the qualitative fullness revealed in lived experience. In addition, the grasp of nature within the world is permeated with the meaning structures by which human organism and world are interactionally or intensionally bound, at the levels of both common-sense experience and scientific reflection. And, it is only within this context that the biological approach to the emergence of meanings as a function of organism-environment adaptation can be understood. The human being is within nature. Neither human activity in general nor human knowledge can be separated from the fact that this being is a natural organism dependent upon a natural environment. The externally real does not, however, at any level of human activity cause a reaction as does a stimulus. Rather it has a significance, and is a being that is acted upon even as it acts upon us. The structures that come to awareness in experience are an interactional unity of such activities.

Further, the relation between organism and environment cannot be understood as one in which two self-contained "things" are put in contact. Rather, to speak of organism and environment in separation is to speak of abstractions from what is, in fact, an organic unity. An environment is what it is in relation to the purposive activities of a biological organism, while the purposes of the organism have developed in the course of its need to deal successfully with the environment. The human organism both creates and responds to its environment. As Mead concisely states this dual aspect, the dependence of the organism upon its environment is generally stated in causal terms, while the dependence of the environment on the organism must be stated in terms of the meanings which appear.[18]

There is a two-fold philosophical sense of purposive biological activity running throughout pragmatism, one ontological, the other epistemic, both of which undercut the level of the biological in terms of the contents of scientific analysis. The dependence of the organism on the environment from which it and its habits have emerged is indeed causal or ontological, but this has nothing whatsoever to do with a causal or reductionistic theory of perception, with causality as expressed in scientific categories, or with a related reductionistic ontology. Rather, it concerns the fact that there is an independent "hardness" or "bruteness" to that which is "there" that will either frustrate or allow to progress the purposive activities of the organism. In this sense one may speak of the adequacy of meanings in terms of the objective categories of the ongoing conduct of the biological organism immersed in a natural world.[19]

The dependence of the perceived environment on the organism is, however, also noetic or epistemic. Such noetic/epistemic dependence involves neither the above excluded features nor objective categories, but rather is an intentional mind-object relationship that can be epistemically or phenomenologically studied from within. In this second sense one speaks of the adequacy of meanings in terms of the appearance of what is meant. The significance of biological habits, not as ontological categories, but as epistemic/phenomenological categories, is that such dispositions, habits, or tendencies are immediately experienced and pervade the very tone and structure of immediately grasped

18 / Mead, *Philosophy of the Act*, pp. 115–116. Dewey's use of the term *transaction* is probably the most adequate in capturing the unity of organism-environment interaction. Nevertheless, since the term *organism-environment interaction* is so central to pragmatism, this terminology will be retained.

19 / Such "causal terms" should not be conflated with, or even related to, a causal theory of perception. If the term *causal* is taken to involve a causal theory of perception or the causality expressed in scientific categories, there results the kind of misunderstanding found in reductionistic interpretations of pragmatic naturalism.

content. Thus, the focus on scientific method itself, far from excluding a descriptive analysis of lived or everyday experience, points directly toward such an endeavor. This is to be expected, for as has been seen, in uncovering, through its focus on scientific method, the essential aspects of the emergence of any objects of awareness, pragmatism is, at the same time, revealing the essential dimensions of the everyday level of experience as foundational for science.

There is an inseparable relationship between the human biological organism bound to a natural environment, and the human knower who through meanings constitutes a world. From the context of organism-environment interaction, there emerge irreducible meanings within the structure of experience. The pragmatic focus on scientific method leads to a biological approach that is not in opposition to a view of human awareness in terms of a field of irreducible meanings partially constitutive of the world, but rather, when properly understood, points to the purposive activity out of which consciousness of meanings emerges. From the context of organic activity and behavioral environment, there emerge irreducible meanings which allow objects to come to conscious awareness. Such meanings are irreducible to physical causal conditions or to psychological acts and processes; yet they emerge from the biological, when the biological is properly understood, for the content of human perception is inseparable from the structure of human behavior within its natural setting.

This interrelatedness of the content of human perception and the structure of human behavior in its natural environment is well evinced in Dewey's dual expressions of meaning in everyday experience. A pre-reflective mode of experience "as far as it has meaning is neither mere doing nor mere undergoing, but is an acknowledgment of the *connection* between something done and something undergone in consequence of the doing."[20] Or, translated from the language of purposive or experimental activity into the language of description of the emergence of objects of awareness:

> An experience is a knowledge, if in its quale there is an experienced distinction and connection of two elements of the following sort: one means or intends the presence of the other in the same fashion in which itself is already present, while the other is that which, while not present in the same fashion, must become so present if the meaning or intention of

20 / Dewey, *Quest for Certainty*, p. 142 (italics in text). Such an acknowledgment need not imply a conscious awareness, but may be embodied in modes of response which have not been brought to conscious awareness.

its companion or yoke-fellow is to be fulfilled through the operation it sets up.[21]

Thus, the irreducibly meaningful behavior of the organism in interaction with its environment is the very foundation of the intentional unity of knower and known. As Peirce cryptically states in indicating this relationship, "Desire creates classes."[22] Human behavior is meaningful behavior, and it is in behavior that meaning is rooted. As Lewis observes, "The earliest cognitions of a mind like ours are continuous with those modes of animal behavior which foreshadow explicit knowledge."[23] Further, the "mode of behavior" man brings to experience, "and which represents its meaning, dictates the explicit concept and implicitly possesses it already."[24]

The above inseparable relationship between the biological organism bound to a natural environment and the knower whose noetic creativity is partially constitutive of the object of awareness, is concisely delineated in Mead's assertion that

> objects about us are unitary objects, not simple sums of the parts into which analysis would resolve them. And they are what they are in relation to organisms whose environment they constitute. When we reduce a thing to parts we have destroyed the thing that was there. . . . We refer to these differences as the meanings these things have in their relationship to the organism.[25]

The focus on scientific method has indicated that experience is permeated by a noetic activity by which the human organism is intentionally bound to the objects of awareness, and that neither the nature into which this organism is placed, nor this organism itself, can be adequately understood in terms of the contents of scientific categories. The focus on biological organism does not lead to causal analyses of human awareness and human knowledge in opposition to an irreducible field of meanings, but to a structure of behavior which, as purposive, provides the experimental activity out of which consciousness of meanings emerges.

---

21 / John Dewey, "The Experimental Theory of Knowledge," in vol. 3 (1977) of *Middle Works*, pp. 114–115.

22 / Peirce, 1.205.

23 / C. I. Lewis, *An Analysis of Knowledge and Valuation* (La Salle, Ill.: Open Court, 1962), p. 260.

24 / Lewis, *Mind and the World Order*, p. 88.

25 / G. H. Mead, *The Philosophy of the Present*, ed. Arthur Murphy (LaSalle, Ill.: Open Court, 1959), pp. 116–117.

Further, if scientific method is indicative of the dynamics of all levels of cognitive activity, then it is indicative of the dynamics of philosophic activity, for philosophy is a cognitive enterprise. And, like science, it is a second-level system of meanings. Thus, in grasping the systematic interconnections within the structure of speculative pragmatism, its assertions must be understood as arising from, yet going beyond in the sense of making meaningful through philosophic interpretation, the immediacies of lived experience. And, in turn, the test for the adequacy of such philosophic assertions must be found in their continual verification in lived experience. Thus, the pragmatic focus on scientific method, far from leading to an antispeculative position limited to a theory of meaning and truth, requires and provides the direction for the understanding of the nature of a speculative metaphysics. As Dewey insightfully notes, "The trouble then with the conclusions of philosophy is not in the least that they are the results of reflection and theorizing. It is rather that philosophers have borrowed from various sources the conclusions of special analyses, particularly of some ruling science of the day."[26] However, this philosophic direction will be put aside until a later time. From the backdrop of the nature of scientific methodology and the approach to the biological to which it leads, the immediately following chapters will explore the nature of that everyday perceptual experience that both reflects and is foundational for the level of scientific activity.

Before turning to this examination, however, two points implicit in the preceding discussions should be brought into focus. First, it may be objected that speculative pragmatism seems to be caught in a vicious circle. The following chapters will examine meaning, perceptual experience, and verification in light of the model of scientific method. But is it perhaps not the case that the previous understanding of the model of scientific method has in fact been guided by a particular perception of these structures of everyday experience? This is indeed the case. It does not, however, imply a vicious circle, nor does it imply a circle at all. Rather, it reflects the cumulative development of insight through the interplay of lived experience and its second-level interpretations.

It was shown that science provides a self-corrective rather than a building-block model of knowledge through the interplay of lived experience and the second-level interpretations of science; that in one sense, the model of scientific methodology makes intelligible the dynamics and priority of lived experience; that nonetheless it is only by understanding the dynamics and priority of lived experience that the nature of

26 / Dewey, *Experience and Nature*, p. 37.

scientific methodology and the status of the objects at which it arrives can be understood. The model of science itself indicates this enrichment of understanding of each level to be gained by viewing each in relationship to the other.

Similarly, the second-level interpretation of experience constituting a philosophic claim is self-corrective through its interplay with the lived experience in which it is rooted. As with a scientific theory, an interrelated network of philosophic claims can only be justified by the workability of the network in providing a unifying and clarifying perspective for the understanding of experience. The philosophic network here presented will provide such a perspective through its ability to get beneath past philosophic distinctions that have left a legacy of false dichotomies and dismembered parts. Thus the adequacy of understanding the scientific object and the common-sense object, each in terms of the other, can only be judged by the workability of the entire philosophical network, and the model of scientific method in which it is embedded, in making intelligible the full range of experience in its various facets. Such a judgment, and the clarification of the criteria in terms of which it should be made, must be put aside till the closing chapter.

As a second preliminary point, since the following discussions of meaning, perception, and verification are basically epistemic issues, the use of the term *epistemology* and the focus on epistemic issues should be clarified. Unless the fundamental sense of epistemology intended in the present work is clarified now, the following discussions will be placed within the very context of epistemology that is being rejected, and they will be judged by their ability to handle problems that emerge only in an alien framework. The following epistemological discussions are not setting the framework for proving an external world or for showing how a subject can bridge the gap to know an object. Rather, such problems emerge as epistemological problems because epistemology has tended to ignore our primordial sense of ontological presence by splitting subject and object asunder before undertaking the epistemological chore of trying to put them back together. Thus, several of the pragmatists at times claim to be wary of the epistemological endeavor, though they are all the time engaged in developing epistemic claims.

What pragmatism houses is a rich and fundamental "existential" view of epistemology, not an epistemological existentialism, but an epistemological point of view on existence as the foundational level of all knowledge. Epistemology is not here understood as an abstract articulation of conditions of our understanding, but as an examination of conditions and structures of our way of being, an examination at once epistemic and ontological. A development of epistemology is possible that opens meanings to the fullness and richness of their epistemic depth at the ground level of lived experience. To investigate the primordial epistemic level grounding any knowledge is to investigate also the structure and process of the being of the knower. It is a task both epistemic and ontological. The structure of human behavior within its natural setting grounds all levels of knowledge, and reflection on this grounding is at once epistemic and ontological. The following discussions of meaning, perception, and verification must be understood as arising from a more primordial level of experience yet to be examined, and to incorporate ontological considerations yet to be discussed.

Two

Activity and the Structure of Meaning

HE CONCEPT of habit is central to pragmatic thought, yet it has been a key source of ambiguities in interpreting the epistemic thrust of the position. Implicit conflations of habit as the basis of meaning and as the basis of belief run throughout pragmatism, for meanings and beliefs alike are understood in a general sense in terms of habits of response. Along with this ambiguity, there is a parallel ambiguity concerning the role of verificationism within pragmatic thought, for it has been taken both as a theory of meaning and as a theory of truth. The meaning of a term is held to lie in possible consequences, but the verification of a belief is also held to depend upon possible consequences in experience.[1] Such ambiguities lead naturally to the issue of whether problems of epistemic reductionism lurk within pragmatic thought. As long as such ambiguities abound, the attempt to extradite pragmatic thought definitively from any reductivistic epistemic tendencies can only begin with one foot already in the enemy camp.

The following discussion proposes to develop the pragmatic concept of meaning in a manner that clearly distinguishes between habit as the basis of meaning, and habit as the basis of belief; between the conditions of possible verification as the structure of meaning, and possible verifying instances as the conditions of truth; between meaning as intensional, and exemplification as extensional; between the logically continuous process of meaning explication operative within the internal structure of any meaning, and the empirically continuous process of

1 / The issue of pragmatic verificationism as related to meaning versus truth goes back to the very origins of pragmatism, and is, of course, responsible for Peirce's changing the name of his own position from pragmatism to pragmaticism "which would be ugly enough to be safe from kidnappers," namely James.

meaning generation within the developing course of experience. The ensuing discussion will turn to the development of the first of each of the above alternatives. And here the distinction between habit as an ontological category and habit as an epistemic/phenomenological category becomes relevant. The language in which meaning as a habit of response is usually expressed too often conflates its epistemic and ontological dimensions, thereby hiding from view its full systematic significance. The following discussion will focus on dispositions or habits, not as ontological categories, but as epistemic/phenomenological categories, as epistemic relational structures which pervade the very tone and organization of immediately grasped content. Before such an examination, however, a few preliminary remarks are in order.

First, though the following discussion of meaning will focus mainly on perceptual awareness, the discussion is intended as indicative of the structure of meaning in general. As will be shown, the difference between concepts and percepts represents two ends of a continuum rather than an absolute difference in kind. The same structure of meaning is involved in both, and the term *pragmatic meaning* will be used as a term that encompasses the meaningfulness of both percepts and concepts. To speak of a percept is to speak of sensory presence as grasped via the vehicle of pragmatic meaning and infused with its structure. The vehicle capable of grasping sensory presence, either directly in experience or through a highly abstract network linked more tenuously to sensory presence, is pragmatic meaning. Pragmatic meaning thus incorporates what may be called perceptual meanings and conceptual meanings. The difference between the two lies precisely in the levels of abstraction within which each operates, and thus the abstract concepts of science, representing one end of the continuum, house the same structure of meaning as is to be found in the most concrete perceptual awareness.[2]

Second, the term *pragmatic meaning* is not to be understood in terms of workability or verifiability as opposed to some other type of meaning from which it is distinguished. Claims such as this are to be found running throughout analyses of the pragmatists in attempts to "save" them from the problems of pragmatic meaning as verification by introducing some other kind of meaning.[3] Rather, the claim is that all meaning is pragmatic meaning in the sense to be developed. Further, such meaning

2 / This will be seen below to be in keeping with pragmatic thought in general.

3 / For example, critics have held, in relation to Peirce, that though he slides back and forth between 'expressions of meaning' and 'expressions of truth,' and though verificational meaning is reductionistic, Peirce avoids reductionism by "a still higher grade of clearness of thought," by ultimate meaning coming after verificational meaning.

is not to be understood in terms of verification or workability at all. As the next chapter will show, the genesis of pragmatic meaning is rooted in the need to get around in experience, or to resolve potentially problematic situations, and the usefulness of such meanings is tested by their workability in achieving these goals. Yet meanings qua meanings are not pragmatic in this sense. Rather, they are pragmatic in the sense that such meanings are constituted by activity.

The *active agent* is used by pragmatism in two senses. First, it is used at the level of the active use of knowledge to change society or the environment. This is a level frequently intended in pragmatism. Yet this level, if erroneously taken as the sole sense of active agent, leads to the often heard condemnation of pragmatism as overly concerned with action, as indicating an antitheoretical attitude that makes knowing only for the sake of doing. The second, and more technically important, aspect of *active agent* indicates the manner in which one knows the world through the structures of the meanings one has created by one's responses to the environment. Here the focus on the role of human beings as active is not on what one should do with knowledge, but on what knowledge is, on human activity or response as built into the very structure of meaningful awareness. Pragmatic meaning is intended to appropriate this sense of activity as constitutive of the structure of meaning. In this appropriation, however, the goal-directed interactional element between humans and their environment, the first aspect of humans as active agents, will be incorporated in the very heart of the internal structure of pragmatic meaning. Thus, the purposive activity that gives rise to the conscious awareness of an irreducible field of meanings is incorporated within the structure of these meanings, and its character, as incorporated within these meanings, permeates the tone and content of any object of awareness.

Such meanings are further pragmatic in that their internal structure incorporates the dynamics of experimental method. This follows directly from the above point, for the structure of human activity incorporated within the internal structure of meaning is precisely the structure of experimental activity. Such an incorporation can be anticipated by following the direction indicated by the previous examination of scientific method. A focus on the relation between scientific method and the internal structure of meaning shows that habit, as an organizational disposition or tendency to act, embodies a vital creativity that arises out of the matrix of more concrete or rudimentary experience, and in turn infuses its meaning into the more rudimentary experience; it incorporates within its internal structure an intensional unity of knower and

known; and it contains within its structure purposive activity as the resolution of a problem within a potentially indeterminate situation. Further, though such an internal structure of meaning will clearly distinguish between meaning and verification, the criteria for truth in terms
of verification are contained within it.

A third and final preliminary point to be noted is that the discussion
of *a* meaning is an artificial isolation within experience for two reasons,
both of which will be developed in later chapters.[4] First, it is an artificial
isolation from a context of meaningful awareness. We do not begin with
atomic meanings and build up a world of objects; rather, any meaningful
content emerges from the backdrop of a meaningful world. Second, even
the focus on concrete perceptual meanings as part of an entire network
is an artificial isolation, for experience spills over the network of pragmatic meanings by which we attempt to hold it. This is not intended as
the claim that perceptual awareness can occur outside the bounds of
pragmatic meaning, but rather that experience is wider than perception
and cannot be enclosed within the bounds of perceptual awareness.[5]
Though this third set of issues will not be developed at present, they
should be kept in mind throughout the following discussion. Otherwise, something isolated from an indefinitely rich matrix for the purposes of analysis will be viewed as an atomic building block. And it is
precisely the vestiges of any notion of knowledge or meaning in terms
of an atomic building block model that the present work adamantly
rejects.

What the above qualifications and postponements of discussions indicate is that the issues first discussed are not the ultimate starting
points, either logically, structurally, or temporally, for the development
of speculative pragmatism. They are convenient starting points among
possible others, and, like any others, must be abstracted out from the
unified context that provides the fullness both of their significance
and of their very meaning. With these preliminary points in mind, the
following discussion can now focus on habit as the basis of epistemic/
phenomenologically experienced relational structures, the characteristics of which permeate every grasp of the world in which we live.

Meanings here are to be understood as logical or epistemic structures

4 / The first point will be developed in chapter 7; the second point will be developed in
chapter 4.

5 / Though experience is wider than perception, this does not mean that experience is
equivalent to the interaction between any two aspects of nature. Some philosophers make
experience too narrow; others at times tend to overgeneralize it. Experience, as here used,
occurs when at least one of the interacting aspects of nature is a sentient organism.

emerging from behavioral patterns. Though they do not exist independent of purpose, they cannot be understood in terms of the categories of psychology or biology. Rather, meanings are to be understood as relational structures or relational patterns emerging from the lived-through response of the human organism to that with which it interacts. Or, in other terms, human behavior is meaningful behavior, and it is in behavior that meaning is rooted. What, however, is meaning as a relational pattern? An answer to this question requires an examination of the internal structure of meaning.

The relational patterns intended cannot be understood in terms of linguistic relationships. Pragmatic meaning is not to be understood fundamentally in terms of language, but rather as that matrix within which language emerges. This is not to say that we have consciously explicit prelinguistic experience. At the level of everyday lived experience, language and pragmatic meaning are separable only by abstraction. Language is the expression of pragmatic meaning; pragmatic meaning becomes explicit and communicable within the structures of language. Meaning, however, is not fundamentally propositional; at its basic level meaning is embodied in the activity of a purposive agent engrossed in the world, and language emerges as an expression of such active engagement. Language is not the expression of a detached, abstract observer. By the time we come to name a thing, it is already experienced as a meaningful thing within a field of action. The unity of the object is brought about by the purposive activity of the human organism as expressive of a vital intentionality, not by a "thinking subject."

This claim concerning pragmatic meaning is meant to indicate also that the meaning incorporated within a language system is not the creative invention of a conscious subject playing a language game, but rather such meaning has both ontological and historical rootedness. Language is the vehicle through which the perceived world, partially constituted by our active engagement with the ontologically real through the flow of history, explicitly emerges within our conscious experience. As Dewey stresses, language expresses meaning, but meaning is rooted in behavior, and if this fact is not recognized, he warns, "the intrinsic connection of language with community of action is forgotten."[6] As Peirce concisely notes the point, meaning enters language by determining it.[7] Such a distinction, though analytic, is of vital importance, lest we forget the fact,

---

6 / John Dewey, *Logic: The Theory of Inquiry* (New York: Henry Holt and Co., 1938), p. 48.

7 / Section 1105, p. 4, *The Microfilm Edition of the Peirce Papers*, Harvard University.

emphasized by Lewis, that meaning "spills over its verbal containers," for meaning "cannot be literally put into words, or exhibited by exhibiting words and the relations of words."[8] As James stresses a similar point, namelessness is compatible with experience of a sense of meaningfulness.[9] Language makes our meanings communicable and precise, but only by abstracting from a concreteness which overflows any bounds it attempts to set. Indeed, just as experience will be seen to overflow the bounds of consistently interlaced meaning structures, so meaning overflows the bounds of linguistic structure.

The relational patterns of meaning, then, are to be understood as emerging beneath the level of language, embedded in human response, and this level must be explored. Such responses cannot be understood in terms of pure patterns of relations. A pure pattern of relationships, devoid of sensuous criteria of recognition, would be a pattern of relationships relating nothing that had reference to experience. As has been seen by an examination of the model of scientific method, any concept, no matter how abstract, must have some linkage with sense experience, and thus must involve criteria for such linkage. As Lewis has well noted, even the employment of nonintuitive noneuclidean geometry involves some criteria of linkage with sense awareness. It is grasped as like intuitive euclidean geometry, but differing in certain ways.[10] Any relational pattern must be a relational pattern among sensuous criteria of recognition. And a pure datum, devoid of some relational pattern, could not be an object of awareness, for, as the model of science has shown, the purposive activity or vital intentionality of the organism enters into the character of every content grasped. Such activity need not imply conscious awareness, for meaning is rooted in behavior that, as human, is pervaded by a vital intentionality at even the most rudimentary level.

There is an intentional unity of knower and known that permeates any grasp of the world around us, and which must be reflected in some manner in the internal structure of meaning. We do not have purely abstract categories of understanding on the one hand, and a brute sensory manifold on the other. Rather, pragmatic meaning, as the inseparable mingling of the sensuous and the relational, is the vehicle by which we think about and recognize objects in the world. Peirce's view that sensuous recognition involves interpretive aspects is found in his view that

8 / C. I. Lewis, *Analysis of Knowledge and Valuation*, pp. 17, 140.

9 / William James, *Principles of Psychology*, I, p. 243. James there states that "namelessness is compatible with existence," but what he is there speaking of is the existence of meaningful differences within experience.

10 / Lewis, *Mind and the World Order*, pp. 217–220.

there are no first impressions of sense,[11] while his view that conceptualization requires criteria of sense can be found in his claim that the "imagery" or sense criteria of meaning must be general, as opposed to singular and determinate in all respects.[12] As Mead states a similar position, "some sort of image with sensuous content . . . must accompany any concept, however abstract this may be, though the image occurs in varying degrees as the cognitive act is of the nature of sensuous recognition or conceptual interpretation."[13] Thus sensuous recognition that makes possible perceptual awareness involves conceptual interpretation; and no concept is possible without some imagery of some sort. Perceptual and conceptual meanings involve the same structure.

Though Dewey may seem to make an absolute distinction in some of his technical discussions, most notably in his essay misleadingly titled "How Do Concepts Arise from Percepts?"[14] yet concepts "arise" from percepts in the sense that an explicit conceptual awareness requires us to abstract out of perceptual experience that which we have previously, though unreflectively, put into it.[15] There is no percept independent of dispositional modes of behavior that provide the structure of experience, and thus the distinction between the concept and the percept is "not fixed but movable."[16] The distinction for Dewey is, like many of his distinctions, a functional one, here based on levels of abstraction. Similarly, James at times speaks of concepts and percepts in ways that seem to indicate an absolute distinction. He frequently speaks of experience as nonconceptual equally in terms of sensible flux, sensational flux, or perceptual flux; holds that percepts differ from concepts in that "percepts are continuous and concepts are discrete" in their meaning;[17] and claims that "We harness perceptual reality in concepts in order to

11 / Peirce, 5.416; 5.213; 7.465.

12 / 5.531 for acceptance of its generality; 5.298-299 for its rejection as a determinate singular. This generality of imagery cannot be related in any way to any type of traditional notion of abstract general ideas. The meaning intended will be developed below in some detail.

13 / George Herbert Mead, "Image or Sensation," *Journal of the History of Philosophy,* I, Part 2 (1904), p. 606. See qualifying comments in previous note.

14 / John Dewey, "How Do Concepts Arise from Percepts?" in vol. 3 (1969) of *The Early Works,* Jo Ann Boydston (Carbondale and Edwardsville: Southern Illinois University Press, 1969–1972), pp. 142–146.

15 / Ibid., p. 145.

16 / Dewey, "Experience and Objective Idealism," in vol. 3 of *The Middle Works,* p. 138.

17 / William James, *Some Problems of Philosophy* (1979), *The Works of William James,* p. 32.

drive it better to our ends."[18] Yet he clearly indicates that as soon as the flow of sensational experiences[19] is recognized in some way, it is already structured through conceptualization. There is no absolute distinction between percept and concept.[20] Indeed, James's stress on the distinction, which is not absolute, seems mainly to show the potential dangers of allowing abstract conceptual meanings to distort the concreteness of perceptual meanings. It is an emphasis on one aspect of scientific method as discussed in the previous chapter. Any abstract conceptual network must both feed upon and make intelligible the concreteness of everyday perceptual experience, not distort it.[21]

The following development of pragmatic meaning, then, as incorporating the inseparable intermingling of the sensuous and the relational as the vehicle by which we think about and recognize objects in our world, flows within the entire backdrop of classical American pragmatism. The sensuous aspect of meaning in terms of criteria of recognized content is, of course, dominant in the pragmatic claim that meaning must be understood in terms of possible consequences in experience. Here issues of meaning and truth tend to merge, and it is precisely here that critics of pragmatic thought find reductionistic tendencies lurking in it. As will be seen, however, a sensuous criterion of recognition cannot be understood in terms of verifying instances, actual or possible, but rather it is that within the structure of meaning that allows for the possibility of verifying instances. Though meaning is derivative from the sensuous, and though meanings themselves can be termed sensuous insofar as they refer to experience, yet meaning, even in its sensory aspect, cannot be reduced to the content of experience. The difference can perhaps best be indicated by stating that meaning, even in its most concrete sensory aspect, provides literally the "sense" or principle or form by which man interprets and organizes the sensory. As such, it is general as opposed to particular.

At this point the introduction of the concept of schemata will help in

18 / Ibid., p. 39.

19 / Pure experience is characterized by James as the flow of sensation or feeling, yet even feelings are interpreted in being experienced. The ambiguities of sensation and feeling within the context of pragmatic thought in general will be discussed in the following two chapters.

20 / In one sense, both concepts and percepts in their immediacy are "mere bits of pure experience." William James, *Essays in Radical Empiricism* (1976), *The Works of William James.* It is, of course, not in this sense that similarity between the two is intended.

21 / James, *A Pluralistic Universe* (1977), *The Works of William James*, p. 122, n. 1 provides a good insight into this intention.

examining the internal structure of meaning. The term *schemata* will
be introduced for two reasons. First, it appropriates from Kant the fundamental insight that concepts are meaningful only if they contain
schematic possibilities for their application to sensible experience. Further, the criteria that make possible the application of a concept cannot
be abstracted from sense experience, but rather must be provided before
meaningful perceptual content can emerge within experience. The pragmatic appropriation of these insights, through the development of what
will here be called *pragmatic schemata* radically alters Kant's understanding of the schema, however. Such a schema is no longer the product of productive imagination as distinct from the understanding as the
faculty of judgment. Rather, both understanding and imagination are
unified and transformed into the creative functioning of habit, as providing a lived or vital intentionality between knower and known. Such an
interactional unity of knower and known, rooted in man's mode of existing in the world in terms of purposive activity or vital intentionality,
will be seen to be incorporated within the internal structure of meaning
through the functioning of pragmatic schemata.

A second reason for the use of this term is that both Lewis and Peirce
flirted with the use of Kantian schemata within their respective pragmatic positions, though neither explicitly developed it in terms of a systematic significance within pragmatic thought. Peirce states of the pragmatist that he will hold that everything in the substance of his beliefs
can be represented in the schemata of his imagination,[22] which is, on the
one side, an object capable of being observed; while, on the other side,
it is a general.[23] Lewis's similar understanding of sense meaning as a
schema provides the basis for his refutation of Kant's synthetic a priori,
for, according to Lewis, the schemata for the application of a concept to
experience must be part of or contained within the generality of the
meaning.[24] Thus, the following discussion of pragmatic schemata can
be seen as growing out of a context of classical American pragmatism, expanded to have intrasystematic significance unrecognized in its
semi-developed form. The development of schemata within the internal
structure of meaning can best begin with the modification of Lewis's introduction of the schema in describing a sense meaning[25] as a rule and

22 / Section 288, p. 95 of Microfilm Edition.

23 / Section 293, p. 14 of Microfilm Edition.

24 / Lewis, *Analysis of Knowledge and Valuation*, pp. 161–163.

25 / As Lewis indicates, there is a generally unnoticed complexity to sense meaning
(*Analysis of Knowledge and Valuation*). The reduction of sense meaning to sensory contents is the basis for the usual reductionistic-phenomenalistic interpretation of Lewis.

imagined result.[26] Such a development will reveal three basic features of perceptual awareness.

First, there is a radical rejection of epistemic phenomenalism.[27] Neither physical objects nor objective properties can be understood as constructed from appearances, for within the structure of meaning appearances emerge *as appearances of* objectivities. Second, a physical object cannot be understood as just a collection of objective properties, for the meaningfulness of physical-object claims includes the meaningfulness of a dynamic concreteness that transcends such a collection of objective properties. Third, the structure of meaning incorporates an interactional structural unity of knower and known that traditional rationalism and traditional empiricism have each tried unsuccessfully to pull asunder. The radically nonspectator character undercuts the subject-object split, and cannot be adequately elucidated within the confines of rationalism or traditional empiricism.

Lewis defines a schema as a rule or prescribed routine and an imagined result. It would seem, however, that there must be incorporated within the schema, not only the prescribed act or routine and imagined result, but also the sensory cues that lead to the instigation of the act. Further, if the schema is part of the generality of meaning, then the schematic result apparently cannot be reduced to the content of any experience, whether imagined or actual. The incorporation of an initiating cue, as well as a generality irreducible to imagined results, lies implicit in Peirce's claim that a habit is best described by describing the kinds of conditions, actions, and intended results.[28] Following this lead, it can be noted that it is habit that gives rise to certain kinds of action in the presence of certain kinds of conditions to yield certain kinds of results. And

26 / Ibid., p. 134.

27 / There are two key questions in resolving the issue of phenomenalism, which can perhaps best be called, for purposes of distinction, the logical or epistemological question and the ontological question. The first concerns the level of complexity of that of which consciousness is aware. Do we build objectivities out of more primitive contents of awareness, or is the perception of objectivity fundamental? The second question concerns the objective reference of the content of awareness: Are the contents of awareness—at whatever level of complexity—either the only reality there is or the only reality that can be known; or is the content of awareness a direct grasp (though not necessarily a "spectator" grasp) of a "hard," external, independent reality? An affirmative answer to the first alternative offered by either the epistemological question or the ontological question places one within the phenomenalist camp in some sense. This chapter is concerned only with the epistemic issue.

28 / Peirce, 5.491. A kind is general, while an instance of a kind is particular. Peirce is very deliberate here in his use of *kind* as indicating a generality.

if the act that arrives at the object or objective property is dependent upon the cue or sensory condition, then different cues will give rise to different acts. Here a problem can be seen: even if we consider only one essential property, so that the application of a physical-object meaning is determined solely by the presence of one property, the concept of a "prescribed" routine leads to an unlimited number of possible actions. Thus, even for the simplified case of grasping one objective property, there is not one act but an indefinite number of acts corresponding to an indefinite number of possible cues or sensory appearances. Yet this indefinite number of cues and acts radiate from one intended objectivity. Precisely what it means to apprehend an object or objective structure, rather than an appearance only, is to have "filled in" the result of a particular act with the results of other possible acts given other possible cues. For example, varying perspectives of an objectivity yield varying cues, and hence varying resulting acts. In a sense, then, there are an indefinite number of cues, acts, and resulting appearances. Yet in another sense, though there are an indefinite number of cues and acts, they are all "part of" the one result—an objectivity having certain characteristics. The difference between an apprehended appearance and an apprehended object is not the difference between internal and external, or between subjective or objective, but rather lies in this difference in levels of meaning organization.

The emphasis on an indefinite number of cues and acts stresses a variability, in that an indefinite number of schemata is needed to exhibit fully the totality of experiences implied in attributing even one character to an object. Yet the variability is limited, and in some sense the totality of the range is brought to bear in the apprehension of an objectivity. Thus, if we are meaningfully to assert the existence of physical objects, or, in other terms, to perceive a world of objectivities, then there must be, in addition to sensory cue, act, and further sensory experience, that which binds into a system the set of possible sensory cues and possible resultant acts that, as a system, gives rise to the resultant objective structure.

In addition to the diversity of specific schemata, then, there must be that which limits the range of varying schemata, and imaginatively fills in the resultant appearance of a particular act with the results of other possible acts, thus giving intended objectivity to that which is produced via the schema. There must be, in short, a "fixity" to meanings. What is fixed is precisely a structure or rule of generation of explicit schemata, and this is habit as a vital intentionality, or as a concrete dispositional tendency. Concrete dispositional meaning or living habit, as a vital intentionality, is the source of the generation of explicit schemata, each of which makes precise for conscious awareness some aspect of the concrete dispositional meaning, some selection from the inexhaustible range of possibilities. This distinction between a concrete disposition and its schematic forms, which together constitute pragmatic meaning, lies incipient in Lewis's philosophy in his distinction between implicit and explicit sense meaning,[29] while in Peirce's philosophy it lies implicit in his distinction between the ultimate logical interpretant and the logical interpretant.[30]

Pragmatic meaning thus includes the total set of possible experiences and possible transformations via appropriate responses to other experiences, as controlled by habit as a rule of generation and organization. This dispositional rule fills in a resultant schematic appearance with the results of other possible acts, given other possible conditions, thereby endowing the result of an act with intentional objectivity. Thus, what is apprehended is not an appearance only, but a perspective of an object. The unity of a meaning thus incorporates an inner dynamics that includes both empirical generalizations and the effects of perceptual relativity or perspectival appearance. The term *image* then, as used concerning schematic criteria for the recognition of sense content, can best be understood as *aspect*. For example, one might say that an ocean presents a turbulent image or aspect. Thus, the image, as criterion of recognition, is a criterion for grasping an aspect or perspective of an object. Things can appear in experience only because we mean that thing. Things emerge in experience via the system of schematic aspects or perspectives, organized by the creative functioning of concrete dispositional activity. Physical objects must appear perspectively, for this is built into the very structure for the possibility of the emergence of physical objects within experience.[31] Although meaning, as dispositional or as a habit, does not fully determine actual behavior, as different circumstances provide for different possibilities of reaching an in-

29 / Although Lewis usually speaks of sense meaning as a precise, explicit schema, yet sense meaning is, for Lewis, intensional or conceptual meaning, and this he frequently identifies as a disposition or habit. He clarifies this dual aspect of sense meaning when he observes that "a sense meaning *when precise and explicit* is a schema" (*Analysis of Knowledge and Valuation*, p. 134). Making precise via schematic perspective is not equivalent to making verbally communicable. This difference will be discussed in the next chapter.

30 / For Peirce, the ultimate logical interpretant is the "living habit," while the logical interpretant, as schematic structure, is "the general idea."

31 / Here it is important to remember the warning earlier that this chapter cannot be lifted out of the entire ontological context to follow. The ontological dimension of a thing is yet to be discussed.

tended goal, habit generates and unifies the range of possibilities of kinds of action given kinds of conditions in achieving the object or intended goal, for habit binds into a system the set of possible conditions and possible acts that, as a system, gives rise to the intended objective structure. Thus, Peirce stresses that while a schematic structure must be understood not as a generalization of imagined instances, but as a product of a predictive rule, distinct schemata are needed to represent alternative possibilities of that rule.[32] As Mead condenses this point, percepts are "collapsed" acts.[33]

Further, habit does more than unify three preexistent elements, sensory cue, act, and resultant structure. Only as habit performs its function, that of unifying sensory cue and reaction, does structure emerge at all. Thus Peirce holds that the general idea or schematic result is the "mark of the habit."[34] Even more significant, perhaps, habit determines reaction, and reaction partially determines the nature of the sensory cue. Habit, then, ultimately partially determines the nature of the sensory cue. As Dewey states, "the so-called response is not merely *to* the stimulus; it is *into* it," or otherwise stated, perception "is the operation of constituting a stimulus."[35] And not only is the conceptual objectivity fixed in its character through the functioning of habit in filling in the results of an act with the results of other possible acts given other possible cues, but the appearance that is apprehended by withholding this filling in is itself partially fixed in its character precisely by that which is being "withheld." Pure sensory presence is "there" as the logically or epistemically final basis and ultimate referent for all cognitive activity. In this sense it is epistemically primitive.[36] Further, a sensory core held apart from particular experiences must be there as part of the schema, if concepts are to be applicable to experience. But such a core is precisely the sensuous core of the schematic criteria for grasp of appearing objects. The core is not isolatable in its purity; it is not, in its purity, apprehended appearance. Thus, though Mead holds that the possibilities of appearings contained within meaning structure always contain a core of sensuous content, he explicitly refuses to equate the two.[37] Rather,

32 / Peirce, 4.478; 4.233.

33 / Mead, "The Mechanism of Social Consciousness," in *Selected Writings*, p. 134.

34 / Peirce, 7.498. This represents a refinement of this quotation as used in chapter 1.

35 / Dewey, "The Reflex Arc Concept in Psychology," in vol. 5 (1972) of *The Early Works*, p. 98; "Perception and Organic Action," in vol. 7 (1979) of *The Middle Works*, p. 19. This will be developed more fully in the following two chapters.

36 / Chapter 4 will show that such purity, as an absolute purity, is a limiting concept within experience.

37 / Mead, "Image or Sensation," p. 606.

sensuous stimulation merges with schematic results of past acts that this stimulus sets going.[38] The sensuous core within schematic structure allows the relation between purpose and stimulus, or between response and object, to exist apart from the actual instances denoted by the meaning. Meaning as dispositional thus serves to bind into a triadic, schematic relation within its own internal structure the factors emerging from organism-environment interaction. Indeed, though the sensory core of any schematic criteria serves as a particular stimulus within the logic of pragmatic meaning, it is itself an epistemic universal that has been determined at a more fundamental level.[39] The sensuous criteria of recognized content within the schematic structure can in none of its aspects be reduced to the content of any experience, whether imagined or actual. Rather, it forms part of the principle or rule of interpretation, as opposed to the manifold of particulars organized by it. Such a universalized sensory core is precisely what Peirce refers to as the *ponecipuum*, or logically primitive criteria for the apprehension of recognized content.[40] Further, as will later be stressed,[41] such a sensory core cannot be understood in terms of atomic contents of separate senses. The experience of the separate senses is gained only through a change of focus by which one takes a highly particularized attitude. Thus, such an experience is not foundational for the emergence of perceived objects, but rather emerges via a reflective focus placed upon perceptual experience.

As has been shown, appearances, with their core of sensuous content, are the bedrock data to which one can work back in conscious awareness. In brief, immediate experience of appearance is not the experience of pure immediacy, but rather is shot through with the dispositional structural orderings of objectivity, for the appearances apprehended in immediate experience are generated indirectly through the functioning of habit. To call apprehension of appearances immediate and the bedrock data of conscious awareness, is to indicate a functional role. As Dewey states of such sensory appearances, "They are primary only in logical status; they are primary as tests and confirmations of inferences concerning matters of fact, not as historic originals."[42] And, as he well cautions, the transformation of these "ulterior check meanings into exis-

---

38 / Mead, "The Mechanism of Social Consciousness," p. 164.
39 / This point will be developed in chapter 4.
40 / Peirce, 7.648.
41 / See chapter 4.
42 / Dewey, *Experience and Nature*, p. 246.

tential primary data is but another example of . . . the fallacy which converts a functional office into an antecedent existence."[43] The immediate experience of appearance, then, is an abstraction from within the meaning structures by which we experience a world of objectivities, and thus it reflects in some sense the structure of these meanings. Only through a change of focus or attention does such a level emerge for conscious awareness.

In brief, appearances are not the building blocks of our perceptual world, but rather are creative abstractions from within it. Like the experience of the separate senses, they are products of common-sense critical vision, in this case a common-sense critical vision concerned with perceptual mistakes, bringing into focus an epistemic level within the structure of meaning that serves a special function in the process of verification. In Dewey's terms, they are the class of irreducible meanings that are employed in verifying and correcting other meanings.[44] In one sense, this level is most devoid of interpretive elements precisely because reference to future experience contained in assertions of objectivity is withheld. In a certain sense, however, interpretation is very much in evidence, since abstractive or reflective attention is a type of interpretive process that yields experience of sense content as "an appearance of." In brief, appearances come to awareness only within a world of appearing objects, for appearances, as generated by schemata, are generated as appearances of intended objectivities because of the functioning of the concrete disposition or habit, as the rule of generation of explicit schemata.

The generality of the schematic content at all levels, then, lies precisely in the fact that, as an aspect of the dispositional structural ordering, it reflects, in its very generation, the generality of such an ordering. In the schematic aspects of meaning, there is to be found the inseparable mingling of the sensuous and the relational as the vehicle by which we think about and recognize objects in the world. This is what Dewey intends when he observes that a concept as a mode of construction or method of action[45] is dispositional in nature, and, as such, has an ideality that cannot be reduced to sense contents or to particular activities.[46]

The concreteness of living habit does more than generate schematic

43 / Ibid.

44 / Ibid., p. 246. Any further discussion of the verificatory function of appearances will be put aside till the following chapter.

45 / Ibid., p. 147.

46 / "How Do Concepts Arise from Percepts?" p. 144.

aspects, however, for it provides the conceptual counterpart of the "that which has" characteristics, and the "that which has" can never be exhausted by any indefinite set of qualitative regularities and relationships which it incorporates. Indeed, far from a set of characteristics constituting the unity and constancy of the intended thing, the unity and constancy of the intended thing provides the unity and constancy of the characteristics. And, as representing a "that which has," or a possible existent individual, there is a second fundamental indeterminateness. The internal logic of perceptual meanings relating schematic forms of possible experiences not only reveals that certain structural and qualitative characteristics are included in the very meaning of the intended object and are, in fact, criteria for delineating that kind of object within experience, but further reveals that indefinite numbers of characteristics are possible, but not essential. An object, as a concrete individual, contains not just those characteristics necessary for its being a particular type of object, but also the indefinite specificity of having or not having other characteristics. Any pragmatic meaning represents an object to which essential characteristics must apply, and to which an indefinite number of nonessential characteristics may or may not apply, though it will cancel out as unreal those characteristics that do not fit consistently within the range constituted by the perceptual unity.

Thus, the specificity of meaning that lies in the disposition or habit as the rule of generation includes within itself a basic indeterminateness, both in relation to the total meaning, and in relation to the specificity of the concrete, existing object denoted. A meaning is indeterminate in that there is, in principle, always more to specify. And its application to the world is further indeterminate, in that its very meaning intends that to which the attribution of a limitless number of nonessential characteristics is always possible. This difference intended between the concreteness of an existing object and a set of objective properties is not the difference between extension and intension. Rather, the intensional meaning contains the meaningfulness of the concreteness of objectivity or "existence" as that which can never be reduced to a set of qualitative aspects or structural relations, for the "that which has" qualities and relations incorporate the concreteness of existence, and this concreteness is built into the very meaning intended, through the concreteness of living habit as generative rule. Thus, meaning identifies an individual existent as an instance of a kind, not as a uniquely concrete individual, but it also provides the meaningful recognition that concrete individuality provides an "always more." We can denote objects, rather than collections of qualities, because the concreteness of our meanings embodies the basis of the concreteness of objectivity, of concrete existence, of "the that which" incorporates certain qualitative possibilities. The living habit thus provides the meaning of the existential dynamical bond.[47]

In no respect, then, is the intensional meaning of dispositions reducible to the denotation of verifying instances. Rather, the meaning must be prior to the very possibility of denotable instances. The meaning of the concreteness of existing objects is included in the concreteness of habit as rule, and is represented in the perspectival aspect of schematic structure. The total meaning intends an object as that to which essential characters must apply, and to which nonessential properties may or may not apply, and these two types of applicability are built into the very sense of the meanings by which we delineate a world of perceptual objects.

The most adequate models to summarize the relationship intended in the above analysis are those of a continuity as the generative basis of discrete cuts within itself,[48] or of a mathematical rule generating a number series.[49] The use of the two models points out diverse but equally important aspects of pragmatic meaning. First, the model of a continuity generating cuts within itself indicates the ontological rootedness of the functioning of meaning, for such a model will be seen to be continuous with the functioning of that ontological reality within which man is immersed, and of which he is a part.[50] Second, the mathematical model indicates the nature of the internal structure of meaning as that of a logical relationship, irreducible to physical causal conditions or to the categories of psychology or biology.[51] What are the similar characteristics of such models?

First, neither a mathematical rule nor a continuum, as the basis for

47 / This point will be developed from an ontological perspective in later chapters. Once again, it must be stressed that the present focus on meaning requires further ontological consideration of that which is meaningfully grasped.

48 / Peirce, 6.170; 6.138. Peirce also develops the relationship as analogous to a mathematical rule when he generalizes from theorematic reasoning as schematic (2.778; 4.478; 4.233 provide the basis for this claim).

49 / Lewis, *Analysis of Knowledge and Valuation*, p. 110.

50 / Peirce relates his synecism and pragmatism while James develops continuity as essentially related to pragmatic method. This will come to the forefront in chapter 4 and on through the following pages.

51 / As stated earlier, habit or disposition cannot here be understood in terms of biological categories, but rather in terms of a phenomenological sense of the lived-through response as it structures emerging content.

the generation of a series, can be reduced to or constructed out of the series, for each is necessary to the formation of the series, and to the character that each member of the series possesses. Like its models, a dispositional rule of generation can neither be reduced to nor constructed out of the series generated, nor can it be separated from that which it generates, for that which is generated represents an aspect of the structural order by which it is generated. As has been seen, not only is the meant objectivity fixed in its character, through the functioning of habit in filling in the results of an act with the results of other possible acts given other possible cues, but the appearance that is apprehended by a change of focus that attempts to withhold this filling in is itself partially fixed in its character precisely by that which is attempting to be withheld. Apprehended appearance is not brute uninterpreted content, but is shot through with the dispositional structural orderings of objectivities, for the focus on appearance is the focus on that which is generated indirectly through the functioning of habit. At every level, human response enters into the very character of the data.

Second, both the number series generated by the mathematical rule and the cuts generated from the continuum have the capacity for indefinite expansion. Just as a mathematical rule may generate an unlimited series of numbers, or just as a continuum may generate an unlimited number of cuts within itself, so a disposition as a rule of organization contains within itself an unlimited number of possibilities of specific schemata to be generated. Furthermore, the inability to exhaust via enumeration all possibilities is not a contingent fact, but is intrinsic to the nature of the generating rule. Similarly, meaning as dispositional is the source of the concrete unity of objectivity as more than a collection of appearances or abstract properties. Such an objective concreteness that transcends any indefinite number of appearances is built into our very sense of objectivity, for meaning as dispositional is the source of a sense of a reality of physical objectivities whose possibilities of being experienced transcend, in their very nature, the experiences in which they appear.

As has been seen in the above discussion, the series of possible schemata for the application of a meaning to experience is fixed prior to the imposition of a linguistic structure. Yet it is fixed not by any eternal ontological order, but rather by the concrete, biologically based, disposition or habit, as the rule of generation of explicit schemata. Such meaning cannot be reduced to the "merely psychological" or "merely biological," for what is bound together into a unity is an irreducibly triadic relationship of factors emerging from organism-environment interaction; it is an irreducibly triadic semiotic structure.[52] Meanings emerge from organism-environment interaction as precise triadic relational or logical structures, unified by habit as a rule of organization and as a rule of generation of specific schemata, and they include activity and temporal reference in the very heart of their internal structure. Only within the backdrop of such a concrete functioning of purposive activity can appearances come to awareness and qualities, properties, or characters of objects gain their stability and acceptability. The intentionally grounded unity of knower and known within the dynamic structure of pragmatic meaning cannot be understood in terms of the alternatives of traditional empiricism or rationalism, for it undercuts the problematics of each.

This living meaning as a rule for the production of schematic aspects is at once a rule for the construction of the conditions for possible verifying instances. The concrete living meaning or vital intentionality contains the conditions for its verification. Such conditions are not collections of actual or possible verifying instances, but rather consist of the relational generality of schematic aspects that set the conditions of recognition for what will count as verifying instances. The if-then orderings of such general relations or conditional resolutions to action are contained in the perceptual meaning. Not only does meaning as dispositional contain an indefinite number of possible kinds of verification in respect to possible kinds of conditions, but each kind is itself a generality that, rather than a collection of, helps give structure to, possible verifying instances. As a "kind," it is contained in, or is part of, a meaning, while an instance of a kind, delineated by such meaning, gives evidence for the applicability of the meaning. Thus, pragmatic meaning is in principle irreducible to verifying instances, actual or possible, because possible conditions of verification, contained in the meaning, are different in their very nature from any number of particular verifying instances, actual or possible.

As a concluding point, note that though all meaning is pragmatic, in the sense developed above, this does not imply that all meaning is fundamentally cognitive. The generic character of meaning is not that it is intellectual or cognitive, but that it is intentional or interpretive. There are many ways of apprehending the world, and an apprehension may emphasize the cognitive, the active, or the emotive response. These are,

---

52 / As has already been seen, each "ingredient" in this triadic relationship is affected in its character by its relation with the others.

however, types of intentional relatedness, and each, as intentional or interpretive, is anticipatory unification embodied within the structures of pragmatic meaning.[53] Each type of intentional relatedness involves the others at least in some minimal sense.[54] The difference lies in the features predominating in experience.

In light of the discussions of the present chapter, the following two chapters will turn successively to the complexities of verification in the emerging context of pragmatic meaning, and to the emergence of pragmatic meanings from a more primordial experience.

53 / Indeed, Dewey cannot even delineate the emotional aspect of responsive behavior as its immediate quality (fear, hope, joy, sorrow, etc.) without reference to the future, to "what the present situation may become" (*Quest for Certainty*, p. 180).

54 / Thus Peirce, late in his writings, draws the emotional, energetic and logical interpretants into a semiotic structure of meaning unified by habit as the ultimate logical interpretant. These are drawn into the internal structure of meaning as the elements of Firstness, Secondness, and Thirdness in his logical or phaneroscopic analysis of the concept (8.305).

Three

Meaning and the Structure of Verification

T HE PREVIOUS chapter attempted to show that the complexities of pragmatic meaning, when examined, point toward a sharp distinction between conditions of possible verification as the structure of meaning and possible verifying instances as the conditions of truth. The present chapter examines the pragmatic understanding of truth in terms of verification to clarify the complexities of the structure of verification that lie implicit in this claim. To do this, the following discussion must first bring into focus what lies implicit throughout the previous chapter: the nature of pragmatic meaning as a priori regulative and as the basis of analytic claims.

The following discussion proposes to show that pragmatic meaning, as developed in the previous chapter, carries the analytic-synthetic distinction beyond the conventionalism of language, beyond the functionalism of decisions of usage, and beyond the distinction between logic and knowledge about the world. Pragmatic meaning founds the absoluteness of the analyticity of an a priori that coerces the mind within any system, but which can be nonetheless exchanged for another system, and which is linked to experience by the method of experimentation, for it founds an a priori analyticity that both arises from the concretely rich matrix of experience and is justified by the intelligibility it introduces into experience.

Before beginning such a development, two points should be noted. First, though the present chapter will deal with the issue of truth in terms of verification, the understanding of the nature of truth cannot be fully established until later chapters, because a complete understanding of the nature of truth as verification requires an explicit development of certain ontological features that are deliberately omitted here.

Second, though specific references will be made to points in Lewis's philosophy, no number of specific references can adequately reflect the extent to which this entire chapter is pervaded by the backdrop of Lewis's "pragmatic a priori." However, the a priori, as developed in this chapter in light of Lewis's own work, will emerge as more systematically comprehensive for pragmatic thought than is evinced in Lewis's development. Indeed, even within Lewis's own philosophy, the import of his pragmatic a priori is usually interpreted as quite limited in scope and as irrelevant to issues that are frequently seen as central, either to Lewis's position or to classical American pragmatism in general. The a priori as here discussed will be found in the thought of Peirce, James, and Dewey as well, though they made little effort to develop it or to relate it explicitly to other issues within the context of their respective philosophies, and its development here will be inseparably tied to most of the key issues of speculative pragmatism. In light of these preliminary points, the ensuing discussion can begin to delineate the context of the a priori within speculative pragmatism.

Empiricism has been given such a broad range of meanings throughout the history of philosophy as to have virtually no defining characteristics that cover all supposedly empirical philosophies. However, the distinction between the a priori, analytic, nonfactual statement on the one hand, and the a posteriori, synthetic, factual statement on the other, has been taken to offer the most inclusive characteristic of empiricism. Yet there has been much controversy within the empiricist camp itself over the adequacy of this distinction. Cases have been made for the existence of the synthetic a priori by several philosophers who, whether or not they call themselves empiricists, fit into the empiricist category on other grounds. This so-called principle of empiricism has also been questioned from another direction in controversies concerning the denial of the long-held absolute distinction between the analytic and the synthetic.

In the midst of this controversy, the a priori that runs through pragmatism can perhaps be said to occupy a unique position. Drawn from a fundamentally Kantian approach adapted to fit the needs of contemporary logic and science, this a priori is coextensive with the analytic, yet cannot be said to be empirically vacuous. It both arises out of experience and has possible reference to experience. The analyticity of the a priori is absolute, founded on meaning relations; all-pervasive, underlying empirical knowledge as well as propositions of logic and mathematics; and experimental, arising from the matrix of experience and justified by its workability in experience. The uniqueness of this point of view explains, to some extent, both the great amount of conflicting criticism that assertions by the pragmatists of an a priori element in knowledge have received, as well as the general ignoring of any analytic-synthetic distinction within pragmatic thought by its critics. This nature of the a priori and of analyticity within pragmatic thought can best be brought into focus by first separating the a priori, analytic claims to which meanings give rise from their origin within the ongoing course of experience. It is to this latter aspect that the ensuing discussion will first turn.

As the previous chapter has shown, meaning structures, which emerge in the context of man's behavioral response to that which gives itself, underlie all perceptual experience and, in fact, make it possible. This relatedness to experience, however, leads to the objection that structures so rich in empirical meaning can arise neither through induction, nor definition, nor linguistic stipulation, and hence require a synthetic aspect. The "fixation" of meaning structures, however, corresponds to none of these alternatives. They arise through the creative fixation of a set of relationships unified by habit as a rule of organization of the related experiences and our possible responses to them. The fixation intended corresponds most closely to the creative process which Peirce calls abduction, though what are here fixed by such creative activity or abductive processes are not empirical hypotheses asserting the applicability of meanings to experience, but rather the very structure of the meanings themselves. And habit, as creatively structuring, always brings a "more than" to the organization of past experience.

Our behavioral responses to the world incorporated within the internal structure of meaning are organized by the creative fixation of habit as a dispositional rule. Genetically, meanings arise through the cumulative effect of past experience and the abductive, creative fixation, within the ongoing course of experience, of dispositionally organized relationships among experiences. But, at any point in the process, a meaning or dispositional rule contains, analytically, all that it has creatively fixated, or, conversely, all that it now has the power or potential to generate within the ongoing course of experience. It is a priori regulative for future experience, for it is legislative for what is to count as an instance of a kind within future experience.

The meanings embodied in our conceptual schemes are built up in the light of past experience. They are drawn from the empirical situation, although the relation between the meanings is statable apart from any particular instance of fact. The origin of our analytic structures, then, is empirical, pragmatic, functional. This genesis of meanings from the context of experience is in no way analogous to the logical reducibility of meanings to experience. The first answers the question as to why we create the meanings we do; the second answers the question as to what a meaning is. Meaning, qua created structure, contains no truth claim as to applicability in experience. Though for pragmatic reasons we must create or fixate meanings with workable applications in the ongoing course of experience, a meaning itself is a deductive system applying to a hypothetical state of affairs, the implications of which we can know about since we create it. Thus, Peirce and Lewis explicitly work toward an understanding of a priori analyticity within everyday lived experience by analogy with logical deducibility within abstract systems of mathematics and logic; Dewey, conversely, understands abstract systems of mathematics and logic by viewing them as emerging from and as continuous with an a priori analyticity operative within rudimentary experience.[1]

Though the relation between meanings is statable apart from any particular instance of fact, the meanings are built up in the light of past experience and chosen for pragmatic reasons. A priori truth as legislative emerges within the context of purposive attitudes of interpretation drawn from the context of past experience. As Lewis summarizes this point, "What is a priori is prior to experience in almost the same sense that purpose is. Purposes are not dictated by the content of the given; they are our own. Yet purposes must take their shape and have their realization in terms of experience. . . . In somewhat the same fashion what is a priori and of the mind is prior 'to present experience' yet in another sense not altogether independent of experience in general."[2]

The rulelike or regulative aspect of the a priori, as well as its emergence within the ongoing course of experience, is expressed in Dewey's claim that "a postulate as a rule of action is thus neither arbitrary nor

---

1 / See especially Lewis, "Logic and Pragmatism," *Collected Papers of Clarence Irving Lewis*, ed. John D. Goheen and John L. Mothershead, Jr. (Stanford: Stanford University Press, 1970); Peirce, 1.232ff; 1.443ff, 4.233ff; Sections 288, p. 95, and 293, p. 14 of Microfilm Edition (these diverse sections need synthesizing in terms of the issue involved); Dewey, *Logic: The Theory of Inquiry*. A comparison of the logical interests of Lewis, Peirce, and Dewey may seem doomed from the start, since Lewis's and Peirce's focus is on abstract symbolic systems, while Dewey develops logic as procedural rules emerging within the context of concrete inquiry by man, the biological organism. However, as will be indicated in this chapter as well as in the next, Lewis and Peirce trace the pragmatic element in logic to its very roots in lived experience, "descending" to the point from which Dewey begins his own logical "ascent" to the understanding of abstract symbolic systems.

2 / Lewis, *Mind and the World Order*, p. 24.

externally a priori. It is not the former because it issues from the relation of means to the end to be reached. It is not the latter, because it is not imposed upon inquiry from without, but is acknowledgment of that to which the undertaking of inquiry commits us."[3] Nonetheless, such a postulate or rule of action "is empirically and temporally a priori in the same sense in which the law of contracts is a rule regulating in advance the making of certain kinds of business engagements. While it is derived from what is involved in inquiries that have been successful in the past, it imposes a condition to be satisfied in future inquiries."[4] Such an a priori element within experience, exemplified for Dewey in the postulational aspect of logic as the theory of inquiry,[5] is not rooted in this abstract level, but again reflects the pragmatic insight that the level of reflective inquiry can provide a clear model for understanding the structures of lived experience. As Dewey carefully observes, insofar as thought does exercise this a priorily regulative aspect, "it is because thought is itself still a vital function."[6] Similarly, though Lewis develops his understanding of the nature of the a priori through work in logic, he holds that such a priori criteria as meanings entertained in advance can be considered in terms of incipient behavior or behavior attitudes.[7]

If that which a meaning generates, or in other terms, contains, is too frequently inapplicable, our meaning may alter through the formation of new habits that creatively fixate inductively accumulated experiences in new ways. But what we then have is a new meaning, or a new rule of generation of conditions of verification, which now necessarily contains at least partially different schematic possibilities. Though the same words may be used, the meanings attached to them are different, for as has been seen in the previous chapter, pragmatic meaning is not fundamentally a relational system among words, but rather among schematic possibilities contained in our dispositional tendencies as ways of acting toward a situation. Thus, Peirce holds that a self-contradictory proposition is not meaningless; it means too much.[8] It "means" something in the predicate, not allowed by the subject as the dispositional rule of generation. However, through a change of meaning, though not necessarily of words, "what is inconceivable today may become conceivable tomor-

3 / Dewey, *Logic: The Theory of Inquiry*, p. 17.
4 / Ibid.
5 / Ibid., p. 18.
6 / Dewey, "Experience and Objective Idealism," p. 136.
7 / Lewis, *Analysis of Knowledge and Valuation*, p. 144.
8 / Peirce, 2.352.

row."[9] Lewis makes a similar point as he continually stresses that though words may remain the same, the meanings frequently change.[10]

If the rootedness of analyticity in the structure of pragmatic meaning is ignored in favor of language, then indeed the analytic-synthetic distinction will seem inoperative, and the a priori–a posteriori distinction will seem to be a functional one only, a characterization given continually to Lewis's distinction, as well as to that of Dewey. However, as has been seen, the same word can both house, and hide, an accepted change of meaning. Lewis's distinction between the intensional and the extensional "all" is instructive here.[11] The a priori proposition and the empirical generalization are usually indistinguishable by their form. Both are universal in intent, and are normally expressed by an 'all' proposition or by one in which the 'all' though unexpressed is obviously understood. The difference between these two is that between the intensional and extensional 'all.' The first expresses in the predicate something logically contained in the subject; the subject concept implies the predicate concept. The second states a factual connection of two classes of objects that are not related intensionally. Dewey makes this same point, noting that the intensional "all" of meaning relationships implies a necessary relation, while the extensional "all" of empirical claims provides a high degree of probability at best.[12] Though the denotation of the subject term in each case may in fact be the same, its meaning in the two cases is different, for in the first case, the schematic possibilities of the meaning contained in the predicate terms are included in the schematic possibilities necessarily contained in the meaning of the subject term.

Thus, though one may carelessly speak of "the same" proposition

9 / Peirce, 8.191, 2.29.

10 / See, for example, *Mind and the World Order*, p. 235. A meaning does not literally change, but rather a meaning is replaced by another meaning, each of which is a logically distinct generative rule. Thus, both Lewis and Peirce speak of meanings as analogous to Platonic ideas. (Lewis, *Mind and the World Order*, p. 269; Peirce's cryptic comments, 6.194). Concepts are analogous to Platonic forms, not in the sense of being metaphysical essences, but in the sense of being fixed, eternal, unchanging (though replaceable) and, indeed, "toward the side of math."

11 / Lewis, *Mind and the World Order*, Appendix F, p. 434.

12 / Dewey, *Logic: The Theory of Inquiry*, p. 296. Some critics hold that this former type of proposition involves a kind of knowledge that eludes experimental method and thus reveals Dewey as inconsistent. In fact, this type of proposition reflects experimental method in its genesis from the matrix of experience, in the establishment of its usefulness in terms of workability in experience, and in its explication of the dynamics of experimental method embedded in the internal structure of meaning.

serving now in one capacity, now in the other, what is involved is not the same proposition but rather two different propositions having the same sentential expression. What is determined by our attitudes of response is not the function of one proposition, but rather the choice between two propositions, the one eternally analytic, and eternally valid if ever valid, though perhaps not always a useful tool for prescribing what will count as an instance of a kind; the other eternally synthetic and subject to the verdict of experience. Thus, what is functionally determined is not whether a given proposition is analytic or synthetic; a specific proposition is either analytic or synthetic and is, eternally, that which it is. What is determined functionally is which of two propositions, the same only in their sentential expression, is to be entertained. The two propositions are, indeed, often difficult to distinguish, for the terms are identical. But, as the meaning of the subject term in one case is a logically distinct and different meaning from the meaning of the subject term in another case, what is involved is the choice between two logically and epistemologically distinct propositions. Thus, though analytic relationships are determined by us in the light of pragmatic considerations, and are often determined prereflectively, yet the analytic and the synthetic proposition are different in kind.

As Dewey indicates the key role of an a priori regulative feature which is distinctively analytic, "All propositions of existential import involve delimiting analytic operations of observation. . . . The operations of observation executed are controlled by conceptions which define the conditions to be satisfied . . . in descriptive determination of kinds."[13] Thus, for Dewey and Lewis, the a priori element in knowledge that regulates in advance the possibility of the emergence within experience of certain kinds of facts or objects is rooted in human behavior, as partially constitutive of the environment in which it operates. Further, for both Dewey and Lewis the distinction between the a priori and the a posteriori corresponds with the distinction between the analytic and the synthetic, and both distinctions are rooted in the absoluteness of the containment of schematic possibilities within the structure of meaning.

Here the fundamental basis of analyticity is not synonymy but containment. The previous chapter showed that a rule of generation cannot be separated from that which it generates, for that which is generated represents an aspect of the structural order by which it is generated. In addition, dispositions cannot be said to generate explicit schemata in the sense of providing a copy—even a partial one. A schema is not a par-

13 / Ibid., p. 243.

ticular copy of a general rule. It is not a copy of anything; nor, as has been seen, is anything in the schema particular. In understanding the relational structure of that which is generated, however, we understand to that extent the rule that generates it. The disposition or "ground" of meaning cannot, it is true, be inspected *an sich*, but it is inspectable in any aspect. Explicit schematic aspects can be continually generated for inspection, though the rule of generation will never be exhausted by the schemata, and hence will never be completely inspected. As was stressed in the previous chapter, there is a basic indeterminateness to meanings, in that there are always more schematic possibilities to be generated.

A disposition as an implicit criterion is concrete, and any attempt to make it clear and explicit requires an abstraction from this concreteness. Any explicit criterion generated by the concrete disposition gains clarity and explicitness at the expense of concreteness. This relationship between concrete dispositional meaning and its schematic aspects within the structure of pragmatic meaning should not be confounded with the relation between pragmatic meaning and language. The relation of language to pragmatic meaning is to a large degree conventionalized abstraction. Hence, an examination of linguistic expression will give no satisfactory understanding of the necessity of analytic statements. The relation of a concrete disposition to the schematic possibilities it generates is not, however, that of conventionalized abstraction, but rather is that of a concrete rule of generation to the organizational structure generated by it. Hence, schematic aspects do give an indication of the necessity of analytic claims.

That the total concrete meaning as a disposition cannot be made fully explicit is undeniable. A meaning is determinate beyond what any number of schematic possibilities can assure with theoretical certainty. What follows from this position is that though a meaning is never fully inspected, it is inspectable in any aspect. And what follows from this is that some propositions may be necessary that we do not recognize to be so; it does not mean that those we do recognize to be necessary, cannot be. If an analytic statement is true, it is necessarily true, though it need not be exhaustive. The fundamental relation for analyticity is not synonymy but containment.

As Peirce puzzled over the problem of containment: "Consider a state of mind which is a conception. It is a conception by virtue of having a meaning, a logical comprehension; and if it is applicable to any object, it is because that object has the characters contained in the comprehension of this conception. Now the logical comprehension of a thought is usually said to consist of the thoughts contained in it, but thoughts are events. . . ."[14] He finds the answer to the puzzle in the distinction between the concrete disposition or habit as the rule of organization, and the awareness of the schematic aspects of that which is organized by the rule, for, as he notes, the living meaning "virtually contains" these aspects.[15] Thus, through the internal logic of the functioning of meaning as dispositional, Peirce can offer a solution to the problem of containment. It is through an understanding of this internal functioning that we can understand the sense in which one can discover that some quality or character is essential to the meaning in question.[16] Similarly, this functioning of meaning makes clear the way in which a meaning of which one is not conscious may be implicit in that meaning of which one is conscious.[17] Indeed, how the meaning implicit in behavior becomes explicit, and what would be recognized as essential when the meaning is examined, is already implicit in the dispositional mode of response. As Peirce concludes, "What we must mean, therefore, by saying that one concept is contained in another, is that we normally represent one to be in the other; that is, that we form a particular kind of judgment, of which the subject signifies one concept and the predicate the other."[18] Such a "particular kind of judgment" is precisely an analytic claim that expresses a deductive relation of containment between generative rule and schematic product, for, "the conclusion is compelled to be true by the conditions of the construction."[19] Indeed, Peirce indicates that the mathematical model of containment represents "the modes in which concepts are, or should be, represented as compounded in definitions."[20]

The ambiguities of James's understanding of the a priori as found in *Principles of Psychology* falls into focus within the context of the above discussion. James holds that there is a coerciveness among necessary and eternal relations that the mind finds between certain of its ideal conceptions, and that these relations among ideal conceptions form a determinate system independent of the order of frequency in which

14 / Peirce, 5.288.

15 / Peirce, 4.233.

16 / Such a discovery requires "a real effective force behind consciousness," or, in other terms, a living habit (5.288).

17 / Thus, "the meaning of a thought is something virtual . . . it lies not in what is actually thought, but in what this thought may be connected with in representation by subsequent thoughts" (5.289).

18 / Peirce, 4.480 n.

19 / Peirce, 2.778.

20 / Peirce, *The New Elements of Mathematics*, ed. Carolyn Eisele (The Hague: Mouton Press, 1976), 3, p. 850.

experience may have associated the conception's originals in time and space.[21] As far as some of nature's realities fit this network, "we can make a priori propositions concerning natural fact."[22] Yet he also indicates that our regulative principles are themselves conditioned by the experiences that they serve to organize.[23] Again, at times he holds that there is a sharp distinction between the way in which we justify the a priori truths of logic and mathematics on the one hand, and the a posteriori truths of physics on the other.[24] Yet there are places where James comes close to holding that physical theories and theories of mathematics are alike not only in being "spontaneous variations," but also in being "rational propositions."[25] What seems implicit here is not an ambiguous vacillation, but a development toward a view that physical truths contain an a priori element, though for physical truths, such an a priori element both arises within the matrix of experience and must be found workable within the context of experience.[26]

Indeed, James's refusal to relate issues of the a priori to the analytic is instructive of his understanding of the a priori. He holds that the analytic-synthetic distinction is an unhappy legacy from Kant that loses all philosophical interest the moment one ceases to ascribe to any a priori truths the "legislative character for all possible experience" that Kant believed in.[27] "We ourselves have denied such legislative character, and contended that it was for experience itself to prove whether its data can or cannot be assimilated to those ideal terms between which a priori relations obtain. The analytic-synthetic debate is thus for us devoid of all significance."[28] Thus, James thinks that the experimental context of a priori truths—the temporal origin of a priori relationships and the testing of their usefulness in terms of their workability in experience—makes the issue of the analytic-synthetic distinction useless, since there is no claim for any a priori truth legislative of all experience in Kant's sense. What we can know, holds James, is only that *if* these things are anywhere to be found, then eternal verities will obtain of them.[29] This if-then, however, is the if-then of containment, which Lewis calls the hypothetical certitude of a priori claims about experience. I can know in advance of any experience, as "eternal verities," that if the subject term

21 / James, *Principles of Psychology*, 2, p. 1255.

22 / Ibid., p. 1269.   23 / Ibid., pp. 1215–1270.

24 / Ibid.   25 / Ibid.

26 / As will be seen in the next chapter, this genesis and workability holds true for even the most fundamental laws of logic.

27 / James, *Principles of Psychology*, 2, p. 1255 n.

28 / Ibid.

29 / Ibid., p. 1257.

applies then certain features must obtain for they are analytically contained in the meaning of the subject term.

Before one can make empirical generalizations about facts, one must have delineated facts through meanings which are prescriptive for what experiences will constitute the experience of particular kinds of facts. Before one can make the empirical claim that a particular kind of fact is there, one must have the structure of the experiences which are to count as exemplifications of the presence of a particular kind of fact. Thus, the analytic structures of meanings provide the tools without which synthetic statements about the nature of experience cannot be made. Yet these tools themselves are fashioned in the light of the cumulative effects of past experience through the creative fixation of experienced uniformities, and are retained in light of their ability to delineate facts and objects in useful ways, in ways that work in successfully organizing the ongoing course of experience. As will be seen later, this does not mean that meanings that work in any sense "copy" the independently real. Dispositional or pragmatic meaning cannot be just a collection of uniformities, for as will be seen in following chapters, uniformities are themselves discriminated as meaningful in relation to basic intents, or fundamental dispositional tendencies to act, or vital intentionalities. From the perspective of a meaning system rooted in active interest and intent, *meaningful* uniformities emerge within experience. Facts, at their very core, will be seen to emerge neither from mind alone nor from the universe alone, but rather from the interaction of the two which constitutes experience. This is not a vicious circle, but rather a cumulative process based on the pragmatic interplay of all levels between meanings and experience. Such a cumulative and self-corrective process has been seen to lie at the heart of scientific method.

The way in which any conceptual structure originates genetically in experience, but is yet logically or epistemically prior to the delineation of what is presented in any particular experience, reflects the difference between the indefinite extendability of the interpretive process as a whole and the unity and completeness of any one particular interpretive structure or concept. Genetically the interpretive process can be extended indefinitely, for the cumulative knowledge process is unending; our concepts, based on previous experiences delineated by previous concepts, become more and more sophisticated. Yet at any point in the cumulative knowledge process, a particular interpretive structure is complete and self-sufficient, having an internal unity that requires nothing beyond itself for its fulfillment. Thus, there is an interrelation of the absoluteness of intensional relationships of meanings, and the functionalism of attitudes of response as the determining factor in the fixation of meanings. The interrelationship within or among meanings may be wrongly explicated in formally false, or invalid, analytic claims. Such meaning interrelationships cannot, however, be shown false by experience. As Lewis has well observed, an a priori claim cannot be shown false by a nonconformity of the kinds it delineates, for its criteria determine what will count as an instance of a kind. It can, however, be discarded because experience shows it not to be a useful tool of organization. This inadequacy will thus lead to the development of new dispositional tendencies or attitudes of response, fixating new a priori legislative meanings to be used in the ongoing course of experience.

Both the origin and nature of the a priori element within experience will take on added significance through further development in later chapters, after more explicitly ontological considerations have been introduced. For the remainder of this chapter, the focus will turn to the more limited consideration of the way in which a perceptual claim, involving the application of a meaning as a priori regulative of kinds of experience and as analytically containing the conditions of its verification, becomes verified or falsified in experience. The empirical or synthetic claim that a meaning applies or does not apply to a segment of experience incorporates the features indicated above. The empirical or synthetic claim that this segment of experience is experience of an x is possible only in light of the implicit analytic a priori regulative claim that x, to be an x, must exhibit certain characteristics, for the meaning of an objective claim contains analytically a set of interrelated characteristics structured according to the established dispositional rule. This element of analytic a priori regulativeness introduces into the verification of empirical judgments a complexity that needs to be explored.

As has been seen, a schematic aspect is structured by hypothetical or conditional resolutions to action. If 'a' and response 'b', then 'c' will result. Further, this relationship can be grasped in terms of perspectives of an object, or as "mere appearance." To grasp this relationship in terms of a perspective of an object is to have filled in the result of this particular act with the results of other acts, given other cues, as unified by habit as a rule of generation and organization. This is the normal functioning within the internal structure of meaning. In times of doubt, however, or for purposes of verification, there are two possible modes of procedure. The first, but less epistemically interesting, is what can best be called "linear verification." Here one helps verify the truth of an objective claim by other objective claims. This point will be relevant in the following chapter. Verification in terms of epistemic levels, however, requires focusing on the schematic relationship not as objective perspective, but as mere appearance. As was seen in the previous chapter, appearances are not historic originals, but emerge within the context of a world of objectivities by a change of focus, usually brought about by the need for verification. The structure of verification in this sense will be explored in what follows.

If schematic structures are contained in the dispositional generative rule, which together constitute pragmatic meaning, then the physical-object claim implies, as the conditions of its truth, the progressive apprehension of experience as structured by these schematic forms. And if these schematic aspects are implied by the physical-object claim, then though verifying instances cannot prove with certitude the applicability of the meaning that generates their possibility, yet a disconfirming instance may seem to prove with certainty its inapplicability by the operation of modus tolens. And since the ingredients of schematic structure are, for purposes of verification, being focused upon as mere appearances, there is no room for claiming that one may be mistaken about the nonoccurrence of the expected result, and must judge the result itself in terms of further evidence. For the very emergence of appearances, as appearances, occurs through the change of focus that withholds from apprehended content any reference to future experience. Thus, the nonoccurrence of the anticipated appearance would seem to show definitively that the schematic form of verification does not apply, and hence, via modus tolens, that the meaning is inapplicable, or, in other terms, the physical-object claim is false. Thus, while empirical truth claims are always fallible, falsity claims would seem to be certain. The following discussion proposes to show that this antifallibilistic consequence is misplaced.

An examination of the structure of meaning has indeed shown that the schematic forms of verification are contained within it. What the genesis of meaning has shown, however, is that what is asserted as holding within schematic relationships are experiential uniformities, and experiential uniformities are expressible as probability claims.[30] Habit creatively structures a set of inductively learned probabilistic relations expressible, via meanings, as the generality of schematic forms or forms

30 / The assertion that such empirical uniformities are to be expressed in probability claims will be discussed in later chapters. Also, the issue as to whether the probability claim is an assertion of mere regularity or is the stronger assertion of causal relatedness must be left ambiguous at this point, but will emerge as central in following chapters. For the present, the assertion that empirical claims of uniformities are probability claims must be taken in a somewhat common-sense fashion.

of possible verification. Thus, the relationships within any schematic form generated by the concrete disposition that contains it, must be understood in terms of probabilistic relations. Any schematic aspect provides a relational structure evincing that if condition 'a' is presented, and act 'b' is performed, then in all probability 'c' will follow. If 'c' does follow, then there is partial verification of the meaning applicability. If 'c' does not follow, however, there is again only partial disconfirmation of the applicability of the meaning, for no one instance in experience can disprove a probability claim, and what is evinced in the schematic structure is precisely a probability claim about experienced empirical relationships.

Earlier a distinction was made between the intensional and the extensional "all." Here it will be helpful to make a distinction between an intensional and an extensional "if-then," though both of these are here contained within the structure of pragmatic meaning. Dewey notes that if-then claims are systematically ambiguous in their meaning. Sometimes they refer to the existential and sometimes to the ideational.[31] Existential propositions refer directly to actual conditions as determined by experimental observation, while ideational or conceptual propositions consist of interrelated meanings that are nonexistential in content in direct reference, but are applicable to existence through the operations they represent as possibilities.[32] Thus, if-then claims sometimes refer to existential circumstances, and sometimes to a logical relation among meanings.

The if-then of meaning relations—the intensional if-then—expresses the relation between concrete dispositional meaning and its schematic forms that together constitute pragmatic meaning. If this is an object of a particular type, then certain schematic forms must necessarily be applicable. If a schematic form logically contained in the meaning is inapplicable, then the application of the meaning is false by modus tolens. No single instance of the nonoccurrence of the expected resultant appearance can prove the prediction contained in the schematic form false, however, for what is asserted in the schematic form is the if-then of existential conditions, an if-then expressive of a probability relation that can never be proven false by a single nonoccurrence of the expected result.

There are two different levels of probability involved in the above structure of verification: the probability of the truth or falsity of the ap-

31 / Dewey, *Logic: The Theory of Inquiry*, pp. 255–256.
32 / Ibid., pp. 283–284.

plicability of a schematic form, and the probability relation contained within the schematic form. Verifying instances give evidence for or against the probability of the truth of the probability claim contained in the schematic aspect. What is confirmed by verifying instances is the probability of the truth of the probability claim, a claim that must be true if the physical-object claim is true, but which can be stated categorically as probably true or probably false only. Confirming instances give evidence for the probability of the truth of the probability claim. And, conversely, disconfirming instances increase the probability that no such probability claim can, in fact, be made.

Further, this same probability factor, built into the internal structure of a schematic form, which prevents the strict operation of modus tolens, also supplies the epistemological equivalent of auxiliary hypotheses within the internal structure of meaning. The epistemological equivalent of auxiliary hypotheses in science is built into the very logical structure of the perceptual judgment, for the nonoccurrence of the expected verification instance may be held to indicate not probable falsification of the perceptual claim, but the prospect of possibilities of explanation in terms of other conditions which must be, but were not, satisfied, for the verification instance to occur. Thus, the probability factor serves a dual function within the schematic structure: it prevents the strict operation of modus tolens in the face of a disconfirming appearance, and it allows for the nonoccurrence of the anticipated result due to other conditions.

It has been indicated above that what can be decisively verified or falsified is only the particular occurrence or nonoccurrence, on this particular occasion, of the anticipated result as an appearance only. Such an appearance is a verification level, not a building block. It emerges within the context of appearing objects, and reflects the structure of these objects. It is not the experience of pure immediacy, but is shot through with the dispositional structural orderings of objectivity. Yet, because of its very nature as an appearance, it has a type of "certainty." Since reference to future experience is withheld, the apprehension of appearance is beyond doubt because to doubt it in the sense that one thinks it may be shown wrong is senseless; indeed, literally so. To doubt it is to put into question something for which there is no more fundamental tool by which it can be questioned. It is "immediate and indubitable," in the sense that the future reference of verification has no meaning in relation to it; it is by its very nature devoid of references to any future experiences that could verify. It is neither true nor false, it can be neither correctly nor incorrectly apprehended, for the verificatory tools for such claims do not apply. To make any of these claims is to place it in a context of other related experiences, and hence to see it, not as an appearance, but as a perspective of an object, or as an appearing object. Hence, such an apprehension must be accepted, for all intents and purposes, as the bedrock data for verification. It has thus a type of certainty which can perhaps best be called *pragmatic certainty*. It functions as the ultimate data in terms of which any claim can be questioned, but it itself is by its very nature unquestionable.

Further, as has already been briefly anticipated,[33] to claim that an appearance is correct or true in the sense of corresponding with or being identical with something independent of experience is equally meaningless, for it is shot through with, and emerges only within the context of, the dispositional structural orderings of pragmatic meaning. The interrelation between genetic origins and logical containments as a cumulative process, developed earlier, helps clarify here the relation between appearances and objects within experience. We take from the matrix of experience complexes that can be presentations of objects, complexes that the dispositional structurings of objectivities makes possible. Yet we know objects only by apprehensions of presentations. This is not a vicious circle, however, nor a circle at all, but rather again indicates a cumulative process based on the experimental interplay between, and mutual clarification of, diverse levels of experience, best exemplified by the relation between science and common sense, but operative in a less clearly distinguishable matrix at all levels of human awareness.

The reciprocal relationship between appearance and object is evinced in the fact that in the process of reinterpretation the very apprehension of appearance as appearance undergoes a process of transformation: now what appears "appears like" the new objectivity rather than the old. Or, more precisely stated, one appearance "disintegrates" and another appearance emerges. Apprehensions of appearances must always be stated in physical object language, not because of the limitations of language, but because appearances, in their very emergence, emerge as "appearing like" or "seeming like" a particular object or objective property, since the very emergence of the appearance in its structure is dependent upon the generative rule that gives rise to the meant objectivity. Mead develops this point in his support of Dewey as opposed to Wundt, noting that as the content loses its objectivity, it loses any semblance of form until a restructuring occurs that restores a perceptual object to a place in the

33 / This will be developed in more detail in following chapters.

world.[34] In the very breakdown and restructuring of objectivity, there is a loss of the form or structure of appearance. This mutual interdependence is built into the internal structure of meaning. Appearances and objects are interdependent epistemic emergents which stand or fall together in terms of the workability of a meaning as a unified whole. Such epistemic emergents emerge only within the context of an ontological dimension that the next chapter will begin to explore. It can be noted here, in anticipation, that such epistemic emergents *are* the independently real as related to humans through the dispositional structures of the meanings by which they are intentionally united with the independently real. The position intended can be captured neither by the traditional epistemic alternatives of realism or idealism, nor by the more recent alternatives of realism or antirealism or of foundationalism or antifoundationalism.

As has been shown, the pragmatic certainty of the experience of an expected appearance verifies, though never completely, the applicability of the if-then of the probabilistic relation of the schematic structure which is contained in the meaning, and thus it helps to verify, indirectly, the applicability of the meaning. Accumulations of instances of such verifications provide the ground for, or the basis of, habits of belief and contingent, probabilistic, but often practically undoubted, perceptual claims. The purpose of the creation of meanings is the establishment of beliefs that allow for successful interaction with a surrounding universe.

Though there is a theoretically sharp distinction between analytic a priori knowledge and synthetic a posteriori knowledge, all knowledge is fallibilistic and contextualistic. Just as all empirical generalizations are subject to error, so the empirical claim of the applicability of a meaning to a segment of experience is always fallible. Both are examples of contingent truths, fallible knowledge. So, also, our explications of meanings, though yielding necessary truths if correctly made, are always subject to error, thus providing only fallible knowledge about necessary truths. The very claim that a relationship between meanings is in fact analytic or synthetic is itself always fallible; we may easily, through failure of analysis, take as synthetic a relation that is in fact analytic. And when experience turns out unexpectedly, requiring a change in our set of beliefs, there is no certainty as to whether experience has overturned an empirical generalization only, or has given rise, on pragmatic grounds, to a new meaning. We can never be certain if, and when, a highly con-

---

34 / Mead, "The Definition of the Psychical," *Selected Writings*, p. 40.

firmed empirical generalization about an object becomes incorporated into the very meaning of the object, related necessarily to the dispositional rule which now has the power to generate it. The cumulative effects of experience can lead to new empirical generalizations about the same meaningful contents of experience, or it can lead to the perception of different contents by the replacement of the meanings in terms of which contents of a particular type can emerge within experience.

Further, we do not, at any level of experience, test beliefs in isolation, but rather as parts of a whole set of claims. Something similar to auxiliary hypotheses in science is operative in our common-sense awareness of the world around us. No part of a relevant corpus of knowledge is immune from change in the face of repeated disconfirming instances, and any part of a belief structure can be held in the face of disconfirming evidence by changing other parts of the structure.[35] Experience reveals that an improvement is necessary, but clearly not which improvement is needed. Whether we change empirical generalizations in the face of disconfirming evidence or restructure a set of meanings that do not adequately capture experience is not itself dictated by the evidence but is rather a pragmatic decision operative within the context of that encompassing intentional unity of man and nature. And, indeed, experience usually proceeds without any awareness as to whether or not we have modified an empirical generalization by counter instances, or have replaced a meaning to avoid having to throw out too much of experience as not real contents of a particular type, for such pragmatic decisions are implicit in modes of response.

At this point it may be asked whether, after such a long excursion, the only conclusion to be reached is that, after all, the supposed distinction between analytic meaning containments and empirical generalizations is nebulous at best, totally useless at worst. The answer here is a decided "no." This sharp theoretical difference, which is always operative within the structure of knowledge, though always elusive for our recognition because of its fallibilistic, holistic contextualistic features, is inextricably woven into the complex fabric of the uniquely pragmatic understanding of a noetic creativity that is rooted in purposive biological activity and constitutive of the nature of experience as experimental.

35 / See Peirce, 4.71 and Section 290, pp. 2–3 of Microfilm Edition; Lewis, *Mind and the World Order*, Appendix A.

Four

Foundational Experience: Epistemic Unity and Ontological Presence

THE PRECEDING chapters have focused on issues of meaning and verification within the context of everyday experience. This chapter will trace this common-sense level to its foundations in a rudimentary experiential matrix from which it emerges. Once again, the direction to be followed is set by an examination of scientific method. If, as has been claimed, the dynamics of everyday lived experience reflect throughout the dynamics of scientific methodology, then, since "the object" of science is an abstraction from a richer or more concrete transactional experience and cannot be hypostatized as absolute, the perceptual object can be expected likewise to be an abstraction from a richer, more concrete experience and hence not something that can be hypostatized as absolute. This more concrete or primordial experience can be reflected upon philosophically through interpretive description. Such interpretive description can be used philosophically to fund the dynamics of everyday lived experience with enriched meaning, and, in turn, the interpretive description must be verified by everyday lived experience. Such an endeavor reflects throughout the dynamics of scientific method. Like the objects of second-level scientific creativity, the objects of second-level philosophical reflections arise out of the matrix of ordinary experience and refer back to such everyday experience. The contents of systematic philosophic creativity, like the objects of scientific creativity, gain their fullness of meaning from, and fuse their own meaning into, the matrix of ordinary experience. But though philosophic and scientific reflections alike are second-level reflective activities, their respective objects are quite different. The object of philosophical inquiry here is the concrete experiential basis for all objects of awareness—be they the objects of common sense or the more abstract objects of scientific reflection. The content of such an undertaking is at once more abstract and more concrete than the content of everyday lived experience: more abstract because it emerges from a second-level philosophic reflection on lived experience; more concrete because that which is clarified by such philosophic reflection is the basis of the everyday level, that prereflective, processive continuity of organism-environment interaction foundational for the emergence of common-sense experience.

James's world of pure experience, as well as his radical empiricism, and Dewey's most primordial experience are interpretive descriptions that direct the manner in which one actively gazes at everyday lived experience. These descriptions emerge from and bring enriched meaningful understanding to everyday lived experience, and they are, in turn, verified by the structures of such everyday experiences. James speaks of the methodological postulate of pure experience,[1] and claims that radical empiricism is also a postulate.[2] By referring to them as postulates, he does not mean that they form a deductive system that can explain away lived experience, but that they are not pure descriptions but rather interpretive descriptions or explanatory hypotheses that explain, take account of, or fund with meaning, the level of everyday experience. Thus, their methodological function reflects the model of scientific method as indicative of the relation between experience and second-level reflection.

James's radical empiricism, pure experience, and pragmatism are intimately interrelated. He holds that the establishment of the pragmatist theory of truth is a step of first-rate importance in making radical empiricism prevail.[3] Conversely, his radical empiricism exchanges the alternatives of dualism or reductionism for a basis of pure experience, and together they provide the foundation for his pragmatism. The relations of continuous transition within pure experience make cognition and pragmatic verification possible.[4] This key relation between continuity and pragmatism is a focus also within Peirce's philosophy, for both the

---

1 / James, *Essays in Radical Empiricism*, p. 81.

2 / William James, *The Meaning of Truth* (1975), *The Works of William James*, p. 6. James states that radical empiricism consists first of a postulate, next of a statement of fact, and finally of a generalized conclusion. All these, however, together form a postulate or interpretive description as here being discussed.

3 / Ibid.

4 / James, *Essays in Radical Empiricism*, pp. 42–43.

functioning of habit and the possibility of verification, the core features of the pragmatic understanding of meaning and of truth, are for Peirce tied to the primitive experience of continuity in the durational present.[5] Dewey's own understanding of primary experience as a unity of activity undifferentiated by any thought distinctions develops as a natural outgrowth from his pragmatic understanding of the model of scientific methodology.[6]

As has already been indicated, this foundational level of experience has at once epistemic and ontological dimensions. It is constituted by a fundamental unity, but a unity with diverse dimensions. First, the unity can be understood as epistemic, as an intentionally grounded epistemic unity of awareness and its field. Such a unity is foundational for the higher-level categorization of experience as either subjective or objective, mind or matter, internal or external. These distinctions represent neither metaphysical givens nor epistemic foundations, but rather derivative epistemic categorizations. They are epistemic distinctions made from a more foundational experience that both undercuts and underlies them. Focusing on this foundational level will show that not only is epistemic activity constitutive of the distinction between mind and matter, subjective and objective, internal and external, but in its radically nonspectator nature it is partially constitutive of the very field of awareness upon which it builds these distinctions. Not only does all experience include both sensibility and activity, but all sensibility, even at its most rudimentary level, involves activity as partially constitutive of its nature.

The second unity is the unity of awareness and ontological presence. As will be shown, we do not *think to* an ontological presence, but rather *live through* it. Awareness *is* awareness of ontological presence. Ontological presence intrudes itself within the field of awareness, and thus there is an ontological dimension within the very heart of experience with epistemic-phenomenological dimensions that can be studied from within experience. The phenomenological features of experience point toward a concrete organism immersed in a natural universe, and belie any interpretation of the field of awareness as subjective contents or as any type of self-enclosed experience. Thus, the objective ontological categories of organism-environment that are used in the analysis of experi-

---

5 / Peirce, see especially 7.671; 6.170; 6.138; 6.143.

6 / Dewey, *Quest for Certainty*, pp. 188–189; "Does Reality Possess Practical Character?" pp. 137–138.

ence are themselves to be justified by the phenomenological dimensions of experience.

These two types of unities will be developed together in the following discussion, for each both requires and implicates the other. Indeed, these two types of unity are dimensions of the unity of knowing and being at its foundations in experience. Yet they must be kept analytically distinct within the context of the discussion, and both must be clearly separated from products of common-sense awareness. When these diverse dimensions are conflated in various ways, as they frequently are, or confused with reflective distinctions within everyday experience, correlative far-reaching confusions abound. First, the categorization of experience into subjective and objective, internal and external, mind and matter, is not recognized as a derived product of epistemic activity. As a result, these products are illegitimately turned into the ultimate "components" that must combine to give rise to experience. This leads to the spurious problem, in some form or another, of how subjective contents can know an objective world. Second, and almost conversely, subjective and objective are recognized as products of epistemic activity, but are then taken as exhaustive of any reality intended. Thus both knower and known dissolve into the phenomenal contents of epistemic activity.[7] Third, the ontological presence which intrudes itself into experience is recognized, but is not adequately distinguished from the epistemic activity within which it emerges. As a result, there are attributed to that which is ontologically independent of experience, features within experience that emerge only as that independent element functions as an ontological dimension within experience. Thus, for example, discrete physical objects, as they emerge within experience through the functioning of pragmatic meaning, are illicitly reified as ontological ultimates. With this cautionary note in mind concerning the importance of recognizing distinct types of analyses within an existential unity of subject matter, and the pitfalls such a recognition is intended to avoid, the ensuing discussion can turn to an examination of foundational experience.

In focusing on an experiential-level foundational for common-sense experience, as opposed to the common-sense level itself, pragmatists have tended to utilize distinctions between sensation and perception, feeling and perception, or apprehensions of givenness and perception. But each of these terms used to contrast a level of experiencing with

7 / The rejection of epistemological phenomenalism seen in the last two chapters still leaves open the question of ontological phenomenalism or subjectivism of some sort. See Chapter 2, n. 27.

perceptual awareness causes problems because of traditional connotations attached to them. The terms 'feeling,' 'sensation,' and 'the given' tend to bring to mind views of experience that are subjectivistic, psychologistic, mentalistic, and atomistic. Thus, Dewey's stress on feeling is at times held by critics to implicate him in a view of experience that is subjectivistic and psychologistic, in spite of his insistence that experience is of and in nature. This subjectivistic aspect of feeling can be found to arise whenever Dewey discusses qualitative immediacy, for he holds that feeling is objectively defined by reference to immediate quality.[8] Lewis's understanding of the given as constituted by some quale or complex of qualia, is characterized by its feeling quality and as subjective.[9] Yet he notes that it is difficult to express that which he intends in any terms not preempted to slightly different use, and carefully shows that by "feeling"there is intended nothing that can be delineated by psychological categories.[10] He stresses that such content is grasped neither by introspection nor by extrospection, but simply by spection, for it reaches a level that cuts beneath the subject-object distinction and beneath the objectively grasped contents of either psychology or commonsense awareness.[11] James's stress on pure experience in terms of sensation[12] tends to lead some interpreters to view pure experience as psychologistic, subjectivistic, similar to the stream of consciousness of *The Principles of Psychology*, and as implying a counterpart to an external world.[13] Yet he clearly indicates that sensation and perception are "names for different cognitive *functions*, not for different sorts of mental *fact*."[14] The former term represents "the words that say the least,"[15] and contains the minimum of subject-object distinction.

Further, such terms tend to imply a level of experiencing that is atomistic and, to that extent, ultimately spectator in at least some minimal sense. As has been seen, the purity of experience for James corre-

---

8 / Dewey, "Peirce's Theory of Quality," *On Experience, Nature and Freedom*, ed. Richard Bernstein (New York: Bobbs-Merrill, 1960), p. 209. (Originally published in the *Journal of Philosophy* 32 (1935).

9 / Lewis, *Mind and the World Order*, pp. 52–53, 121. Qualia, for Lewis, are "subjective" only in the sense that one cannot speak of unsensed qualia because qualia are, by their very nature, emergents within the context of interactive awareness (*Mind and the World Order*, p. 63).

10 / Ibid., p. 127 n.

11 / Lewis, *Analysis of Knowledge and Valuation*, p. 444.

12 / See chapter 2; James, *Essays in Radical Empiricism*, p. 46.

13 / This is only one strand to be found in *Principles*.

14 / James, *Principles of Psychology*, 2, p. 651 (italics in text).

15 / Ibid., 1, p. 218.

lates with the degree of the sensational or the felt. The concept of pure sensation tends, however, to indicate the grasp of simple quality in its isolation from all others, to indicate the atomic unit. As James states, "the nearer the object cognized comes to being a simple quality like 'hot,' 'cold,' 'red,' 'noise,' 'pain' apprehended irrelatively to other things, the more the state of mind approaches pure sensation."[16] Yet though he tends to equate sensation and pure experience, pure experience, with its focus on experienced relations, represents, for James, the contradictory of atomic units, and is ultimately misunderstood if such experienced relations are seen as relations among "separate sensations." Peirce characterizes Firstness in terms of qualities of feeling, and notes of pure feeling, sensation, or qualitative immediacy, that it is absolutely simple,[17] yet, the experience of such "absolutely simples" is for him inseparable from the experience of continuity.[18] The interpretation of Lewis's 'given' in terms of atomic units abounds throughout the literature, though he characterizes the given, before the abstractive, objectifying activity of mind, as a Bergsonian duration.[19] Regardless of how frequently the classical pragmatists anticipate such potentially misleading interpretations of their respective positions by explicit disclaimers, their use of terminology continually draws interpreters in these directions, as they point out that various pragmatists could not ultimately escape the trap of the atomistic, psychologistic, subjectivist view of experience they were explicitly claiming to avoid.

Additionally, in their writings the terms chosen to indicate a level of experiencing foundational for common sense tend to be used in more than one way, which further complicates interpretation. Thus, Dewey uses *feeling*, and its correlate, *qualitative immediacy*, in three distinct senses. He uses it to indicate grasp of appearances within a perceptual context; to indicate the pervasive quality of a context; and to indicate a level of experiencing that is more rudimentary than perceptual consciousness.[20] Further, Dewey uses *primary experience* in two senses,

16 / Ibid., 2, p. 651.

17 / Peirce, 6.236.

18 / See, for example Peirce, 6.132. As will be seen in later chapters, there is a continuity inherent in Firstness that is distinct from, though interrelated with, the continuity of Thirdness.

19 / Lewis, *Mind and the World Order*, p. 58.

20 / Here the level of appearance, for Dewey as for the other pragmatists, emerges from a sophisticated focus taken within the context of perceptual awareness and hence must not be confounded with that level of experiencing that is more rudimentary than perceptual awareness.

which he frequently does not clearly distinguish. It sometimes indicates the realm of everyday perceptual awareness prior to the second-level interpretations of science or philosophy. Here primary experience is the "crude or macroscopic experience of everyday life."[21] However, Dewey also uses primary experience to indicate the level of experience here being discussed, a unity of activity undifferentiated by any thought distinctions. As Dewey so well summarizes this usage, experience "'is double-barrelled' in that it recognizes in its primary integrity no division between act and material, subject and object, but contains them both in an unanalyzed totality. 'Thing' and 'thought', as James says in the same connection, are single barrelled; they refer to products discriminated by reflection out of primary experience."[22]

Similarly, James uses the terms *sensation* or *feeling* in dual senses, both to indicate the grasp of appearance within the context of perceptual awareness, and to indicate pure experience as prior to perceptual awareness and to subject-object distinctions. Further, his own use of *pure experience* is frequently ambiguous because of the language used. For example, pure experience is at times used to indicate "pure" pure experience, while pure experience is usually used to indicate "relatively" pure experience,[23] though the qualifying terms are seldom incorporated into the discussion. Thus, *pure experience* is understood in two different ways, and characteristics of one are frequently transferred illegitimately to the other by his critics.[24] Lewis's use of *givenness*, to indicate both that processive continuity that is foundational for perceptual consciousness and that apprehension of appearances as a verification level within the structures of perceptual awareness, has been a source of much confusion.[25] A further distinction between "the given" and given passages of experience usually goes unnoticed because of the similarity of terminology, though it is an important distinction within his position.[26] Peirce's use of *Firstness* as involving both simplicity and feeling can be found to correlate in some sense with just about all of the above usages of the various terminologies.

21 / Dewey, *Experience and Nature*, pp. 15–16.

22 / Ibid., pp. 18–19.

23 / See especially *Essays in Radical Empiricism*, p. 46.

24 / These two senses do not correlate with the two senses of primary experience used by Dewey, though there is a correlation between "relatively pure experience" and Dewey's primary experience as a unity of activity undifferentiated by any thought distinctions.

25 / This confusion is largely responsible for the phenomenalistic, reductionistic interpretations of his position.

26 / This is to be found throughout *Analysis of Knowledge and Valuation*.

Thus, the present analysis proposes to avoid the terminology of feeling, sensation, or givenness, as well as pure experience or primary experience, in portraying a rudimentary level of experiencing foundational for the emergence of a perceptual world, in order to avoid both the historically misleading burden of meaning these words carry, and the ambiguities to which they give rise. Instead, a term will be introduced that will avoid these problems, both because it does not contain a history of psychologistic or atomistic connotations, and because it can be incorporated unambiguously into the context of terms used to indicate other facets of experience.

Experience as wider than perception and as the context within which perception emerges will be discussed, by using the concept of *anteception*. This term is taken from Peirce's terminology, *antecept* and *antecipium*,[27] which he introduces only briefly and obscurely within his writings. No claim is made that the concept as here used corresponds to Peirce's own intended meaning. In fact, what little evidence there is available within his writings to interpret his use of *antecept* and *antecipium* would seem to indicate that such is probably not the case. Thus, though the term is borrowed from Peirce, any specific meaning one may hold it to imply within Peirce's philosophy is left behind. As the above discussion anticipates, however, the term is intended to capture the basic thrust of the writings of the pragmatists in dealing with this level of experiencing. The term *anteception* as opposed to *feeling* or *sensation* is intended to stress that the difference between perceptual content and anteceptive content is not the distinction between physical and psychical, external and internal, or matter and mind, but rather between epistemic levels by which humans interact with that which is there. Precisely to cut beneath these traditional distinctions, pragmatists introduced their own terminologies of rudimentary experience—terminologies weighted, unfortunately, with the very historical traditions they are rejecting.

The experiential level termed *anteception* is constituted by the durational continuity of rudimentary experimental activity constitutive of organism-environment interaction. Anteception is an indefinitely rich matrix within which the process of perceptual awareness and cognition in general are rooted, and from which they emerge, and its character enters into their structure and content. Such durational continuity of rudimentary experimental activity is what will be called the *anteceptive*

27 / Peirce, 7.648.

field, and its boundaries the *anteceptive horizon*. The term *field* was used earlier to indicate the epistemic correlate of awareness; awareness and field form an inseparable unity. Here, it is "thickened" to include an ontological dimension. An anteceptive field by its very nature evinces the ontological presence of an independently there otherness. Further, such a thickened field is intended to indicate not a fixed static entity, but rather a field of action constituted by rudimentary organism-environment interaction. The term *horizon*, rather than *boundary*, is introduced to emphasize that the boundaries of a field (of activity), like a horizon, approach and recede in relation to activity and that, like a horizon, the boundaries are relative to a perspective. A horizon is a horizon from a perspective. Further, a horizon does not enclose, but opens outward.

Such a field, as constituted by rudimentary organism-environment interaction, is "there"; it is what we always experience, but we always experience it through the complex web of meanings we have woven into it through the dynamics of experience as experimental, as manifested in the vital intentionality of meaning as dispositional. The field is that primordial processive activity within, or upon, which we project the meaningful background for the delineation of objects, and which is foundational both for the human mode of being, and for the human mode of knowing, both at the levels of everyday lived experience and of scientific theorizing.

Anteception by its very character involves already what James imputes to "relatively" pure experience, a minimal interactive unity, an interactive unity from which subject and object emerge as epistemically grasped entities. Idealized anteception, like James's truly pure experience, is a limiting concept. Idealized anteception, like pure experience, is the "instant field of the present,"[28] but as James has well noted, "there is literally no such object as the present moment;" it is "a postulate of abstract thought," for the "passing moment" is the minimal fact.[29] If the purity of experience, which is but another name for feeling or sensation,[30] is a relative purity, then so also is the purity of sensation or feeling relative. If "the instant field of the present" as pure experience is a "postulate of abstract thought," then brute sensation or feeling is also a postulate of abstract thought.

Idealized anteception, like truly pure experience, is a philosophic ab-

28 / James, *Essays in Radical Empiricism*, p. 36.
29 / James, *A Pluralistic Universe* (1977), *The Works of William James*, p. 128.
30 / James, *Essays in Radical Empiricism*, p. 46.

straction or limiting concept analogous to that of a moment within process, or a point on a line. It represents the idealized moment of organism-environment interaction, and the pure concrete having, within such a moment, of the indefinitely rich universe within or upon which the dynamics of experience as experimental operate to create a world of perceived objects. Brute anteception would be interaction at an instant. But, the concept of interaction at an instant is an abstraction from the reality of process, and brute activity is an abstraction from the continuity of a dispositional tendency or vital intentionality. Such an abstraction represents the limiting point of the boundary of consciousness; the postulated 'moment' of the brute "having" of the stuff of immediate experience in that idealized instant before past and future enter into the very grasping of that which is had. This philosophic idealization is not an unreal one; it is the idealized moment of brute contact with that which we always experience through the dispositional activities expressive of the dynamics of experience as experimental. As James states, the idealized moment of pure experience "reduces to the notion of what is just entering into experience. . . . It is what is absolutely dumb and evanescent, the merely ideal limit of our minds."[31]

An idealization or limiting concept similar to James's is found in Peirce's characterization of brute sensation as an ideal limit indicating the boundary of consciousness.[32] Yet, again, such an idealized moment, because of its association with pure sensation, tends to imply the grasp, in that idealized instant, of an atomic sensory unit, though again this is not Peirce's intention. Idealized anteception, however, is intended to indicate unambiguously precisely the opposite. In that idealized moment before past and future enter into the character of what is grasped, what is there in the immediate interaction is an indefinitely rich matrix or complexity of a qualitatively rich spatial continuity, within which, however, the potentiality neither for separability nor for order are to be found. For within such a matrix there would be an indefinite richness but no sense of the temporal pulsations or directional flows or incipient activities, which are the source of both order and discreteness within experience.[33] To be orderable, or to be capable of displaying qualitative

31 / James, *Pragmatism* (1975), *The Works of William James*, p. 119.

32 / Peirce, 5.213; 7.465; Murray Murphey, *The Development of Peirce's Philosophy* (Cambridge: Harvard University Press, 1961), p. 416.

33 / Though there are both epistemological and ontological dimensions, the focus here is not on the ontological features of that which enters into experience *in its character as independent,* for already these "pulsations" are a product of interaction.

distinctness, is to pass beyond the static spread-outedness of the moment of idealized anteception to the durational spread-outedness of temporal flow, which reflects the pulsations of rudimentary experience within which directional order and qualitative distinctness can begin to emerge. As Peirce stresses, "Time as the universal form of change cannot exist unless there is something to undergo change and to undergo a change continuous in time there must be a continuity of changeable qualities."[34] Yet Peirce characterizes such a qualitative continuity as that immediacy that mind has "practically extinguished,"[35] for mind separates and orders. That such qualities cannot be taken as subjective is evidenced through the bringing together of two claims by Peirce, "Not only is consciousness continuous in a subjective sense. . . . Its object is ipso facto continuous. In fact, this infinitesimally spread out consciousness is a direct feeling of its contents as spread out."[36] Further, though "everything which is present to us is a phenomenal manifestation of ourselves," this "does not prevent its being a phenomenon of something without us, just as a rainbow is at once a manifestation both of the sun and of the rain."[37]

Similarly, the limiting concept of brute sensation or brute feeling for James does not draw one within the subjective, but rather throws one outward onto the universe. The focus on sensation as opposed to the focus on objects in the world is not, for James, the difference between internal and external, psychical and physical, but between modes of focusing on one and the same "stuff." The approach toward pure feeling gets closer not to mental content but to the grasp of surrounding environment as it "feels." Feeling is not a psychological category here but an epistemic level indicating "the minimum of grammatical subject, of objective presence, of reality known about, the mere beginning of knowledge."[38] Relatively pure experience represents for James "the immediate flux of life,"[39] but such a flux as it concretely occurs contains already a phenomenological dimension of human thrown-outness onto the universe through a primordial intentionality. As James succinctly expresses this, such a flux of life,

> immediately present now in each of us is a little past, a little future,
> a little awareness of our own body, of each other's persons, of these sub-

34 / Peirce, 6.132.   35 / Ibid.
36 / Peirce, 6.111.   37 / Peirce, 5.283.
38 / James, *Principles of Psychology*, 1, p. 218.
39 / James, *Essays in Radical Empiricism*, p. 46.

limities we are trying to talk about of the earth's geography, and the direction of history. . . . Feeling, however dimly and subconsciously, all these things, your pulse of inner life is continuous with them, belongs to them, and they to it. You can't identify it with either one of them rather than with the others.[40]

In the immediate flow of experience, in the immediate "feel" of temporality, knower and known cannot be distinguished because the flow belongs to both. Feeling, here, as an epistemic level, incorporates also an ontological dimension of human thrown-outness onto the universe and the intrusion within experience of both its brute otherness and the temporally rooted corporeal intentionality of one's own body. In brief, incorporated, at this primordial level, is a sense of the denseness of both sensor and what is sensed. At the level of anteceptive experience, the primordial unity within which both things and ideas come to be, sensor and sensed, are inseparably intertwined. Yet, though there is a fundamental unity, there is also a sense of the intertwining of two distinct dimensions: the independence of what is sensed and the role of human activity in the sensing.

Anteceptive experience must be understood, in its ontological status, as an inseparable unity of organism-environment interaction, the phenomenological dimensions of which reveal themselves in anteceptive experience. If this is ignored, the epistemic distinction within experience of subjective and objective, as ways of interpreting anteceptive experience, is confounded with the ontological status of organism-environment interaction, and the thick noetically creative organism whose thinking makes such distinctions dissolves into an ephemeral "subjective series" constructed from pure experience. This confusion brings into question the entire fabric of the position intended. Thus Lewis carefully notes of his major focus on epistemic issues, that while the "order of knowing" is at the forefront of his analysis, the "order of being" is always lurking in the background and cannot be forgotten.[41] Lewis's somewhat brief but crucial discussions of the ontological dimensions of a natural being immersed in a natural environment as ingredient in the very texture of the emergence of perceptual awareness are virtually ignored.[42] As Lewis expresses the intrusion of ontological presence within experience, "if independent factuality did not force it-

40 / James, *Pluralistic Universe*, p. 129.
41 / Lewis, *Mind and the World Order*, Appendix D, pp. 425–426.
42 / Lewis, *Analysis of Knowledge and Valuation*, Introduction.

self upon us, we should have to invent it in order to exist as beings who think."[43] Such an invention, however, is unnecessary, for it "does not need to be assumed nor to be proved, but only to be acknowledged."[44]

This intertwining of organism-environment interaction at the heart of experience is well expressed in Dewey's claim that "experience is *of* as well as *in* nature. . . . Things interacting in certain ways *are* experience; they are what is experienced. Linked in certain other ways with another natural object—the human organism—they are *how* things are experienced as well. Experience thus reaches down into nature; it has depth."[45] Mead's description of the ontological dimension of experience is well capsulated in his claim that, in becoming an object, something has the character of "actually or potentially acting upon the organism from within itself." He calls this character that of having an inside.[46] And such an acting upon the organism cannot be understood in terms of passive resistance, but as active resistance, resistance to our organic activity.[47] Thus, the phenomenological description of the characteristics found at the heart of experience provides the ultimate basis for, and the justification of, the use of the pragmatic ontological category or organism-environment interaction in understanding the ontological dimensions of the field of awareness.

The distinctions between subject and object, mind and matter, internal and external, are epistemic categorizations emerging from or derivative from, the foundational epistemic unity of anteceptive experience that forms the epistemic foundation for such distinctions. They are the products of conscious activity as the function which makes such categorizations or distinctions.[48] But this function itself emerges within the context of a concrete purposive organism immersed in a natural universe, an organism whose behavior is permeated by a vital intentionality constitutive of noetic creativity. Thus, though the subjective, as opposed to the objective, is a derivative epistemic distinction rooted in the foundational epistemic unity of anteceptive experience, anteceptive experience itself is ontologically rooted in the interactive unity of a concrete, noetically creative biological organism immersed in a natural world.

43 / Lewis, "Realism or Phenomenalism?" *Collected Papers*, p. 339.

44 / Lewis, *Analysis of Knowledge and Valuation*, p. 361.

45 / Dewey, *Experience and Nature*, pp. 12–13 (italics in text).

46 / Mead, *Philosophy of the Present*, p. 137.

47 / Ibid.

48 / James, of course, develops the view that consciousness is a function, not a stuff. *Essays in Radical Empiricism*, pp. 3–19.

Such a foundational ontological and epistemic unity at the heart of experience is expressed by Peirce in a telling criticism of Kant: "That time and space are innate ideas, so far from proving that they have merely a mental existence, as Kant thought, ought to be regarded as evidence of their reality. For the constitution of the mind is the result of evolution under the influence of experience."[49]

Indeed, the fundamental horizons of anteceptive experience are spatial and temporal, though, as will be seen, the temporal perhaps emerges as the key dimension. Within the context of these spatial and temporal horizons, one can begin to speak of the beginnings of horizons of meaning, or the beginnings of partial ordering within the context of anteceptive experience.[50]

As has been shown, the minimal anteceptive experience always involves a durational flow. Anteceptive experience is not the experience of pure immediacy, for it is filled with the rudimentary vital intentionality of the temporal structure of human behavior as anticipatory. Such a minimal anteceptive experience is experimental, for it involves an anticipation of a next experience to come, something for which we are waiting, an expectation set in motion by the temporal stretch of human activity. It is instrumental, for it is activity guided by direction. Every field of awareness is "permeated by initiation, direction or intent, and consequence or import."[51] At its most rudimentary level, such expectation, rooted in the experience of anteceptive flow, may be the expectation not of some specific complex, but of a general sense of more to come as, in the anteceptive flow, the processive present contains within itself a future emerging within the temporal spread-outedness of the present. Indeed, there is no span of time so short "as not to contain something for the confirmation of which we are waiting."[52] Even the most rudimentary conscious experience, then, "contains within itself the ele-

---

49 / Peirce, Section 14, Article 23, p. 33 of Microfilm Edition. Peirce asserts that the pragmatist cannot deny a doctrine of innate ideas (5.504). What Peirce means is that the pragmatist must hold to the embeddedness within behavior of dispositional tendencies. However, dispositional tendencies are always "tendencies in relation to" or a "readiness to act in a certain way under given circumstances" (5.480). Thus, what is emphasized by innate ideas is the interactional element in experience.

50 / This context may point the way toward a unifying perspective for understanding James's seemingly contradictory claims in which he holds both for a "chaos" of pure experience and for the apprehension of a common, objective space-time order (*Principles of Psychology*).

51 / Dewey, *Experience and Nature*, p. 85.

52 / Peirce, 7.675.

ment of suggestion or expectation," and thus the object of experience "even with an infant is homogeneous with the world of the adult."[53]

Such rudimentary expectation enters into the very character of the anteceptive field. James's use of the term *pure experience* to indicate both the limiting point of experience at an instant and the indefinitely rich durational matrix of relative purity tends, at times, to obscure the radical nature of his nonspectator theory of knowledge. Not only is consciousness, the active function, the source of the distinction between inner and outer, but it is partially constitutive of the very character of the stream of pure experience that provides the stuff of such interpretation, for relatively pure experience reflects, in its very nature, the rudimentary pulsations of a vital intentionality. And the mode of focusing on, or abstracting from, or delimiting within, the stream of pure experience reflects the character of meaningful objectivities that we interpret the experience to be an instance of, for, "as a matter of fact we can hardly take an impression at all, in the absence of a preconception of what impressions there may possibly be."[54] This sense of "what impressions there may possibly be" emerges within the cumulative process of grasping the "stuff" of pure experience in ways that work in the context of the anticipations of future experience contained in our meaning structures. Here, at the most primordial level of experience, is to be found that same interplay of experiential genesis and a priori legislation which was found to be operative at the level of fully developed pragmatic meaning. Peirce summarizes such a position in his claim that "when a feeling emerges into immediate consciousness it always appears as a modification of a more or less general object already in the mind."[55] James expresses this cumulative interplay in his rhetorical question, "Does the river make its banks, or do the banks make the river?"[56] James's answer is clear: each helps mold the other. What reveals itself as the stuff of the stream of relatively pure experience is not just a content revealed, but rather the product of a "taking" which can fulfill the anticipatory structure of human experience as experimental. In short, the stuff of experience that comes to awareness within the context of pragmatic meaning is itself partially constituted in the taking, and the taking will remain a taking only if it works.

---

53 / Dewey, "The Existence of the World as a Logical Problem," in vol. 8 (1979) of *The Middle Works*, p. 95.

54 / James, *Pragmatism*, p. 119.

55 / Peirce, 6.141–6.142.

56 / James, *Pragmatism*, p. 120.

Thus, the anteceptive field, within which both things and ideas come to be, is itself partially constituted in its character by the vital intentionality of purposive organic response. Such purposive organic response infuses the features of its creative, vital intentionality into the very fabric of the anteceptive field, and its anticipatory character demands the function of verification as the fulfillment of expectation.

In the temporal pulsations of the anteceptive durational flow within which perceptual experience develops, order has not yet emerged as fully constituted within the matrix of the anteceptive field. It has what can perhaps be called a *partial order*, or, in James's terms, it is, conversely, a *partial chaos*.[57] It is a partial-chaos, or only partially ordered, not because there is a lack of relationships that full blown perceptual experience must provide, but because there is an overabundance of relationships, an indefinitely rich relational field from which perceptual awareness must select and, in the process of selecting, organize. A total lack of order, or in Peirce's terms a universe of chance, is "simply our actual world viewed from the standpoint of an animal at the vanishing point of intelligence. There would be neither memory nor expectation."[58] For partial order to emerge within an anteceptive field, there must be a durational present that allows for the operation of memory and expectation. As has been seen, such a durational present cannot be understood in terms of discrete moments of a sequence, but only in terms of an unbroken continuum as a process, and with depth.

In the context of such a primitive temporal matrix awareness is not yet focused around "enduring objectivities." Within such a primitive field of awareness, assimilation of similar anteceptive experiences establishes the experience of repetition. Such experienced repetition can be attributed neither to that which is there independently of the vital intentionality of organic response alone, nor to response alone, but to emergents within a durational continuity that belongs to both, or within which both are intertwined. In the anteceptive constitution of "brute" repeatability, the only reference to future experience is that of "it has been seen before and may be seen again." However, such constituted experience of repetition emerges within the context of similar anticipations and similar tendencies to act in light of a particular content grasped. Thus, the emergence of repetition within experience, of the

---

57 / James holds to a total chaos of first impressions, but first impressions are a limiting concept. Thus, relatively pure experience would seem to provide a "limited" or "partial" chaos. James develops toward this view of a "partial" chaos.

58 / Peirce, 6.406. Memory, like expectation, depends on a law of organization, a dispositional tendency operating in a durational temporal flow. This will be indicated below.

awareness of repeatable content, occurs within the context of the rudimentary dynamics of experience as experimental.[59]

This process of establishing repeatability at its most fundamental level is precisely the process of forming the "sensory core" of the schematic structure.[60] The welter of anteceptive experience is taken up into a perspective by the schematic structure, and the sensory core of the schematic structure becomes the criteria for grasping a portion of anteceptive experience as an instance of a kind, and as representative of an appearing object. Thus, the core of the schematic structure, as criterion for grasping sensory cue, is the criterion by which anteceptive content is transformed into stimulus to action toward an object.[61] Such stimuli to action do not come in atomic bits; they are cut from the continuity of anteceptive experience and reflect the character of the "cutting activity." Further, as has already been seen, what is thus cut from the concretely rich matrix of anteceptive experiences is not what can be understood as the contents of any separate sense. The concreteness of anteceptive durational pulsations becomes creatively organized as possibilities of acting toward an object relative to anteceptive content grasped via schematic sensory core, and the unity of the schematic core incorporates the unity of a portion of a diversely rich qualitative continuity, not the unity of a self-enclosed content of a particular sense. Even the most minimal anteceptive experience is complex. At no level of experience are "pure simples" to be found.

Further, as has been shown, such a sensory core, precisely as the core of the schematic image, is never experienced in its purity, but rather emerges within experience as the criterion of recognition of appearing objects. The closest one can come to grasp of sensory core within our perceptual world is grasp of appearance, with its core of sensory content. Such a grasp of appearance is derivative from a world of appearing objects, for it reflects the structuring of objectivities embedded in pragmatic meaning. "What is there" is grasped only as it emerges from the transactional matrix of anteceptive experience via the structures of pragmatic meaning.

In the chapter on pragmatic meaning, only the epistemic aspects of

59 / To take experienced repetition as independent of the intentional link of knower and known is to confuse the categories of process epistemology with the remnants of those of substance metaphysics. The correlate to this is a spectator theory of knowledge at least in some minimal sense. Repetition is an epistemic emergent, not a metaphysical given. The epistemic status of repetition, when not recognized, leads to interpretive problems in virtually all the classical American pragmatists.

60 / See chapter 2.

61 / This is of course not to be confused with stimulus-response activity.

perceptual awareness were discussed. Now, however, such an analysis can be rounded out by a more direct discussion of the ontological presence manifested in perceptual awareness via the structures of pragmatic meaning. And here anteceptive content, perceived object, and apprehended appearance will be shown to be three different levels of focusing on one and the same ontological presence. That which intrudes itself inexplicably into experience is not bare datum, but rather evidences itself as the over-againstness of a thick universe "there" for my activity. This externally real from a certain particular place does not, at any level of awareness, cause a reaction as does a stimulus. Rather, even in the most rudimentary anteceptive flow, it has a minimal significance, and is acted upon as it acts upon us. The structures that come to awareness in experience are an interactional unity of such activities.

Meanings are structured sequences of possible experiences ordered in certain ways. To know reality of any type is to recognize sequences of possible experiences by relating given experience to possible experiences in a way anticipated by some meaning pattern. Thus, the object of awareness is the independently real, and yields knowledge of the independent nature of the real, in the sense that we know the nature of the independently real when we know its ability to enter into our experience in a certain way. This ability to enter into our experience in a certain way is the nature of the independently real. How a thing appears in what is chosen as the "standard situation" becomes a revelation of the "real" characteristics of its being, which in turn manifest themselves in varying ways in varying perspectives. These perspectival characteristics are incorporated in the varying schematic forms within the internal structure of meaning, and certain schemata are taken as indicative of the "standard perspective," or, in common parlance, as indicative of the "real" character of the property or object.

Abstract knowledge claims do not constitute our main access to the natural universe; concrete experience does. The beginning infiltrations of meanings as embodied in human activity are, however, immediately present in even the most rudimentary anteceptive grasp. Conversely, the semiotic relationships embodied in pragmatic meaning are not the products of the free play of nonreferential signs expressed in language, but rather are contoured within limits by the historically grounded dynamic forces which are there in their own right. Thus, Peirce can make the seemingly paradoxical claim that "the object of final belief, which exists only in consequence of the belief, should itself produce the belief."[62]

62 / Peirce, 7.340.

It can be seen again that this position undercuts the dichotomy of foundationalism or nonfoundationalism and along with it, the closely related dichotomies of realism or antirealism and objectivism or relativism since each, in its own way, represents the alternatives of an absolute grounding of knowledge or skepticism. The present position provides an orientation within which these sets of alternatives cannot work. The objects that come to awareness do not exist independently of or prior to human activity, nor can we work back in experience to a direct grasp of anything that is as it is prior to its emergence within the context of experimental activity. Yet the concretely rich anteceptive field provides the source of, as well as the touchstone for the workability of, the meaning structures which yield the framework of any knowledge. Further, this concretely rich anteceptive matrix incorporates an ontological presence as one aspect ingredient in it. At the very heart of the temporal stretch of human behavior as anticipatory is a creativity, expressive of the experimental nature of experience, that is at once unified with that ontological presence but that renders its grasp in terms of any absolute grounding impossible. The unity denies the arbitrariness of antifoundationalism or antirealism, or relativism. The temporally founded creativity denies the absoluteness of foundationalism or realism or objectivism. The full significance of this orientation in undercutting these popular but self-defeating dichotomies will be seen in later chapters, but the beginnings of its relevance are to be found in the character of the anteceptive field.

As has been shown, the indefinitely rich matrix which constitutes the anteceptive field involves a spatial-temporal continuity, so rich in qualitative diversity and directional activity that no pattern or order is possible without discrimination. Such directional flows in their temporally rooted concreteness emerge within the context of rudimentary organism-environment interaction, and thus emerge as an intertwining of the rudimentary creative pulsations of the human organism projecting toward a future and the dynamic activities operative in the surrounding natural universe. At the very heart of such an anteceptive field is the experience of temporality, processive continuity, the spread-outness of durational flow. And at the very heart of such an anteceptive grasp of temporality is the experience of the generative activities inherent in the dynamics of the multitudinous directional flows that must be ordered through discrimination. Thus, here is found the concrete experience for understanding the extensional "if-then" built into the internal structure of meaning as expressive of causal relations. Although lawlike regularity can account for the workability of the if-then relational generalities asserting probabilistic claims within the schematic aspects of pragmatic meaning, their emergence within the internal structure of meaning from the anteceptive field accounts for the understanding of such law-like character as the exemplification of causal forces. Acceptance of a uniformity of nature cannot provide a sense of causal relatedness; the sense of causal efficacy at the heart of anteceptive experience provides, however, a basis for belief in uniformity.[63]

The structure of human behavior as anticipatory implies an antecep-tive sense of the future. Such an anteceptive sense of the future is not an induction from past experience, but is at the heart of experience in the durational present. Indeed, it is the experience of the durational present, as past flowing into future, which founds our very sense of the past. Thus, the very possibility of inductive assimilation is rooted in the sense of the durational present as incorporating a sense of both past and future. This sense of the durational present both requires and makes possible the tem-porally founded structure of human behavior as anticipatory.[64]

Some writers hold that brute shock provides an example of an experi-ence devoid of inference, expectation, or connection. But shock presup-poses expectation, regardless of how rudimentary. The anteceptive sense of the future, even if it contains no specific expectation, contains a vague sense of anticipatory possibilities as "fitting" and excludes some vague range of possibilities, one of which is actualized in the "brute" sense of shock. The experience of shock illustrates not a denial of the inher-ently anticipatory, experimental nature of experience, but rather the frustration of irrepressible anticipation as constitutive of experimental activity.

The structure of human behavior as anticipatory both requires and makes possible the emergence of a priori structures of knowing within experience. Such a priori structures begin their formation in the context of anteceptive experience, for "a priori character is no exclusive func-tion of thought. Every biological function, every motor attitude, every vital impulse as the carrying vehicle of experience is thus a priorily regu-lative in prospective reference; what we call expectation, anticipation,

63 / See previous chapter. The question of the probability factor still remains. This will be dealt with in later chapters.

64 / Thus, to speak of spatial-temporal order as "innate" and as the result of evolution (see nn. 49, 50), is not to indicate the ordered content of some particular mathematical sys-tem. It indicates an anteceptive sense of the spatial-temporal continuity that both requires and makes possible the structure of human behavior as anticipatory. This anteceptive sense founds not only the possibility of any abstract system that conceptually orders, but also the very possibility of the genesis of rudimentary meanings, and the very emergence of a rudi-mentary partial order or partial chaos as the foundation for the possibility of such meanings.

choice, are pregnant with this constitutive and organizing power."[65] Even the most rudimentary anteceptive experience contains within itself these elements of suggestion or expectation. Further, this a priorily regulative feature rooted in activity "makes possible the subject-matter of perception not as a material cut out from an instantaneous field, but a material that designates the effects of our possible actions,"[66] or, in other terms, gives rise to our "sense of the experientially possible but not experientially now actual."[67] The temporal stretch constitutive of a priori analyticity within the structure of pragmatic meaning is rooted in the temporal stretch of human behavior as anticipatory.

Further, the principle of consistency, and the if-then ordering of ordinary inference that explicates our meanings in accordance with it, is itself rooted in the structure of behavior. Our fundamental ways of behaving toward the world around us, that are made explicit in our accepted logic, are those ways of behaving that have lasted because they work.[68] The final ground of the validity of the principle of consistency, as well as the validity of ordinary inference, is firmly rooted in a pragmatic, evolutionary-based direction toward survival. As Lewis notes, such fundamental logical principles are rooted in a "pragmatic imperative"; if they are rejected, then thought and action become stultified.[69] Thus Dewey can hold that the serial relation in logic is rooted in the condi-

---

65 / Dewey, "Experience and Objective Idealism," p. 136.

66 / Dewey, "Perception and Organic Action," p. 13.

67 / Lewis, *Analysis of Knowledge and Valuation*, p. 17.

68 / Chapter 3 noted in relation to James, that the experiential genesis and endurance through workability of the a priori in common sense and science do not ultimately contradict the dynamics by which the most fundamental principles of logic are accepted. In light of the discussion of the "if-then" relation in the previous chapter, the question might arise whether the implication relation here being discussed is that of the intensional or the extensional "if-then." Apart from purposive selectivity as a priori regulative, there is no discrimination of extensional "if-then" relations, but an indefinitely rich concrete matrix upon which purposive selectivity must operate. Thus, any grasped extensional if-then always is contained in the a priori regulative aspect of anticipatory structure, even at the most rudimentary level. The if-then of a priori implication in any transaction, no matter how primitive, is always logically prior to the discrimination of meaningful extensional relationships. The if-then of the relation of human activity to anticipated ends, as the foundation of ordinary inference, must be understood as the intensional if-then, for only from this backdrop can the if-then of experienced causal relationships come into focus. Thus, Lewis stresses that even the "extensional logic" of material implication is a system of intensionally related meaning containments. A later chapter will show that the extensional if-then of real relations is itself not expressible in the "extensional" logic of material implication.

69 / Lewis, *Our Social Inheritance* (Bloomington: Indiana University Press, 1957), p. 100.

tions of life itself. Indeed, rationality is precisely "the generalized idea of the means-consequence relation as such."[70]

Dewey can deny a fixed difference between logic and the methodology of scientific and practical inquiry, for all are rooted ultimately in the pragmatic interaction of organism and environment. Any inquiry develops in its own ongoing course the logical standards and forms to which further inquiry must submit. Moreover, inquiry, in its emergence in the context of basic human response to situations, may generate problems in its own development, and thus logic becomes autonomous in solving the problems necessary for its own advancement.[71] The implication relation, and the principle of consistency in which it is rooted, are the fundamental tools for the explication of creatively generated meaning relations, whether at the level of abstract logical systems, or at the level of concrete perceptual awareness,[72] and these principal tools by which meanings are logically related are themselves rooted in the anticipatory structure of human activity. Indeed, it is precisely the if-then implication relation rooted in the temporal spread of primitive anteceptive experience and incorporated in the dispositional generation of schematic forms within the internal structure of meaning that diverse symbolic systems are attempting to capture in getting at the "truth" of implication.[73]

Thus, the sense of temporality and its felt dynamic activities or directional flows in the durational continuity of a rudimentary unity of knower and known which is incorporated within the heart of the internal dynamics of pragmatic meaning, allows for the emergence of the common-sense object, for any common-sense beliefs about the world, and for verification or falsification in the temporally rooted structure of human behavior as anticipatory. The sense of temporality is the foundation for the possibility of a priori claims relative to a conceptual perspective, for the meaningfulness of explanations in terms of causal re-

70 / Dewey, *Logic: The Theory of Inquiry,* pp. 387, p. 10.

71 / Ibid., p. 4.

72 / For a system of logical relationships, as for any system of meaning, there is a difference between the validity of properly explicated meaning relationships and the experiential reasons, in terms of its usefulness, for accepting that particular system of meaning.

73 / Thus, Lewis develops his system of strict implication to avoid the paradoxes of material implication, and holds that some logic is true, not in the sense that, like any other of many possible abstract logical systems, it is self-consistent, but in the sense that the choice of some logical systems will prove more useful than others in being applicable to ordinary inference. Some logical systems are better able than others to explicate, at the abstract symbolic level, that anteceptive sense of implication rooted in the heart of the temporal spread of human activity as anticipatory.

latedness, and for the possibility of scientific experimentation yielding evidence of any kind.

In the pulsations of anteceptive experience, the organism begins the rudimentary constitution of a priori possibilities, and thus it begins the rudimentary constitution of itself as a processive system of possibilities of acting toward that otherness that intrudes itself within experience. Again this is not to say that the organism relegates some anteceptive experiences to the subjective, as opposed to the objective. Such activity presupposes the function of consciousness as grasping experience in terms of the derivative epistemic distinctions of subjective and objective. This function already presupposes a thick dynamic organism creatively structuring its experience. Only through the possibilities of acting in relation to its environment, which are incorporated in the vital intentionality or purposive activity of an ontologically rich, creative, active being, can experienced content be separated into the epistemically based distinctions of subjective and objective.

To relegate to the subjective is already to have a self. To constitute a self is not to engage in a process of epistemically relegating bits of anteceptive experience to the "internal" or the "subjective." Rather, to constitute oneself is a process in which human being and knowing are brought to bear most directly on the development of each. To have a self is to have a reflexive epistemic ability by which one can come to know the thick, dense ontological reality that constitutes the active, ever-growing, ever-developing system of creative possibilities that reaches out both to structure its everyday experience in terms of what belongs to "my inner experience" and what belongs to the "external world," and to permeate the anteceptive field itself, from which such structurings emerge, with the character of its anticipatory pulsations. Such a center of activity is guided in its development by the interactive unity of its creative possibilities with that ontological "otherness" which intrudes upon it, and also by the opening up of new possibilities or the closing of old ones, due not to the intrusion of ontological presence, but due to the directive force of one's own (and hence, indirectly, at least in part, society's own) interpretation of what potential lies within this particular center of creativity.[74] I, as knower, am constituted by an ontologically rich, dense, system of possibilities, partially molded by an interaction with a dense ontological "otherness." As I am *knower of* these possibili-

---

74 / This statement touches on the social nature of the individual, a theme which will be explicitly developed in chapter 7, which will show that James's supposed "rugged individualism" does not contradict but rather requires the social character of the individual as

ties, an interpreter of them, my interpretation enters into my under-standing of what these possibilities are, and hence influences the way I develop or direct them toward a future. In this sense, the constitution of the self is a task at once ontological and epistemic. The foundational constitution of the self begins, like the constitution of any meaningful awareness, with the rudimentary grasp of temporal pulsations in ante-ceptive experience, developing into the common-sense grasp of oneself in terms of types of potentialities, dispositional tendencies, or habits of response. And this constitution of the self must be prior to the very pos-sibility of the derivative epistemic task of relegating experience to the subjective or internal as opposed to the objective or external in terms of two different meaning networks by which experience is organized. Un-less I have begun to develop a self both ontologically and epistemologi-cally at a foundational level, I cannot begin to make this self the "con-tainer" for what does not workably fit into the external world, but which does workably fit when relegated to "my subjective contents."

I cannot know the immediacy of "I" in its creative functioning, for to know is to interpret, bring meaning, have so-called "immediate experi-ence" through mediation.[75] But though I cannot know the immediacy of the "I" functioning in its immediacy, I can have an anteceptive sense of this functioning. As Mead states, the immediacy of the "I" functioning is "felt" in the breakdown and reconstruction of a situation. The objec-tivity of the situation breaks down as a segment of a meaning system fails to work, and in the span of time before the new objective situation has emerged, there is, in Mead's terms, a "feel," or an anteceptive sense of the immediacy of the "I" functioning in its immediacy as a creative

---

emphasized by the other pragmatists. This common acceptance by all the pragmatists of the importance of the social will be assumed in the development of a pragmatic metaphys-ics in chapter 6, though such a common acceptance cannot be clarified until the discussion of pragmatic community in chapter 7. Here, however, it can at least be briefly noted that once the notion of the atomic unit falls by the wayside, the very opposition between indi-vidualism and communality becomes questionable.

75 / As Mead notes, there is "an attitude of observing oneself in which both the ob-server and the observed appear. To be concrete, one remembers asking himself how he could undertake to do this, that, or the other, chiding himself for his shortcomings or pluming himself upon his achievements." Though one finds both a subject and an object, "it is a subject that is now an object of observation and has the same nature as the object self." In brief, it is not a true "I," but a "me." No reflection can ever yield a true "I" for reflection can only yield an *object of* reflection ("The Social Self," *Selected Writings*, p. 142). The self, as both knower and known, as both constitutor and constituted, includes both the "I" and the "me" as functionally distinct aspects. This claim, incorporated here, is to be found through-out Mead's writings.

system of possibilities.[76] In this span of time, as a meaningful context disintegrates, there is a return to anteceptive experience. This elusive but real anteceptive sense of the immediacy of "I" creatively functioning relates, it would seem, to James's hunt for the middle term in the reasoning process,[77] or, in Mead's terms, the search for the copular phase.[78]

Such an understanding of the thick ontological dimension of the person as a dense system of possibilities creatively acting toward a world, shows also that our experience of other ontologically thick persons, whose commonness and uniqueness are manifest in their creative interactions, is a primary fact of experience. We do not begin with subjective contents as constitutive of our own person, and then from the outward behavior of another being "infer" that this, "like me," is a person having "subjective contents" or "inner intents and motives." The ontological depth and density of other persons with whom I interact is something I experience; I do not think or infer to them, but rather I interact with them. The unique ontological activity of the human organism that is not my own intrudes itself within my experience as its own kind of ontological presence.

As has been shown, the rich matrix of anteceptive experience is taken up into the structure of perceptual awareness. Anteceptive experience, at the level of perceptual awareness, is not, however, totally confined within the structurings of perceptual meanings. As has already been noted, perceptual awareness cannot be understood in terms of isolated percepts. Rather, as James has so well observed, perceptual awareness incorporates both a focus and a fringe. I am aware of my pen, for example, as an object resting on a desk littered with papers, and located in a study filled with reference books. My perception of the pen is fringed in this way. This fringe, nonfocal and undelineated, permeates the perceptual focus of the pen with all sorts of anticipations and expectations. When anticipated experiences in dealing with the pen in its contextual setting do not occur, then I may become explicitly aware of the fringe itself. Any aspect of a fringe is capable of becoming the focus of a perceptual awareness, which would then have its own fringe of nonfocal awareness.

In both of these aspects, however, focus and fringe, primordial or anteceptive experience has been incorporated into the structure of perceptual awareness. The fringe of nonfocal awareness occurs within the con-

---

76 / Mead, "Definition of the Psychical," pp. 25–59.
77 / James, *Principles of Psychology*, 1, Chapter 9.
78 / Mead, "Definition of the Psychical," p. 58.

text of perceptual structure and at any time can become the focus of perceptual awareness. The changing contexts of focus and fringe occur within the structures of pragmatic meaning.

At this point the focus-fringe relation may seem to function in a verificatory way without resorting to a change in epistemic levels.[79] This function, however, can best be understood as guiding the projection of correct interpretations, rather than as part of the logical structure of verification, or of a restructuring in case of falsification. For example, the fringe of desk and littered papers may prevent me from wrongly interpreting the pen I see from across the room as a piece of plant root because the sense of fit would be wrong. The plant root doesn't fit the fringe of my perceptual awareness, though were my perceptual awareness fringed with the backdrop of the table and plant parts to be found in my hothouse, I might immediately interpret that object as a piece of plant root. And if I wrongly interpret the pen as a piece of plant root, the correction may occur because of the emerging sense of lack of fit, given the nature of the fringe. In the process of restructuring or reinterpreting the "plant root" as a pen, however, there is a breakdown and restructuring of the appearance.[80] Thus, while the relation of appearance and object is a logical one grounded in the internal structure of meaning and essentially ingredient in the issue of verification, the relation of focus and fringe is the impetus for the correct meaningful grasp of some focal object, or for the beginning of verificatory or restructuring activity. Thus, though the concept of fringe is relevant for the issue of verification, it is not ingredient in the logical structure of verification.

What is important about the relation between focus and fringe for the purposes of the present discussion is that any aspect of any fringe can become the focal object, now surrounded by a new fringe. Yet the rich matrix of the durational flows which constitutes the anteceptive field, because it embodies the concreteness of an indefinite rich matrix, can never be exhausted in the meaning structures within which it emerges for conscious perceptual awareness. Rather, its richness spills over its meaning containers, it overflows any demarcations set by conscious awareness, both in terms of focus and fringe. Its overflow cannot become

79 / This relates to what is briefly referred to in chapter 3 as linear verification and as not essential in understanding the structure of verification.

80 / As was seen in chapter 2, in perceptual awareness we are aware of the thing that appears, though when expectations are frustrated, when verification requires a reflective change of focus, appearances, rather than things appearing, become the content of awareness. In changing to the verification level of appearances, both the focus and fringe within perceptual awareness are "removed" by a withholding of judgments concerning future experience or contextual reference.

the focal point of explicit awareness because it eludes the structures of that which allows the anteceptive field to come to explicit awareness.[81] Yet the spillage, the overflow, is there in experience, and its pervasive but unfocused and unfocusable tonality pervades both focus and fringe. Anteception is not merely a foundation for the emergence of perception. Rather, perceptual awareness, in addition to having a focus and fringe, is pervaded by an anteceptive tonality. Though a fringe can be made the focal point of another perception, experience always is richer and thicker than anything that can become the object of focus or the object of conscious awareness. Anteceptive concreteness overflows perceptual awareness, and lends its tonality to the tonality of a perceptual context.

This added ingredient would seem to correlate with what Dewey calls the quality of a situation. For Dewey, a pervasive quality characterizes a situation and the objects within it. Such a pervasive quality, however, is not itself an object, nor can it become an object. It is not a quality *in* a situation, but a quality *of* a situation.[82] Similarly, anteceptive overflow fuses its own character into the tonality of the concreteness of the perceptual context. There are thus three irreducible dimensions of a situation or experiential context: focus, fringe, and anteceptive tonality. Though these three aspects are present in both James and Dewey, each tends to conflate fringe and tonality, but in diverse directions. This can best be indicated from the perspective of Dewey's characterization of James's concept of fringe. Dewey objects that "the 'fringe' of James seems to me to be a somewhat unfortunate way of expressing the role of the underlying qualitative character that constitutes a situation—unfortunate because the metaphor tends to treat it as an additional element instead of an all-pervasive influence in determining other contents."[83] Dewey here would seem to deny the role of the fringe as a possible object of perceptual focus. The fringe has here collapsed into a pervasive quality which cannot become an object of perceptual focus.[84]

---

81 / There is a qualification here. The chapter on "world" will show that what overflows within our world may be caught from the perspective of a conceivably different world, but then there would still be an irretrievably vague and ultimately uncapturable, though different, overflow.

82 / The ambiguities of Dewey's use of the term *quality* were indicated earlier in this chapter.

83 / John Dewey, "Qualitative Thought," in vol. 5 (1984) of *The Later Works*, p. 248, n. 1.

84 / This view gains support from some of Dewey's writings (see, for example, *Experience and Nature*, p. 227), while it is contradicted by other of his claims (see, for example, *Experience and Nature*, pp. 235–236). He never adequately distinguishes quality and fringe, thus allowing for his ambiguity of usage.

James's own discussion of fringe seems to indicate precisely the reverse. Any aspect of a fringe can become the object of perceptual focus, now surrounded by a new fringe. As James stresses, one and the same content may be at one time the "kernel" and at other times the fringe.[85] Thus, the tonality, or what Dewey calls the pervasive quality, which cannot become such a focal object, is merged with the concept of fringe as that which is vague relative to a particular focus, but can become the topic or focus. Indeed, the doctrine of the fringe frequently leads James not to what eludes the network of pragmatic meanings, but to the way perceptual awareness relates to the functioning of concepts. As he explicates the implications of his doctrine of the fringe, "the geometer, with his one definite figure before him, knows perfectly that his thoughts apply to countless other figures as well, and that although he *sees* lines of a certain special bigness, direction, color, etc. he *means* not one of these details."[86] James holds that in light of his analysis of the fringe, he must decide in favor of conceptualism over nominalism, affirming the mind's ability to think things, qualities, relations, and so forth, abstracted from the perceptual experiences.[87] Here the concept of fringe leads not to that which eludes being grasped by the structures of perceptual awareness, but to the contrast of a specificity or concreteness grasped by perceptual meanings with the abstractness of the conceptual. Even James's discussions of the fringe that seem to come closest to the concept of tonality or pervasive quality, those that speak of suffusions, overtones, halos, and the importance of the vague and the inarticulate,[88] yet point, in the context of his discussion, always to that which can be made explicit, which can become the focal object or "topic of interest."[89] Thus, Dewey captures the pervasive quality or tonality, but tends thereby to lose a distinctive dimension of the fringe as a possible object of focal awareness. James, however, in making full use of the fringe as presently vague but as a possible topic of interest or focus, tends to conflate this functioning of the fringe within the structures of pragmatic meaning with a functioning of tonality as that which is irreducibly and irretrievably vague. His attempt to express both of these functions in the language of fringe does not allow him fully to discriminate two distinct dimensions within experience, though his discussions nevertheless tend to point in this direction.[90]

85 / James, *Principles of Psychology*, I, p. 271.
86 / Ibid., p. 446.   87 / Ibid., pp. 446–447.
88 / Ibid., pp. 249, 451–452, n.   89 / Ibid., p. 250.
90 / This does not represent a real disagreement but a difference in emphasis. Their respective tendencies to conflate in diverse directions perhaps have their roots in their di-

The above discussion has attempted to show that anteceptive tonality, as pervasive of a conceptual context of focus and fringe, is a third
contextual aspect that is irreducible to the other two. Yet it is not totally
independent of the other two, for the structure of a perceptual context
fuses its character, both in terms of focus and fringe, into the concreteness of anteceptive tonality. Thus, meaningfully delineated experiences
emerge within a context of what can perhaps best be called fused anteception. This fused anteception provides the contextual tonality. Fused
anteception, or contextual tonality, functions both to render unique and
unify the total context. The irreducible, irretrievable vagueness of the
concrete anteceptive experience, which spills over the meanings by
which it is caught, which is an overflow of that within experience which
cannot be captured as repeatable within the structures of pragmatic
meaning, renders an experiential situation or context unique: the experiential context that it concretely is, and no other. Yet, in its unique here
and now, anteceptive content is fused with the character of focus and
fringe, and, in pervading them, unifies them. Thus, anteceptive tonality,
as fused into contextual tonality, renders an experienced context at once
more unique and more cohesive than it would otherwise be.[91]

Such an anteceptive presence is not something open to verification or
falsification within everyday experience, for it eludes the meaningful
anticipatory structures within which verification or falsification can
take place.[92] Nor can its elusiveness be captured by making a previous
fringe a topic of focal awareness. Fringe includes a scheme of relations,
influences, anticipations—all of which may become explicit; but fused
anteception, that is, anteceptive content at the level of everyday awareness, eludes the meanings embodied in everyday experience; it cannot
be made explicit. Anteceptive content not only underlies the emergence
of both focus and fringe, but it overflows them as well. Thus, it not only
provides the generative matrix for their possibility, but it also enters into

---

verse interests. James approaches these issues from the perspective of his psychological interests, while Dewey approaches them from the direction of his concern with the unification of experience by the activity of the human biological organism immersed in the reality
of a qualitative world.

91 / Thus, though not all experience is confined within the structures of pragmatic
meaning, yet all experience is what it is because of such meanings.

92 / The philosophical claim that there is such an anteceptive presence must be verified,
like all philosophical claims, by the workability of the philosophic network in which it is
embedded in providing an integrative, clarifying perspective for understanding experience.
And the claim of such a workability will be strengthened or weakened depending upon
whether or not, in approaching experience with this perspective, one thinks it helps illuminate a "sense of what is there" in an experienced context.

their contextual tonality. Any context experienced includes a focus and a fringe, both of which are dispositional organizations of anteceptive experience as grasped through the structures of pragmatic meaning, plus an anteceptive overflow, and the reciprocal relation between these three aspects gives rise to an experiential contextual tonality that eludes explicit breakdown or explicit analytic understanding. Just as the scientific object gains in precision by abstraction from the richness of everyday perceptual experience, so the everyday perceptual object gains in precision by abstraction from an anteceptive field of indefinite concrete richness that both overflows and underlies its emergence.

The present chapter has explored the anteceptive field as a durational continuity of rudimentary organism-environment interaction undifferentiated by any thought distinctions, and has traced it through to its emerging character within the level of everyday lived experience. The following two chapters will, in turn, explore the nature and context of a full blown metaphysics within the structure of speculative pragmatism, and develop the content of such a speculative pragmatic metaphysics.

Five

From Pragmatic Meaning to Process

Metaphysics

T HE CLAIM is frequently made that the general methodology of pragmatism, by its very nature, excludes the possibility of speculative metaphysics, for any pragmatic metaphysics must be at once faithful to the experiential limits of meaningfulness and knowledge imposed by a pragmatic epistemology, and in harmony with the scientific spirit of pragmatic philosophy in general. In the following analysis, three questions must be kept in mind. First, how can pragmatists meaningfully discuss metaphysical issues? Second, how can they be said to know anything in the area of metaphysics? And, third, how do the answers to the problem of meaning and the problem of knowledge in a pragmatic metaphysics relate to the generally scientific spirit of pragmatic philosophy? The following discussion will deal with these questions, beginning with the last question first, for it pervades the other two.

The preceding chapter has shown that primordial processive activity can be philosophically reflected upon through interpretive description; that such interpretive description can be used philosophically to fund the dynamics of everyday lived experience with enriched meaning; and that it is in turn verified by everyday experience. The content of such an undertaking is at once more abstract and more concrete than the content of everyday experience. It is more abstract in that it emerges from a second-level philosophic reflection on everyday experience. But that which is clarified by such philosophic reflection is the more concrete basis of everyday experience, that anteceptive processive continuity of organism-environment interaction that is partially constitutive of our everyday experience. Such an endeavor reflects throughout the method of scientific experimentalism.

But the model of scientific method indicates further that a more speculative level can be reached that focuses not on the pervasive textures of experience, but on the pervasive features of the independently real in its character as independent of experience. This speculative endeavor, which is rooted in the previously analyzed levels of experience, and which will be seen to reflect the dynamics of scientific experimentalism, goes beyond both common sense and anteceptive experience to that independent element which enters into all experience. The categories of such a speculative metaphysics emerge as philosophically reflective structures or tools for delineating the interwoven pervasive textures of the concrete, independent reality which provides the concrete basis for all experience. As second-level explanatory tools, they are a step more abstract than the second-level philosophic interpretive descriptions of anteceptive experience. But that to which they are applied and within which they delineate is one step more concrete than anteceptive experience, in the sense that it is the concrete basis for all levels of experiencing. It is that "thereness" upon which or within which the intentionality of purposive activity operates in giving rise to the interactional unity that is experience.

Before turning to an examination of the nature and context of such a speculative endeavor, the clarification of some terminology will be helpful. In the following pages, the terms *metaphysical* and *ontological* will be used interchangeably. In none of the classical pragmatists is there to be found any systematic distinction between these two, though several of them tend to use the term *metaphysical* as a negative term, as indicative either of the meaninglessness of some past philosophical squabbles or of the illicit reifications to be found in various past philosophies, be they the reifications of mathematical ideas or Newtonian particles or mind-matter distinctions. Even here, however, the several pragmatists deny the validity of metaphysics in favor of ontology, only to proceed with their own developments of positions that they self-label as metaphysical. The present work can proceed in either of two ways. It can follow the trend of labeling as metaphysical the products of what it sees as the errors of past philosophies, reserving the term *ontological* for the present position. Not only is this one strand to be found in the writings of the pragmatists, but it is also in line with the distinction as made in some other contemporary positions.

An analogous situation is found in the writings of the pragmatists concerning epistemological issues, however. Several of them condemn epistemology as the study of the illicit problems caused by the problematics of the modern world view, yet proceed to focus on epistemic concerns. As was pointed out in the first chapter, speculative pragmatism, as well as the backdrop of classical American pragmatism in which it is rooted, *is* concerned with the issues of epistemology, but with an epistemology that reaches the richness of meanings at their foundation in experience. Similarly, these positions *are* concerned with issues of metaphysics, though with a metaphysics that reaches the richness of the independently real in its foundational concreteness. The position intended is traditional in its endeavor; it is concerned with metaphysical speculation; it is consciously speculative, although its speculations cannot be grasped within the distinctions, dichotomies, and presuppositions of past metaphysics. Thus, the present essay will follow the second strand to be found in the pragmatists—the indiscriminate use of *metaphysics* and *ontology*—for, the negative sense of metaphysics to be found in the pragmatic attacks on past positions notwithstanding, this alternative seems best in keeping with the spirit of pragmatic philosophy.

There is a further ambiguous understanding of metaphysics or ontology, and a correlative ambiguous use of 'reality', to be found in pragmatic thought. These two sets of ambiguities can best be clarified in the context of the nature and function of metaphysical or ontological categories as they will be used in the development of speculative pragmatism. And, since it is in the philosophies of Lewis and Peirce that these ambiguities relate most directly to the issue of metaphysical categories, the following discussion can best proceed from the direction of their respective positions.

Lewis notes that "as it turns out, the problem of metaphysics is 'the problem of the categories'."[1] In the context of Lewis's technical terminology, however, 'categories' indicate the most fundamental principles of ordering by the mind. They exhibit our meaningful attitudes, not that which is delineated by such meanings. Categories are deeply embedded —though nonetheless alterable[2]—a priori structures that reflect the purposive attitudes in terms of which we approach the independent ele-

---

1 / Lewis, *Mind and the World Order*, p. 10.

2 / Because they are so deeply embedded in our way of organizing experience, they change more slowly and are harder to elicit as alterable ways of organizing experience. Thus, what is delineated by them is more likely to be illicitly reified. For example, one would speak of the category of substance or the category of physical object, but the concepts of table, chair, etc.

ment; they would not seem to provide information about the independent element in its character as independent.

Lewis does state that the categories are "the principles which formulate criteria of the real."[3] But by reality he means here that experiential content that has been subsumed under its proper category. Thus, he says, "the problem of distinguishing real from unreal, the principles of which metaphysics seeks to formulate, is always a problem of right understanding, of referring the given experience to its proper category."[4] And again, "metaphysics is concerned to reveal just that set of major classifications of phenomena, and just those precise criteria of valid understanding, by which the whole array of given experience can be set in order and each item (ideally) assigned its intelligible and unambiguous place."[5] Finally, he notes that the categories impose no limitation on that independent element which gives itself within experience, "but, as principles of interpretation, nevertheless condition it as a constituent of reality."[6] The reality thus "produced" is not independent reality in its character as independent of our projected meanings, but rather is a reality that emerges from the projection of meanings upon that which is independently there and which reveals itself through such meanings. In this sense, *metaphysics* is a description of the basic contours or delineations made within our lived experience. This reality that emerges from fundamental categories that classify experience in various ways can best be termed *worldly reality* and will be discussed later in the context of "world."

If perceptual awareness and knowledge in general emerge within the context of meanings or categories projected onto an independent element, then certain conditions must hold of this independent element for such a process to be possible. In short, the universe must be one that allows for the experiential situation as pragmatism interprets it. Lewis himself recognizes this second sense of metaphysics and reality in his analysis of the issues of realism, idealism, or phenomenalism. Here it is clear that Lewis sees metaphysics as related to the independent element, not to the categorizations that yield our structured experience.[7] Similarly, he holds that there are "metaphysical presuppositions which are essential to epistemology, for example, the nature of knowledge itself presupposes a reality to be known which transcends the content of any

---

3 / Lewis, *Mind and the World Order*, p. 14.
4 / Ibid., p. 11.
5 / Ibid., p. 12.
6 / Ibid., p. 14.
7 / Lewis, "Realism or Phenomenalism?" pp. 336–337.

experience in which it may be known."[8] This transcendence relates, according to Lewis, not to a noumenal aspect but to a "thick" aspect, an "always more" to experience.

A similar ambiguity is to be found in Peirce's position, though it is a bit more elusive. Peirce holds that a perceptual content is interpreted in the abductive perceptual judgment containing anticipatory regulative claims, and a perception of objective reality or objective fact results. In this sense of the real, Peirce holds the real to be the outcome of opinion.[9] Categorial analysis, however, stands on a different level, providing the conditions for the possibility of such an experiential situation. Focusing on the fact that such an analysis of the knowledge situation itself presupposes certain features of the universe that make possible such an experiential situation, Peirce establishes his metaphysical categories not merely as "simple and irreducible" conceptions of phenomenal analysis but as "real constituents in the universe."[10] In the last analysis, however, Peirce, like Lewis, confounds levels of interpretation. This confusion is evinced in his statement, "Metaphysics is the science of Reality. Reality consists in regularity. Real regularity is active law. . . . Thirdness." Thus, "metaphysics, as I have just remarked, treats of phenomena in their Thirdness."[11] Peirce then goes to deliberate pains to elaborate a metaphysics that gives equal play to Firstness, Secondness, and Thirdness.[12]

The above context shows that Peirce's argument commits the fallacy of equivocation. Worldly reality can be seen, in a sense, as an affair of Thirdness, for it is only through the application of concepts in interpretive perceptual judgments that there is an objective reality as known; and, concepts and judgments do indeed belong to the category of Thirdness. To understand the possibility of this being so, however, ontological reality is characterized by Firstness, Secondness, and Thirdness.

The latter sense of reality, as used by Lewis and Peirce, will be the topic of discussion of this chapter as well as the next. And the corresponding sense of metaphysics or ontology will be the content of the categories that would seem to be applicable to that independent reality

8 / Lewis, "A Comment on the Verification Theory of Meaning," *Collected Papers*, p. 333.

9 / Peirce, 5.407.

10 / Peirce, 5.82. Though Peirce poses the possibility of this change from phenomenology to metaphysics as a question in this passage, his affirmative answer is clear throughout his philosophy.

11 / Peirce, 5.121—5.124.

12 / Peirce, 6.342.

if experience and knowledge as we have them are to be possible. This is not a categorial set of the same level as any categorial set that is applied to the independently real to give rise to our worldly reality.[13] The categories, as truly metaphysical, stand above or beneath[14] any context of noetically related reality emerging within experience via the anticipatory structures of common sense or scientific categories. The categories, as truly metaphysical, are tools for rendering intelligible and describing the pervasive textures of that independently real universe within which such meanings function and which makes possible their emergence within experience.

Like any system of meanings, the categorial system of meanings that constitutes a metaphysical interpretation must arise out of the matrix of experience, provide an organizing perspective that directs the way we approach experience, and in turn must be verified by the intelligibility it introduces into the ongoing course of experience. As Peirce indicates, metaphysical endeavor is like "that of the special sciences," except that it "rests upon a kind of phenomena with which everyman's experience is so saturated that he usually pays no particular attention to them."[15] Thus, James compares the method of science and metaphysics as ideal systems of thought yet allows for a disparity of content,[16] while Dewey points out that philosophy, like science, legitimately theorizes about experience, but can legitimately begin not with the contents of science, but with the "integrity of experience."[17]

The use of the term *category* for delineating the independent ontological conditions for the possibility of the emergence of the basic contours within experience via the categories embedded in ordinary purposive activity, though confusing if not properly understood, points out something of importance. We cannot get outside our intentional relatedness to the independently real to examine it in its character as independent. The characterization of the features of independent reality as independent of human experience can itself be only a categorization within experience to make experience more intelligible. Within lived experience, a grasp of reality—any kind of reality—results from the application of meanings or categories to the given data at some level in ways that make the data intelligible, or, in other terms, in ways that work.

---

13 / This statement will be modified and refined in the concluding chapter.

14 / These alternative descriptions correlate with the alternative perspectives of "abstract" or "concrete" in describing the categories of metaphysics, as discussed above.

15 / Peirce, 1.282; 6.2.

16 / James, *Principles of Psychology*, 2, p. 671.

17 / Dewey, *Experience and Nature*, pp. 37, 19.

But, to understand the possibility of this being so, independent reality must be characterized by certain metaphysical categories. In brief, the radically nonspectator position of speculative pragmatism cannot be abandoned in the quest for "metaphysical knowledge" that somehow can transcend the meaningfulness that can emerge only through some interpretive structure. Like all understanding, its content is housed within the structures of pragmatic meaning and emerges within the context of experience as experimental. The categories of metaphysics, however, require a more speculative focus on the context of lived experience. Thus, Peirce can hold both that his metaphysics is "metaphorical"[18] and that it is scientific.

With these general features of metaphysical categories in mind, we can now turn first to the issue of the meaningfulness of the specific categories to be used, and then to the justification for the claim that they are applicable to the independently real. The first of these issues can best be approached by examining the implication of the pervasive features to be found within the internal structure of pragmatic meaning. Such a structure of meaning grounds in lived experience a primordial grasp of time as process. What occurs within the present awareness is not the apprehension of a discrete datum in a moment of time, but rather the time-extended experiential sense within the passing present of a readiness to respond to more than can ever be specified. This sense provides the experiential basis for the meaningfulness of a process metaphysics.

Further, such a pragmatic understanding of meaning leads to a realism as opposed to nominalism, a realism not of eternal essences but a "process realism" in which there are real modes of behavior that govern what occurs. Laws cannot be understood as some shorthand for what occurs. Laws, which outrun any number of actualities are, as modes of behavior, the source of the structures emerging in what occurs. Here, however, a problem is frequently held to arise, for the rooting of meaning in experience may seem to make any assertion of realism as opposed to nominalism meaningless. The question is often posed, "How can any experience of what occurs provide a meaningful experiential content for the concept of unactualized possibilities, of a reality of potentialities which outruns any experienced actualities?"

Peirce, in discussing the potentialities of lawfulness, notes the manner in which the potential is grasped through the actual when he observes that what would be is learned through observation of what hap-

---

18 / Peirce, 5.119. Peirce characterizes our knowledge of "the premises of nature" as an "imaginative" comparison with fundamental features of experience.

pens to be.[19] What this indicates is that the particular content of any particular law can be ascertained only by reference to actual occurrences. After a certain number of experiments in which a series of actual events takes place, one has discovered the content of a law, and exemplifies this extra knowledge by prediction. We learn what would be by what is, and in turn verify what would be by what is. Thus, Peirce views the existence of scientific prediction and verification as proof of realism. The issue at hand, however, is not merely the question of how one establishes the particular content of a particular law, but the very meaningfulness of the assertion that the potentialities of lawfulness are something real over and above the actual instances that we interpret as their exemplifications. If any law has content only by reference to the actual, what can we even mean by the assertion of the reality of potentiality as something distinguishable from the actual? The answer is to be found neither at the level of the sophisticated elaboration of logical relationships[20] nor at the level of sophisticated scientific experimentation and prediction,[21] but rather at the more fundamental level of the epistemic foundations for such endeavors. And the epistemic foundations must provide an answer for the question: How can any experience of what is actual provide a meaningful content for the concept of unactualized potentialities, of a reality which is not actual?[22]

That relations are given in perception will not by itself handle the problem at its most fundamental level, for whatever is given is actual. Even if actual relations are given, how do we get from this to a meaningful concept of the unrealized potentialities of actual relations? Even if in anteceptive experience we experience the generative or causal activity inherent in dynamic directional flows, how do we get from the meaningfulness of actual generative activity to the meaningfulness of that which is not actual but "could become so"?

Earlier the model of a continuity generating discrete cuts within itself was seen to provide the characteristic of something actual that contains unactualized possibilities in its very nature. There is no experience of abstract continuity however, rather there is the experience of that which is continuous. Such an abstract model must gain its experi-

19 / Peirce, 6.327.

20 / As has been seen in another context in the previous chapter, logic cannot answer the question but can only try to capture the answer found within concrete experience.

21 / As seen in the previous chapter, predictive reliability alone cannot in any way establish even the sense of efficacy.

22 / The characterization and interrelation of the various features discussed here will be developed and refined in the following chapter.

ential content from the concreteness of experience. The concrete meaning of continuity is gained by reference to the experience of the durational present. And the concrete meaning of genuine potentialities, of that which is not actualized, is gained by reference to the experiential awareness within the durational present of habit or dispositional tendency as potentially generative of an indefinite number of possible schemata, and as a readiness to respond to more than can be specified or actualized. The meaningfulness of process realism and of the real potentialities that it implies is gained by a sophisticated elaboration of or abstraction from the reference to the primitive experience of unactualized possibilities, as this occurs through the actual functioning of habit in the durational present. A disposition or habit as a rule of generation has been seen to be something whose possibilities of determination no multitude of actually generated instances can exhaust. The awareness of habit as a disposition or readiness to generate or to respond to more than can be specified gives a concrete meaning to the concept of a process realism,[23] of a real lawfulness which governs unactualized possibilities. Human dispositional tendencies to respond are precisely lawful tendencies of behavior, potentially capable of structuring emerging activities via pragmatic schemata.

The preceding chapter showed that the primitive sense of creative habits as vital pulsations is fused into the very character of the anteceptive field. Thus, in anteceptive experience a vague sense not just of generative activity but of generative tendency is directly felt in the temporal stretch of human behavior as anticipatory. As habits develop into the generative source of pragmatic schemata, the sense of unrealized potentialities implicit in the sensed creativity of habit becomes more focused, as more and more possibilities are incorporated into its character as potentially generative of pragmatic schemata.

Thus, the meaningfulness of the claim that the potentialities of real relationships can never be exhausted by any number of actualities is rooted ultimately in the sense of the unactualized creative potentialities of habit, as experienced in the temporal continuity of the durational present. The meaning of the potentialities of which pragmatism speaks, and for which it is so frequently criticized, is to be found in the awareness of the actuality of habit as that which can never be exhausted by any number of exemplifications. That readiness to respond to more than can ever be made explicit, which is there in the functioning of habit,

---

23 / It should be clear that the realism under discussion here is the realism that lies in opposition to nominalism, not the type of realism that is placed in opposition to idealism.

is immediately experienced in the passing present and gives experiential content to the "more than" of objectivities that can never be exhaustively experienced, to the concept of unactualized possibilities of being experienced that pervade every grasp of the world around us, and that belie any attempt to deny the meaningfulness of assertions of potentialities. The claim that there are ontologically real causal forces operative in the universe that creatively structure emerging facts, that the universe contains potentialities irreducible in principle to actualities, that process realism prevails, gains its explanatory meaningfulness in the concreteness of experience, for dynamic generative potentialities are immediately experienced in the functioning of habit through the passage of time.

Further, the sense of unactualized possibilities embedded in meaning as dispositional brings a sense of real alternatives—the could do or could be otherwise—into the heart of perceptual awareness as it emerges from anteceptive experience. It provides an experientially meaningful basis for the rejection of deterministic hypotheses, and a recognition of what Lewis refers to as a "primordial sense of probable events."[24] This primordial sense of probable events leads to a sense of the empirical relationships incorporated within the internal structure of meaning as probability claims.[25]

Both the sense of unactualized potentialities and of alternative possibilities is something that is dubitable in principle, and that in fact has been doubted at the reflective levels of science and philosophy, but that is so fundamentally ingredient in our sense of the temporal stretch of the anticipatory nature of experience as it emerges within the structures

24 / Lewis, *Analysis of Knowledge and Valuation*, p. 320.

25 / The relationships represented in schematic aspects cannot be expressed by the logical relation of strict implication, which can, however, express the relation of concrete dispositional meaning to the generation of schematic aspects, for strict implications can be known a priori by reflection on meanings, while the schematic relationships are representative of anticipated experiential sequences. Nor can these relations be expressed by material or formal implication, for the sense of potentialities embodied in them requires the meaningfulness of counterfactual assertions, while material or formal implications do not allow for such meaningfulness. Lewis refers to the consequences of a claim, in this sense of consequence, as "natural consequences" or "real consequences." (*Analysis of Knowledge and Valuation*, pp. 226 ff.) Chapter 3 showed that these empirical "if-then" relationships are creatively unified by habit as a principle of organization and hence of generation, via schematic aspects, of that which it has organized.

Peirce's own difficulty of "if-then" formulation in his now famous example of the unscratched diamond leads him to a nominalistic thesis based implicitly on the logic of material implication (5.403), a conclusion which he must later emphatically repudiate (5.457).

of pragmatic meaning, that it can be doubted only by ignoring the sense of ourselves as active beings, the sense of the pervasive features of creative anticipation in the flow of time.

At this point the objection may be raised that though these subtle tones of experiencing within the internal structure of meaning make the above metaphysical issues meaningful, there is no basis for a claim that they are in fact features of the metaphysically real, and hence they provide no basis for claims of metaphysical knowledge. The following discussion will turn to this issue. This discussion will make explicit from another direction what has already been developed in the previous chapters.

All the pragmatists understand the human being as a natural organism in interaction with a natural environment. One of the most distinctive and most crucial aspects of pragmatism is its concept of experience as having the character of an interaction or transaction between organism and environment. Experience is that rich ongoing transactional unity between organism and environment, and only within the context of meanings that reflect such an interactional unity does what is given emerge for conscious awareness. Such a transactional unity is more than a postulate of abstract thought, for it has been seen to have epistemic or phenomenological dimensions. That which intrudes itself inexplicably into experience is not bare datum, but rather evidences itself as the over-againstness of a thick world there for my activity. If experience is an interactional unity of our responses to the ontologically real, then the nature of experience reflects both the responses we bring and the pervasive textures of that independent reality or surrounding natural environment. In such an interactional unity both poles are manifest: the ontological otherness onto which experience opens, and the active organism within whose purposive activity, expressed in pragmatic meaning, it emerges.

There is thus a three-directional openness in experience. What appears within experience reflects the structure of experience, the structure of the independently real or the surrounding natural universe, and the structures of our mode of grasping that independently real, for what appears within experience is a structural unity formed by the interaction of our mode of grasping and that which is there to grasp. The structure of our mode of grasping the independently real, as well as the structure of experience as an interactional unity of the two poles, has been discussed in previous chapters. Here the concern is not with meaning or with the interactional unity constitutive of experience, but with the conditions for the possibility of such meanings and experience that are provided by the independent element in its contribution to what emerges in the interactional unity.

The pervasive textures of experience, which are exemplified in every experience, are at the same time indications of the pervasive textures of the independent universe that, in every experience, gives itself for our responses and provides the touchstone for the workability of our meanings. Though analyticity within selected meaning systems is about meaning relations, meanings are about experience. Relatedness to possible experience is built into the very structure of meaning relations by that same schematic element that provides analytic containments within any system of meanings. And the most pervasive features of experience, which are there in every experience, must be embedded in the internal structure of meaning if meaning in general is to be applicable in experience and relevant to the grasping of the independently real. There is an elusive coerciveness at the basis of meaning selection that cannot be selected or not at will, but rather must be acknowledged within the structure of any meaning. Thus, the being of man in the natural universe and the knowing by man of the natural universe are inseparably connected within the structure of experience.

Lewis, then, can hold at once that the content of knowledge is the ontologically real, that the ontologically real has an independence from mind, and yet that the content of knowledge is partially dependent upon the knowing mind. As Lewis well indicates, insistency on rejecting one or the other of the above alternatives stems from a failure to reject once and for all the presuppositions of a spectator theory of knowledge.[26] What appears within experience is also the appearance of the independently real; there is no ontological gap between appearance and reality.

26 / Lewis holds that "the history of philosophy since Descartes has been largely shaped by the acceptance of the alternatives: either (1) knowledge is not relative to the mind, or (2) the content of knowledge is not the real, or (3) the real is dependent on mind. Kant, and phenomenalism in general, recognizes the relativity of knowledge, the dependence of the phenomenal object on the mind, and hence the impossibility of knowing the real as it is in itself. Idealism, taking the relativity of knowledge as its main premise, argues to the unqualified dependence of reality upon mind. . . . Realists in general seek to reconcile the possibility of knowing reality with its independence of the mind by one or another attempt to escape the relativity of knowledge" (*Mind and the World Order*, p. 154). Although Kant is considered the beginning of "the rejection of the spectator," he himself was not immune to some of its presuppositions, for Kant, in attempting to justify the absoluteness of the Newtonian or modern world view in some sense, was still caught up in the problematics emerging from the absolutizing of scientific content based on an inadequate understanding of scientific method.

Further, it is at the same time "to me" to whom it appears, and it reflects my intentional or interactional link with the externally real. What appears within experience, then, opens in one direction toward the structures of the independently real and in the other direction toward the structures of our mode of grasping the independently real. Or, in other terms, what appears within experience is a function of both in interaction and thus mirrors neither exactly, though it reflects characteristics of each. As Lewis captures the import of this interactional unity, "It may be that between a sufficiently critical idealism and a sufficiently critical realism there are no issues save false issues which arise from the insidious fallacies of a copy theory of knowledge."[27]

The failure to recognize this interactional "reflecting", and as a result to substitute for it a mirroring either of the ontologically real alone or of our selective activity alone, leads to the contemporary dichotomies of realism–antirealism, foundationalism–antifoundationalism, or objectivism–relativism. Further, the failure to recognize that this reflecting that constitutes the structure of experience, not only is not a mirroring of an independent pole alone or a selective activity alone, but also is not a reflection of itself,[28] leads to the failure to see that the categories of metaphysics must undercut not only the distinctions both of science and common sense to get at the ground of their possibility in anteceptive experience, but must also undercut the interactional unity of anteceptive experience to get at the character of the independent pole that such unity in part reflects. The failure to recognize these implicit distinctions in Dewey's position leads to criticisms, on the one hand that he cannot reconcile his discussions of process and physical objects, and on the other hand that he anthropomorphizes the universe in general. Similarly, James is at times accused of fundamental inconsistencies both between his discussions of objects and process, and between his discussions of objective reference and pure experience. There are to be found in the metaphysical claims of pragmatic philosophy no illicit reifications of objects of awareness and no conflicts either between the structures of objectivities and the fundamental nature of process or between experience and objective reference, for an implicit recognition of this three-directional openness within experience is always operative, though it is, admittedly, at times so implicit as to be difficult to discern.

Thus, the claims of speculative metaphysics emerge as speculative extrapolations from the pervasive features of experience to the character

27 / Lewis, *Mind and the World Order*, p. 194.

28 / As Dewey so succinctly notes, experience does not experience itself. *Experience and Nature*, p. 21.

of that which enters into the texture of every experience. Further, there is no anthropomorphizing of nature. This move from the character of experience to the character of the independent pole is not fashioning the independent pole in the likeness of human experience, but rather showing the natural conditions within which human experience emerges. Failure to recognize this three-directional openness of experience leads to interpretive problems and to various charges of inconsistency in relation to all of the classical pragmatists.

Such an experiential openness is difficult to discern from the frameworks of other philosophical stances. For example, those who focus on the aspect of alternative conceptual schemes in Lewis's philosophy as the basis for viewing him as an analytic philosopher have at times been led to note a "nonconformity" in his thought, since for Lewis certain fundamental principles, such as the if-then order of causal relationships and the processive order of time, are not partially determined by alternative conceptual schemes, but rather are necessary for the very possibility of the applicability of any conceptual scheme to experience. Yet this awareness of such a coerciveness at the basis of meaning selection has led either to claims of problems in Lewis's "analytic" position, or to the assertion that such fundamental principles, which are categorial in the sense of being illustrated in every possible experience, imply a heritage from Kant of a fixed, unalterable a priori necessity of the mind. This "problem" from the framework of analytic conventionalism cannot be solved by bringing in the baggage of Kantian fixed categories of the mind, for in addition to contradicting Lewis's explicit and emphatic rejection of fixed, necessary categories of the mind, it ignores a critically important aspect of Lewis's position toward which this element of coerciveness, when properly located, directly points. Such coerciveness does not close us within the phenomenal, forever cut off from the noumenal by necessities of mind, but rather throws us outward toward the features of the ontologically real, and in so doing, negates conventionalist claims.

By eliciting the phenomenological categories and subsequently applying them to the ontologically real in its character as independent of our mode of experiencing, Peirce reflects an awareness of precisely such a three-directional openness.[29] Peirce's phenomenology, or description of the "phaneron," is an attempt to work back, as closely as possible within experience, to the level of what is there in the pervasive textures

29 / Thus, Peirce's phenomenology, in providing categories as "classifications of all that is in any way present to mind in experience" also provides the epistemic categories for analyzing the structures of meaning as well as the metaphysical categories for delineating "modes of being."

of experience. Such phenomenological description provides only an inroad to the categories of a metaphysical explanation, for what is there in the conscious apprehension of the "phaneron" is already shot through with the structurings of organism-environment interaction.[30] Though Peirce describes his phenomenology as a science of what appears, precisely as it appears, its content is grasped within the context of, and reflects the pervasive features of, meaningful experience. The categories of metaphysics, then, can be given content only by an "imaginative"[31] extrapolation from experience, because "man is so completely hemmed in by the bounds of his possible practical experience . . . that he cannot, in the least, *mean* anything that transcends those limits. For let him try ever so hard to think anything about what is beyond that limit, it simply cannot be done."[32] Peirce's "phaneron" provides the foundation for precisely such an imaginative extrapolation. There is an intimate interrelation between Peirce's metaphysical and phenomenological categories. There is no existential or ontological gulf between these categories, for there is no such gulf between noumena and phenomena, between underlying metaphysical reality and that which gives itself in experience.

The metaphysical categories provide, then, the independently real conditions for the possibility of the knowing process as interpreted in a pragmatic philosophy. Yet these categorizations of independent reality themselves arise within the knowledge process. If the knowledge process is characterized as one in which alternative sets of categories emerging within the context of temporal experience can be applied to the given data, then apparently there must be alternatives to the metaphysical categories taken as indicative of the character of independent reality. This is precisely what the pragmatists hold. Peirce nowhere indicates that his categories are absolute or eternal and in fact states quite clearly that though his selection seems the most adequate, alternative series of categories are possible.[33] Similarly, though Lewis speaks of metaphysics as providing the presuppositions for an understanding of the knowledge situation, he notes that though a presupposition is logically prior, the idea of necessity must be given up.[34] Nor is such a presupposition known by some "higher" type of knowledge, but rather it is

30 / Peirce, 1.287.

31 / Peirce, 5.119.

32 / Peirce, 5.356.

33 / Peirce, 1.525; 1.526. This point can be further elaborated only after the development of the concept of "world." It will be reintroduced in the concluding chapter.

34 / Lewis, "The Structure of Logic and Its Relation to Other Systems," *Collected Papers*, p. 378.

an interpretive structure that gains, within lived experience, "partial and inductive verification."[35]

At this point, one may object that speculative pragmatism has become involved in an arbitrary circle with no firm roots anywhere. Though a pragmatic metaphysics attempts to understand the pervasive textures of the independent element which enters, along with a meaning element, into our sense of empirical reality, what this independent element is like can be determined only from experience; and how we understand experience will in part be influenced by the metaphysical categories in terms of which we approach it. A pragmatic metaphysics can be only tentative and responsive to experience, while at the same time legislating for the analysis of experience. This type of procedure, however, is not peculiar to metaphysical investigation, but rather is continuous with the methodology of science that pervades all levels of knowledge, from the most prereflective dynamics of experimentalism embedded in the anteceptive field to the most sophisticated metaphysical knowledge, for our meanings at all levels have arisen out of the context of temporal experience, yet are held legislative for the meaningful delineation of future experience. Such a self-corrective method is not viciously circular, nor is it circular at all, but rather it is a cumulative process based on the pragmatic interplay, at every level, between meanings projected and that independently real which determines their workability. This type of mutual feedback is surely not arbitrary; it reflects the understanding of scientific method as indicating a self-corrective rather than a building-block enterprise.

The failure to recognize this interaction between meaning and perceived fact leads to the question of whether pragmatism is offering an empirical justification of the metaphysical categories or a type of a priori deduction of them. If a dichotomy is made in this way,[36] then the problems attributed to the method do in fact arise. If the method is empirical, then we cannot know that the categories have universal application to the independently real, or that they hold of the independently real in its separation from noetic activity. Alternately, if the method reduces to a rational assertion, the categories have universal application "by fiat," but seem somewhat arbitrary in their application. The categories of speculative metaphysics are drawn from the phenomenological

35 / Ibid.

36 / This entire line of questioning is based on the false alternatives of "rationalism or empiricism" founded in a spectator theory of knowledge and rejected by the method of science.

analysis of experience, and in this sense are rooted in experience. As attempting to describe the independently real that provides the concrete basis for all experience, they must be "guided through" experience toward the real by philosophical extrapolation of the pervasive textures of experience. Such categories or interpretive tools, as objects of second-level reflection, are then held universally applicable to the independently real because we make them interpretive tools for the understanding of their data.

Speculative metaphysics, then, is an endeavor rooted in and verified by lived experience. It provides a speculative analysis, via extrapolation from the pervasive features of lived experience, of what that independent reality must be like, in its character as independent, to give rise to the anteceptive level of experience and to the meanings by which it becomes known to us. It thus offers an "explanation" of lived experience by providing a speculative examination and integration of the features of that independently real universe that presents itself in the immediacy of organism-environment interaction, that is "open to"[37] certain meanings, and that is known only through such meanings.

The above discussion has shown that the meaningfulness of potentialities and alternative possibilities is rooted in the experience of durational flow. The structure of meaning both requires the continuity of temporal flow, and grounds in everyday experience a primordial grasp of processive continuity. The passage from felt temporality as the basis for meaningful experience to process metaphysics as the basis for understanding its ontological character is to be found in all the pragmatists. James's radical empiricism, pure experience, and pragmatism are through and through interrelated with a process metaphysics. As seen in the previous chapter, pure experience does not enclose one within the subjective, but rather leads outward toward a processive universe. When James asks, "How far into the rest of nature may we have to go in order to get entirely beyond its overflow?"[38] his answer is clear. One may "go into the heart of nature," one may grasp the most pervasive textures of its most characteristic features through a metaphysics of experience, and one will not get beyond its overflow. Man is a natural being in interaction with a natural universe. And at the heart of nature is process. Conversely, process metaphysics reinforces the pragmatic understanding of knowledge, for "when the whole universe seems only . . . to be still

37 / The nature of this "openness to meanings" will be further clarified in the following chapters.
38 / James, *Pluralistic Universe*, p. 129.

incomplete (else why its ceaseless changing?) why, of all things, should knowing be exempt?"[39]

Lewis's similar passage to process metaphysics can be found in his claim that the "absolutely given" as independent of noetic activity is a "Bergsonian duration." "The absolutely given is a specious present, fading into the past and growing into the future with no genuine boundaries. The breaking of this up . . . marks already the activity of an interested mind."[40] As Mead states of the universe at the "boundary" of experience or the "outer edge" of constitutive activity, "At the future edge of experience, things pass, their characters change and they go to pieces."[41]

The role of dispositional meaning in transforming the processive universe into a context of meaningfully structured objects is evinced in Dewey's assertion that "structure is constancy of means, of things used for consequences, not of things taken by themselves absolutely."[42] Further, the "isolation of structure from the changes whose stable ordering it is, renders it mysterious—something that is metaphysical in the popular sense of the word, a kind of ghostly queerness."[43] Indeed, it has been seen that for all the pragmatists, the structures of objectivities grasped by the knowing mind do not reach a reality more ultimate than the processive interactions of anteceptive experience, but rather the lived-through anteceptive grasp of felt temporality opening onto a processive universe is the very foundation for the emergence within experience of meaningful structure.

Pragmatism, in attempting to unite meanings freely created with the coercive thereness to which such meanings are applied and from which they have emerged, has at times emphasized meanings freely brought, and at times the speculative examination of what is there to coerce. It has failed, however, adequately to emphasize and distinguish the epistemic and ontological unity at the heart of experience as a three-directional openness that provides the corridor from one to the other, though this is always implicitly operative as its context. The last two chapters each have attempted, from different perspectives, to illuminate this pragmatic corridor. The following chapter can now turn to the exploration of the process metaphysics that emerges via that corridor.

39 / James, *Essays in Radical Empiricism*, p. 37.
40 / Lewis, *Mind and the World Order*, p. 58.
41 / Mead, *Philosophy of the Act*, p. 345.
42 / Dewey, *Experience and Nature*, pp. 64–65.
43 / Ibid., p. 65.

Six

Processive Concreteness and Ontological

Activity Modes

THE USE of the writings of the various pragmatists in developing the subject matter of the present chapter must frequently be extricated from two ambiguous contexts. First, distinctions between features of the natural universe as independent of man and features of world as that natural universe relates to man are never clearly and explicitly distinguished in pragmatic philosophy, though a technical concept of world that is founded upon such a distinction is implicit in the writings of the pragmatists.[1] But such a concept of world is indeed only implicit in the context of their writings, and thus they tend throughout to conflate the two dimensions. This is well illustrated in Mead's continual emphasis on the reality of perspectives. Though Mead holds to the objective reality of perspectives,[2] yet he asserts that "the conception of the world that is independent of any organism is one that is without perspectives."[3] Precisely what this chapter proposes to deal with is a universe independent of any organisms, and thus independent of any perspectives, among other worldly emergents. Within the present structure, however, a world independent of organisms is impossible, for a world, by definition, is encompassed within the horizons of organisms. Perspectives and other products of organism-environment interaction enter into world, not into universe in its character as independent of organisms. This distinction in no way implies a discontinuity between man and the indepen-

1 / This concept of "world" will be the topic of the following chapter.
2 / Mead, *Philosophy of the Present*, pp. 161–175.
3 / Mead, *Philosophy of the Act*, p. 165.

dently real universe. Rather, the general catagorial features of the natural universe independent of man's activities will provide the categorial features for understanding man and the emergent features of world. Though the term *world* will be found sprinkled throughout this chapter as pragmatic philosophers use it in reference to their own respective claims, whenever it is used it will delineate, according to speculative pragmatism, not a world at all, but the independent pole in its character as independent, a processive concreteness that is the matrix within which human experience and worlds may emerge.

Mead comes close to stating the problem of the present chapter when he asks, concerning the independently real, what meaning attaches to the claim that there must be some such universe which we never totally encompass in our perception or theories, "which is independent of all the worlds of perception and scientific theory, that would explain all of them and yet would not transcend them in the sense of being of a nature which could not appear in perception or scientific theory, and would be independent of observation and perception and thought, and would itself include these."[4] Mead's answer indicates the direction his ontological discussions tend to take throughout his work, for his answer does not draw him toward a speculative analysis of the independently real in its character as independent and as foundational for the possibility of worlds, but rather he finds the meaning of the independence he seeks in the relation between the hypothesis needing testing and a "world within which we are living and acting successfully except at the point which has become problematic."[5] In brief, he has changed·the problem from the nature of the independently real as independent and foundational of worlds to the problem of the nature of verification in relation to any "world that is there." This latter dimension, as it relates to various issues, is usually the focus of Mead's ontological discussions.

This central focus of Mead's thought arises from the very understanding of scientific method that set the directions for speculative pragmatism, for Mead, throughout his writings, is concerned to show that scientific content arises from reflection upon, and is answerable to, everyday experience, or, in Mead's terms, "the world that is there." Usually in Mead's writings, when he comes close to getting beneath the level of world and focusing on independent reality in its character as independent, he finds in this focus a danger of absolutizing the contents of science and backs away, never clearly and explicitly focusing on the

4 / Ibid., pp. 277–278.
5 / Ibid., p. 280.

character of an independent reality as foundational for the worlds of both common sense and science. Thus, paradoxically, though Mead writes much on metaphysics, his position will be far more relevant for the following chapter. Though the present chapter will draw from Mead's work, it will do so cautiously, for there are few places in Mead's discussions where an initial focus on the independent nature of the universe is not transformed into a discussion of worldly features and relationships.

A second and somewhat related though different problem of ambiguity of context is to be found in James's discussion of the features of the ontologically real in its character as independent, for James switches back and forth almost continually, and in seemingly unnoticed fashion, between reality and pure experience. Some interpreters of James hold that this is what James must do, since for him to do otherwise would contradict his doctrine of pure experience which denies any dichotomy, either epistemically or ontologically, between experience and reality known. Yet, James does attempt at times to articulate the features of the independently real in its character as independent. His development could perhaps be more clearly made if he did explicitly distinguish between pure experience and the character of the independent pole that enters into such experience. Of course, pure experience, which provides the foundation not only for everyday experience but also for scientific and philosophic reflection, contains no distinctions between experience and reality. Philosophic reflection, however, though rooted ultimately in pure experience, can and should, for purposes of philosophical clarification, make the distinction between pure experience as a primordial interaction with the independent pole, and a reflective philosophical attempt to characterize the nature of that independent ontological pole that intertwines with the organism in giving rise to pure experience. Though James at times focuses on ontological concerns as relevant to the present chapter, he usually tends to slide almost immediately from such a focus into a discussion of pure experience. Thus, in the present framework, he fails to recognize explicitly and systematically a level of metaphysical speculation that can undercut not only common sense and scientific experience, but also anteceptive experience.

Occasionally, however, James comes close to indicating that the switch from independent reality to experience is intended as an analogy by which to understand the features of the independently real. Thus, he states that "for pluralism, all that we are required to admit as the constitution of reality is what we ourselves find empirically realized in every minimum of finite life. Briefly it is this, that nothing real is absolutely

simple, that every smallest bit of experience is a *multum in parvo* plu-
rally related, and that each relation is one aspect, character, or function,
. . . and that a bit of reality when actively engaged in one of these relations is not by that very fact engaged in all the other relations simulta-
neously."[6] Thus, James's comments will be relevant when they can be
seen not as a confounding of the characteristics of the independently
real with characteristics of pure or anteceptive experience, but when the
context is such that the latter can be read as an analogy for understanding the former. Indeed, given the experiential path that leads toward and
limits the meaningfulness of metaphysical discussion, such analogies
would seem unavoidable. But they must be accepted as analogies, not as
attempts to read anthropomorphic features into the natural universe
that is prior to and foundational of the very possibility of human experience. With these preliminary points in mind, we can now turn to the
content of a metaphysics within the context of pragmatic philosophy.

If pragmatic philosophy tends toward *a* pragmatic understanding of
the nature of experience as experimental, then the pervasive features of
such experience, as carried into the categories of metaphysics, would be
expected to provide characteristic features of *a* metaphysics of pragmatism. And, indeed, though Peirce is the only classical American
pragmatist who explicitly develops a set of categories for the metaphysical characterization of the independently real universe within which experience emerges, the other pragmatists, whatever their terminologies,
attribute to universe the features represented by the three Peircean categories. All the pragmatists, through their respective terminologies, converge toward a process metaphysics that can be characterized in terms of
the categories of Firstness, or quality, diversity, spontaneity, unity, possibility; Secondness, or interaction, over-againstness, shock, presentness,
actuality, existence, discreteness; Thirdness, or dispositional tendencies,
potentialities, lawful modes of behavior. These general categorial features will be used in the present development of speculative pragmatism,
though not necessarily either in any of the specific terminologies previously used, or in any of the precise interrelationships previously developed within pragmatism.

Because Peirce's categories of metaphysics are the most developed
within pragmatic thought, the ensuing discussion will use them to
bring to light several key points. First, the concept of process, though
more fundamental than the three Peircean metaphysical categories and

6 / James, *Pluralistic Universe*, p. 145.

the key to understanding their interrelationships, yet remains implicit and obscure within Peirce's categorial discussions, resulting in his various attempts to understand his position in terms of the false alternatives based on the historical tradition of substance philosophy and spectator theory of knowledge. Though such confusions are not to be found in some of the other pragmatists, they are yet important as illustrations of the kinds of interpretive problems that have plagued critical understandings of their positions and that this chapter hopes clearly to expunge from the context of speculative pragmatism. Second, the categories must be understood as analytic tools for discriminating aspects of a complex, concrete, inseparable unity, not as tools for separating distinct "realms of being." No category represents a content that "is" or "can be" apart from the others. Though Peirce at times seems to develop his categories in terms of levels of primacy, their function reveals that no category can be understood as more fundamental than the others. The search for the "more fundamental" is again a legacy of substance philosophy. Third, such a discussion will show why the present position, though in keeping with the spirit of the Peircean categories, will have to alter some of Peirce's terminology, as well as that of some of the other pragmatists, and to alter, as well, some of the "content" of the three fundamental categories.

Turning to the first point, there is a peculiar lack, in Peirce's metaphysical categories, of any category of process. As has been shown, the anteceptive sense of temporality is the condition for the very possibility of Peirce's phenomenal analysis of experience that yields the phenomenal categories of Firstness, Secondness, and Thirdness, and the condition that makes possible the experience of the features grasped in his phenomenological descriptions. Process is the experiential character that accounts for the very possibility of these features. Yet the experience of durational flow does not emerge as the content of any phenomenological category for Peirce. As that experience that yields the possibility of his categories, it is discussed by him in brief and scattered contexts, but not in the context of his phenomenological analysis of experience. Similarly, Peirce does not develop an ontological category of process. Rather, process is the ontological characteristic that accounts for the features grasped by the categories of metaphysics. Process is not itself a categorial feature for Peirce, but is implicitly that which is understood through categorial delineations of its features. Though process must be a metaphysical category, opposed, for example, to the metaphysical category of substance, yet the development of the metaphysical categories will be seen to be *categories of* process, modes of its activity. The term *mode* as here used must of course be severed from its link with substance philosophy. Modes of activity are manners or ways of behaving constitutive of the nature of processive concreteness; the ontological activity modes are ways or manners in which process functions. Just as Peirce's triadic categorial phenomenological divisions are distinctions made within the durational concreteness of experience, so it will be seen that the categories of ontological activity modes, as categories of process metaphysics, are distinctions made within the processive concreteness of the independently real universe. Ontological activity modes, as they grow out of classical pragmatism, and are redirected in the context of speculative pragmatism, will be seen to be analytically discriminated aspects of the *activity* of processive concreteness. Other metaphysical categories will develop within speculative pragmatism as derivative, in some sense, from ontological activity modes as fundamental categorial distinctions. To be "derivative from" emphatically does *not* mean to be less real or less ontologically "ultimate" than, but rather to be understandable in light of, these other distinctions.

Because the pervasive, fundamental role of process is not made adequately explicit in relation to the categorial features of reality as expressed by some of the pragmatists, they themselves at times have problems breaking out of traditional distinctions, or fail to utilize adequately novel emerging distinctions. Perhaps the best example of the difficulty of breaking out of old distinctions when the ultimacy of process is relegated to the background is to be found in what is probably Peirce's most explicit statement of his self-proclaimed idealism. Like most of Peirce's claims on most issues, he proceeds here by showing that the other alternatives are wrong. Peirce's most clear-cut assertions of idealism arise from a rejection of two other positions which he falsely thinks to exhaust the possibilities. But the alternatives from which he begins are rooted in a tradition of substance and kinds of "stuff," while his search for an answer stems from an emerging framework of process and function.

Peirce regards dualism,[7] materialism, and idealism as three conflicting theories, each of which gives a definite answer to the question of the nature of the universe.[8] He attempts to solve this problem by determining what kind of law governs the universe, physical law or law of the

7 / Peirce, 6.24. Peirce calls this position "monism" or "neutralism," but both Peirce's definition of and rejection of the position indicate that what is involved is dualism: the irreducibility of two totally distinct "entities," mind and matter.

8 / Peirce, 6.24.

mind. That Peirce expresses the alternatives in terms of laws rather than either ultimate substances or types of stuff may not at first glance seem a significant move, for the manner of operation of "mind stuff" would surely be different from the manner of operation of "material stuff." However, as Peirce clearly indicates the nature of the problem for himself, "the distinction between psychical and physical phenomena *is* the distinction between final and efficient causation."[9] In short, Peirce is not asking the type of question provided by a substance metaphysics; he is asking a question concerning the behavior of the universe, and mind and matter are names of differing types of functions or processes operative in the universe. Peirce's question here can be seen to follow from his pragmatic orientation which asserts that what a thing is, is determined by its activities or behavior, not by any underlying substance that determines or causes the behavior. Indeed, Peirce's answer to the question of the stuff of the universe would probably be similar to James's answer to the question of the stuff of experience: "There is no general stuff of which experience at large is made. . . . If you ask what any one bit of pure experience is made of, the answer is always the same: 'it is made of that, just what appears.'"[10]

With this initial clarification of the distinction between the law of mind and the law of matter as types of activity, Peirce analyzes the possible choices: dualism, materialism, or idealism. Peirce objects to the first alternative because separating reality into two types or chunks of being leaves each type operating according to a single law: the law of efficient causation or the law of final causation.[11] Here we begin to make contact with the second point to be developed through the focus on Peirce's position, for clearly the separation of final and efficient causation as modes of behavior cannot be given the degree of separation at times indicated by Peirce's writings, and the division of mental and physical simply in terms of final and efficient causation may in fact be inadequate in understanding the position intended.

Peirce's rejection of materialism gives a further insight into the nature of his self-proclaimed idealism. Peirce argues against materialism that it "blocks the road to inquiry,"[12] since law itself needs an explanation.[13] Again, materialism cannot account for the many processes that are characterized by growth and increasing complexity, nor can it ac-

9 / Peirce, 7.366 (italics added).
10 / James, *Essays in Radical Empiricism*, pp. 14–15.
11 / Peirce, 7.570.
12 / Peirce, 6.64.
13 / Peirce, 6.12.

count for the "living spontaneity" which faces us when we gaze outward.[14] Thus, for Peirce materialism omits Thirdness and, in so doing, omits spontaneity which belongs to the category of Firstness. Again, the operation of one categorial feature is clearly inextricably interwoven with the others.

After rejecting dualism and materialism, Peirce accepts the only remaining alternative, idealism. What does this mean for him at this point? It means that the ontologically real that enters into the character of experience cannot be accounted for solely by mechanistic laws that leave no place for spontaneity, and that there must be something more to nature than blind action and reaction. It means that laws must be accounted for in terms of the process of cosmic evolution, and that the richness of lived experience must be able to find its place within the metaphysically real. It means that no part of the universe is totally characterizable either by the law of mind or the law of matter, either by final causation or efficient causation, and that mind cannot be completely separated from the activities of nature as a distinct mode of being, nor can the activities of nature be conflated to the activities of mind.

A reflection on those characteristics that Peirce is concerned to attribute to the universe seems to indicate that he is headed toward a temporalistic, pluralistic "idealism" without a block universe. This idealism holds the law of mind to be in some yet-undetermined sense more fundamental than the law of matter, but nonetheless views humans and their higher faculties as quite unessential to the processes of the universe. In short, Peirce here seems heading toward a naturalism that reintegrates human and nature, not by reducing the human as does the materialist, nor by assimilating nature to mind, as does the idealist, but by presenting an enriched nature within which are to be found the operations of those processes with which human activities are continuous. Thus, Peirce concludes that "all phenomena are of one character, though some are more mental and spontaneous, others more material and regular. Still all alike present that mixture of freedom and constraint which allows them to be, nay, makes them to be, teleological or purposive."[15]

Peirce, in his search for a metaphysical label, is here caught in what might be called the "Cartesian trap." If not dualism, then either all becomes mind or all becomes matter in the mechanistic sense of the

14 / Peirce, 6.553–6.554.

15 / Peirce, 7.570. Purpose, for Peirce, is that form of final cause most familiar to our experience.

nature or external world that remains when one cuts off the mind half of the Cartesian offering. What Peirce did not recognize in his survey of the metaphysical alternatives is that he had gone the path not of choosing among old alternatives, but rather of providing a framework that rejects the logic of the original questioning in terms of which both the problem and all its possible alternatives arise. What Peirce did not always clearly see, and did not have adequate language to express, is that he had not asked the kind of question for which these alternatives could provide a satisfactory answer. In keeping with his pragmatism, he had asked a question concerning the behavior of the universe, and, believing that the "loose play" and "temporal directedness" of final causation and the spontaneity it allowed were necessary for understanding the activity of the universe, he found the only available conclusion to be that "the one intelligible theory of the universe is that of objective idealism, that matter is effete mind, inveterate habits becoming physical laws."[16]

Though Lewis speaks much less frequently and less directly to metaphysical issues, his position incorporates Peirce's three categories and, similarly, is rooted in a switch from substance to process philosophy in a way that leaves him in search of a metaphysical label. The last chapter showed that for Lewis possibility and potentiality are conditions required for knowing. The possibility involved here is the range of independent but possible-to-actualize alternatives or what Peirce calls Firstness. The potentialities indicated by the possibility of knowing an independently real world,[17] the if-then relations or "real connections"[18] that are also required for knowing, are the potentialities of Thirdness. For Lewis, as for Peirce, the reality of Thirdness does not lead to "the supposition of 100 per cent correlation."[19] Finally, as has been seen, independent factuality, which forces itself upon us, is also a condition for the possibility of knowledge.[20] For Lewis, then, possibility, actuality, and potentiality stand above any context of the noetic structuring of experience, though we can only come to know these conditions from within the experiential process in which we find ourselves.

Lewis notes that the ontological problem of the status of objects can be stated as, "Whether an object is merely a bundle of attributes—that

16 / Peirce, 6.25.

17 / Lewis, *Analysis of Knowledge and Valuation*, p. 211.

18 / Ibid., p. 227.

19 / Ibid., p. 229; Peirce, 1.402.

20 / See chapter 4. *Factuality* or *facticity* should not be confused with *facts*. The former terms indicate the "brute thereness" of the independently real, while the latter term will be seen, in the next chapter, to represent meaningful worldly emergents.

and the surd of existential fact," or whether something more is required. That more is needed is evidenced in his statement that we here "make connection with something to be found in traditional discussions of substance: one must either find in the object something which persists unaltered, or one must penetrate to some lawlike or predictable mode of such alteration."[21] Quality and surd existence, then, are not sufficient; objects require either unalterable substance or lawful alteration. That the latter is the alternative accepted by Lewis is evident both from his focus on lawfulness as built into our knowledge of objects, and in his assertion that "any discussion of substance will be avoided as 'unhelpful'."[22] Lewis, then, excludes the concept of substance and opts rather for lawfulness as a type of behavior embodied in process. As he states, "An object is an event; some continuous volume in space-time comprising a history of enduring. Characteristically, the process of change in this kind of event is never too abrupt or too pervasive. . . ."[23]

Nonetheless, Lewis, in his search for a metaphysical label, is trapped, like Peirce, in the historical alternatives that present themselves, failing to recognize the full significance of his switch from substance to process. Lewis concludes that his metaphysical convictions "are, as it happens, realistic,"[24] because "the nature of knowledge itself presupposes a reality to be known which transcends the content of any experience in which it may be known."[25] Here, Lewis embraces realism not because there is a fully structured independent reality that mind mirrors in adequate knowledge, but partially because the first two Peircean categories are not adequate to express the operations of independent reality in its character as independent. Precisely because of the nature of Lewis's realism, he rejects the realist alternatives of representation or identity when he discusses epistemological alternatives. Instead, he states that pragmatism and objective idealism are the two alternatives that allow for a reality that transcends the content of experience.[26]

Lewis's realism tends toward the idealist position because what is real are not discrete individual substances, but rather lawful relations— for Lewis, relations among events. However, Lewis rejects idealism both on epistemological and metaphysical grounds. Speaking within the context of epistemology, he notes that while for objective idealists there is a

21 / Lewis, "Realism or Phenomenalism?", p. 341.
22 / Ibid.
23 / Ibid.
24 / Lewis, "Comment on 'The Verification Theory of Meaning'," p. 333.
25 / Ibid.
26 / Lewis, "Experience and Meaning," *Collected Papers*, pp. 264–265.

deductive relation between a real object and an experience of it, for the pragmatist there is an inductive relationship.[27] And, within a more metaphysical context, he holds that "idealism, taking the relativity of knowledge as its main premise, argues to the unqualified dependence of reality upon mind."[28] Thus, he further embraces realism because it recognizes that the reality known is independent of mind in its brute thereness, yet he explicitly rejects the realist efforts to "reconcile the possibility of knowing reality with its independence of mind by one or another attempt to escape the relativity of knowledge."[29]

When Lewis speaks within the context of epistemology, he readily notes that his assertions are not merely a modification of idealism or of realism, but rather are a switch to pragmatism. When ontological issues are explicitly discussed, however, Lewis fails to explicitly recognize that if pragmatism presents, in matters of metaphysics, its own "principle of orientation in the search for positive conclusions,"[30] then traditional metaphysical alternatives are not satisfactory. Thus, Lewis, after attempting to claim affinities with several metaphysical positions but identity with none, accepts metaphysical realism as opposed to idealism or phenomenalism as the lesser of the available evils, never explicitly recognizing the possibility that he has redirected all the available alternatives into a path leading toward a distinctively pragmatic metaphysics of cosmic activity. Both Peirce and Lewis could well have heeded James's admonition in relation to the "intellectualist" position, that the real way out of its problems "far from consisting in the discovery of such an [intellectual] answer, consists in simply closing one's ears to the question."[31] Both Peirce and Lewis remain trapped in the alternatives offered by the questions of the very substance metaphysics they are attempting to repudiate.

Indeed, no sooner does Peirce embrace idealism as the lesser of the available evils than he attempts to qualify his acceptance, for "the truth is that pragmaticism is closely allied to the Hegelian absolute idealism,

---

27 / Ibid., p. 265.

28 / Lewis, *Mind and the World Order*, p. 154.

29 / Ibid. The present discussion is not concerned with the correctness of either Peirce's or Lewis's characterizations of traditional positions, but rather with the ways in which their interpretations of them lead to a better understanding of their own positions.

30 / Lewis, "Pragmatism and Current Thought," *Collected Papers*, p. 79. Peirce refers to this "principle of orientation" toward metaphysical conclusions embedded in pragmatism as "the ulterior and indirect effects of practising the pragmatistic method." Such metaphysical conclusions concern issues of necessity, contingency, lawfulness, change, and chance (5.496).

31 / James, *Pluralistic Universe*, p. 131 (bracketed expression not in text).

from which, however, it is sundered by its vigorous denial that the third category . . . suffices to make the world, or is even so much as self sufficient."[32] Peirce thus embraces objective idealism with reservations that lead to his assertion that his position is that of "conditional idealism."[33] Idealists, according to Peirce, have been correct in embracing the doctrine of final causation, but misunderstanding its nature, have endowed it with force or Secondness which leaves no room for chance. Thus, we see that "chance," or Firstness, requires not only Thirdness, but also Secondness.

In the earlier discussion of Peirce, the issue was stated in terms of materialism, dualism, and idealism. Within the context of these alternatives Peirce was driven to an "idealism" modified by the insertion of the category of Secondness, and, indirectly, Firstness as well. This, however, leads directly to his realism, for though efficient causation belongs to the category of Secondness, the final causation indicated by Peirce's idealism belongs to the category of Thirdness, and Peirce's realism is concerned with the reality of Thirdness. And the nature of Thirdness requires the reality of Secondness, and indirectly, Firstness as well.

Peirce states the issue of realism in an apparently straightforward way: "Whether laws and general types are figments of the mind or are real."[34] That Peirce intends more by realism than is indicated by this seemingly straightforward question becomes evident from his discussion of realism and from his objections to nominalism. Indeed, his objection to nominalism gives the first glimmerings of the complexity of his realism. Peirce asserts that all modern philosophy has been nominalistic.[35] This includes not only Locke, Berkeley, and Hume, but Leibniz and Hegel as well. Since Peirce criticized Hegelian idealism because it emphasized Thirdness or "laws and general types" to the exclusion of Secondness, Peirce's realism cannot be understood merely by saying that Thirdness is real.

The danger of pulling the position of pragmatic metaphysics first in one direction, then in another, oblivious to the radical change in perspective that has vitiated the traditional alternatives, a danger lurking in the attempts of Peirce and Lewis to find an adequate metaphysical label, is clearly recognized and elucidated in James's discussion of the

32 / Peirce, 5.436.

33 / Peirce, 5.494.

34 / Peirce, 1.16. Here it should be noted again that the realism under discussion is that type of realism which is contrasted with nominalism. It is not the realism that lies in opposition to idealism.

35 / Peirce, 1.19.

misunderstandings of his own path between monistic idealism and atomism. As he concludes, "The whole question revolves in very truth about the word 'some'. Radical empiricism and pluralism stand out for the legitimacy of the notion of *some*: each part of the world is in some ways connected, and in some other ways not connected with its other parts. . . . Absolutism, on its side, seems to hold that 'some' is a category ruinously infected with self-contradictoriness, and that the only categories inwardly consistent and therefore pertinent to reality are 'all' and 'none'."[36] As can be seen, at this point Peirce's realism, like his idealism, involves the lawfulness of final causality. They are diverse labels intended to capture his own attempt to avoid the extremes of absolutism or atomistic nominalism, neither of which allow for "some."

As has been shown, to avoid these extremes, Peirce's realism must in some way involve Secondness. Yet when we turn to Peirce's own often asserted affinity with the scholastic realism of Duns Scotus, we find Peirce objects to the assertion of the interrelationship of Secondness and Thirdness.[37] Nonetheless, the strong interrelation of Secondness and Thirdness is undeniable for Peirce. He holds that an efficient cause, detached from a final cause in the form of a law would not even possess true efficiency, "it might exert itself, but something would follow only post hoc, not propter hoc."[38] Conversely, Peirce claims that the category of Thirdness "can have no concrete being without action, as a separate object on which to work its government."[39] Thus, efficient causation, in the sense of actualization of a possibility, requires the rational causality of Thirdness to provide the potentialities, while Thirdness requires the concrete action of Secondness. Yet, though Thirdness is not real without Secondness, Peirce holds that Secondness does not contain any Thirdness at all; it is the individual, brute, blind, and unintelligible, for the "would-be" of Thirdness is never contracted to the "is" of Secondness.[40]

If the "concrete being" of Thirdness as dependent upon Secondness is approached in the light of the traditional problems of contraction or concretion or ingression of any sort, Peirce's position may well be untenable. But since Peirce is trying once again to deal with his position in terms of traditional alternatives, it may be that what underlies his difficulty is a radical change in perspective, such that the entire framework within which these traditional alternatives arise is rejected. If Thirdness and Secondness are intimately interrelated, if Thirdness cannot be "imag-

36 / James, *Pluralistic Universe*, pp. 40–41.

37 / Peirce, 8.208.   38 / Peirce, 1.213.

39 / Peirce, 5.436.   40 / Peirce, 8.208.

ined" without Secondness, yet Thirdness does not contract into Secondness, then another mode of interrelation is obviously called for. Before pursuing this direction, however, clarification of some terminology will be helpful.

Peirce uses the term *possibility* to characterize not only Firstness, but also Thirdness. This is understandable, for since Secondness comprises the domain of the actual, the possible, in a broad sense, must include both Firstness and Thirdness. Although Firstness clearly indicates the possibility of the mere "may be," while Thirdness indicates the potentialities of lawful modes of behavior, he indiscriminately interchanges the terms *possibility* and *potentiality*, at times speaking of the possibilities of Thirdness and of the potentialities of Firstness. Speculative pragmatism will refer to the possibility of Firstness, as opposed to the possibility of Thirdness, as either negative possibility, as opposed to positive possibility, or possibility as opposed to potentiality. The former set of terms has a more limited but more immediate advantage, for it will help indicate the relationship between possibility and generality, though the latter set of terms will, in the long run, be more frequently used. When there is no need to distinguish between Firstness and Thirdness, the term *possibility* will be used to cover both.[41]

Generality also serves a dual function that can tend to get conflated, as the general is that which is opposed to the singular. Since Secondness is the category of the singular or the individual, generality must in some sense characterize both Firstness and Thirdness, both negative possibility and positive possibility. Thus Peirce holds that "generality is either of that negative sort which belongs to the merely potential, as such, and this is peculiar to the category of Firstness, or it is of the positive kind which belongs to conditional necessity, and this is peculiar to the category of law."[42] Further, Peirce equates generality and continuity.[43] Thus, the continuity of Firstness, as a "mere maybe" is the negative continuity of negative generality.

That the ontological basis for the experience of Firstness cannot be sheer diversity but rather diversity "overlaid" with some continuity was indicated in chapter 4.[44] Such a continuity is part of the very being of the

41 / These occasions will be obvious for the reader.

42 / Peirce, 1.427. Here is an instance in which Peirce uses the term *potential* when what is intended is the possibility of Firstness.

43 / Peirce, Vol. 8, p. 279.

44 / There it was noted that such a qualitative continuity involved the continuity of Firstness as opposed to the continuity of Thirdness. This provides the basis for Peirce's characterization of Firstness not only as diversity, but also as unity. A discussion of Peirce's

qualitative diversity that presents itself in the diversity of qualitative experience, for it is from a qualitative continuum that specific qualities can emerge within experience. What characterizes the general, as opposed to singular or the individual, for Peirce is that the laws of excluded middle and noncontradiction do not apply to the general.[45] Apparently, then, one could hold the rich evolving universe, in its element of negative generality, to be general in the negative sense that no determination can be made.[46] Firstness would seem to display a negative generality in that it is limited by nothing whatsoever. As Peirce states the position, Firstness is essentially indifferent to continuity.[47] But though indifferent to its continuity, it is a continuum of negative possibilities, a substratum of "chance." This can best be clarified by turning briefly to Peirce's cosmological account.

The use of Peirce's cosmological account to understand the functioning of the categories may at first glance seem a bit misplaced, for such an account is frequently considered to be either the black sheep or the white elephant of Peirce's philosophic productivity. Further, to view the ontological problem of the relationship of the categories in terms of the cosmological problem of the origin of the categories may be held to be a type of genetic fallacy at the metaphysical level. Yet only if the emergence of Thirdness from Secondness and Firstness is recognized, can the status of Thirdness be adequately understood. Furthermore, as has been well noted by some critics, the sequence traced in its initial stages is an objective logical sequence, not a temporal one at all. Thus, Peirce's cosmological account provides the logical key for understanding the interrelation of the categories. And Peirce's cosmological account, in which the random actions and reactions of the substratum of chance gradually tend to take on habits that in turn limit future interactions, reveals a relation not of contraction or concretion or ingression of any sort, but rather of emergence. This should be expected, for contraction,

---

identification of quality with Firstness will be postponed till the latter part of this chapter for reasons that will become clear then.

45 / Peirce asserts that the general is that to which the law of the excluded middle does not apply, while the vague is that to which the principle of noncontradiction does not apply (5.448). He then explicitly identifies continuity with generality (see n. 43). And, as will be seen, for Peirce as well as for the present position, whatever is general or continuous is to some degree vague.

46 / Peirce illustrates, in contrast, the positive generality of Thirdness in his example of the triangle: though it is true that "a triangle in general is not isosceles nor equilateral; nor is a triangle in general scalene," yet a triangle in general is triangular, and the generality of triangularity does limit the possible alternative of further determination (5.505).

47 / Peirce, 6.205.

concretion, and ingression are the concepts of substance philosophy, while emergence belongs to the nature of process.[48]

Although Peirce goes into detail in various places concerning the cosmological account, the best summary is an insightful analogy which he provides:

> Let the clean blackboard be a sort of diagram of the original vague potentiality. . . . I draw a chalk line on the board. This discontinuity is one of these brute acts by which alone the original vagueness could have made a step toward definiteness. There is a certain element of continuity in this line. Where did this continuity come from? It is nothing but the original continuity of the blackboard which makes everything upon it continuous.[49]

The discontinuity can be produced upon that blackboard only by the reaction between two continuous surfaces into which it is separated. Thus, what is a singularity or discreteness in the containing continuum is itself a positive generality in relation to the discrete cuts potentially "in" it. In brief, Secondness, or bare brute action and reaction, is a distinct analytic element within the ongoing process of a concretely rich processive continuum. There is no such thing as disembodied interaction, however, and actuality, as it contextually occurs in the passing present, is characterized by the brute hereness and nowness of the shock of interaction or efficient causation "acting upon" the substratum of "negative continuity" or negative possibility, in accordance with the limitations placed upon it by the positive possibilities of lawfulness.

The importance not only of these three categories but also of their mode of interrelation can be seen from the one metaphysical requirement for knowledge that Lewis is forced to make within the context of his otherwise purely epistemological discussion. This one assumption which knowledge as predictive requires is that though "any possibility is a possible actuality, it is not possible that all possibilities should be concomitantly real" or, in other terms, actuality must be a "limitation of the all possible."[50] In short, Secondness must provide the tool for

48 / The objection may be raised that Whitehead's philosophy is a process philosophy that involves the concept of ingression. But, as Mead has well pointed out, Whitehead's ingression of eternal objects into events is an attempt to get contingency from a space-time rigidity that does not adequately allow for contingency and emergence (Mead, *Philosophy of the Present*, pp. 43, 49). This criticism is repeated in various ways throughout much of Mead's book.

49 / Peirce, 6.203.

50 / Lewis, *Mind and the World Order*, pp. 367–368.

progressing from the may-be or spontaneity of Firstness to the would-be or potentiality of Thirdness.

Here we see the manner in which acts or Secondness can be characterized both as privative brute, blind or unintelligible, and as that which gives reality to laws and general types. Secondness, as distinct from Firstness or Thirdness, is brute action and reaction. In this sense, it is the acting compulsion of blind force or efficient causation. Secondness is a mode of behavior of the concrete processive continuum—the mode of behavior that is characterized by brute interaction. Thus, existence, or actuality, or individuality, as an analytic element within processive concreteness, is a mode of behavior of the general; it is the mode of behavior characterized by interaction. And it is the interaction, not that which interacts, which is individual, brute, and blind. But, this brute, blind interaction of the general processive continuum is precisely what turns negative possibility into positive possibility, mere "may-be" into "would-be." Thus, Secondness is that which makes possible the very reality of Thirdness.

We can see now why Peirce insists that Thirdness does not contract into Secondness—Thirdness is not the kind of "thing" that can be in Secondness. Indeed, if one insists on using spatial language, saying that Secondness is in Thirdness is more accurate than that Thirdness is in Secondness, for a continuum may be said to contain its cuts, potential or actual, but the cuts do not contain the continuum.[51] Thus, Peirce can say that Secondness does not contain any Thirdness at all, for an

51 / For Peirce, "A true continuum is something whose possibilities of determination no multitude of individuals can exhaust" (6.170). The objection may be raised that there is a sense in which the cuts do contain the continuum, since the possibilities inherent in the continuum cut are partially dependent upon the possibilities inherent in the continuum from which it is cut. This objection depends upon viewing the cut not in its aspect of discreteness or Secondness, but in its aspect of continuity or Thirdness. Thus, Peirce can hold that final causality is operative in nature and that things tend toward a final cause. Present processes tend to realize a future that is inherent within them as present possibilities. As Peirce observes, "Final causation is that kind of causation whereby the whole calls out its parts" (1.220). This whole is not some idealistic type of "ens necessarium" which "draws" the processes of nature, nor is it any "whole of nature" trying to realize itself, but rather the whole is any continuum of natural processes that "calls out" a determinate range of parts; the rationality of final causality is the rational force of continuity; to say that processes are governed by final causes is to say that potentialities are real, for final causes within nature are precisely continuities that govern their possible cuts or actualities, but that no number of actualities can exhaust. Although the primordial state tends to suggest a representation of the First category alone, yet it implicitly contains Thirdness in the form of the law-taking tendencies of Firstness as a continuum. Thus, the continuity of Thirdness is not something "other than" the continuity of Firstness. Further, Peirce indicates that the law of habit-taking can be understood in terms of Secondness as well as Firstness (6.601). Here,

"*existing* thing is simply a blind reacting thing" though "existing *things* do not need reasons: they are reasons."[52] Here, then, can be found the radical significance of Peirce's view that synechism, realism, and pragmatism are intimately linked.[53]

With the above sketch in mind, the ensuing discussion can now turn to the significance of some changes in categorial delineations that will be found in speculative pragmatism. One of the big confusions in philosophy is the muddling of the concepts of existence and reality, and intertwined with this confusion is the problem of their respective relations to the concept of actuality. Within the context of the present discussion, the confusion involved in the first set of concepts can be found to emerge by confounding the category of existence, as an analytic aspect of processive concreteness, with existence as processive concreteness. As an analytic aspect of processive concreteness, existence is characterized as the bare reaction event, brute force, or over-againstness. As has been noted, however, there is no such thing as disembodied interaction, and that which interacts is a portion of a spatio-temporally real, existing processive concreteness that includes not just Secondness, but Firstness and Thirdness as well. Thus, processive concreteness, as that which comprises the natural universe, is spatio-temporally real, and it exists. Any slab of concreteness, however, in its reality, as it exists, must be understood in terms of analytic distinctions, including the category of Secondness, if its behavior is to be adequately grasped.

Dewey's confounding of concrete existence and an analytic category for grasping it in its aspect of Secondness can begin to be seen in his most general statement concerning existence, which is that "every existence is an event." Events and existence are used interchangeably.[54] This is of course consistent with Peirce's use of the category of Secondness or bare reaction event as the category of existence. Dewey also claims that nature is "a complex of events"[55] and that existence consists of "events . . . characterized by beginning, process and ending."[56] Further, events "have" potentialities, for as he notes, "Common sense has no great occasion to distinguish between bare events and objects; objects being events-with-meanings. Events are present and operative anyway; what

---

again, no categorial content can be understood apart from its interrelatedness with the others.

52 / Peirce, 4.36; 5.107 (italics not in text).

53 / Peirce, 6.169 ff.

54 / Dewey, *Experience and Nature*, pp. 63, 240–241.

55 / Ibid., p. 66.

56 / Ibid., p. 92.

concerns us is their meanings expressed in expectations, beliefs, inferences, regarding their potentialities."[57] For Dewey, as for Peirce, the
event is the category of existence, but there is no bare reaction event,
but events characterized by beginning, process, and ending. Thus, existence as it concretely occurs, includes the analytic aspects of existence
or events, plus guiding potentialities of Thirdness as well as the beginnings and endings that contain an element of the spontaneity of Firstness.

A related categorial confusion is found in Lewis's claim that an object
is an enduring event.[58] To say that an object is an event would seem to
indicate that objects belong to the category of Secondness. Clearly, however, Lewis is using *event* in a different sense from that which indicates
the category of Secondness. An event, in Peirce's technical terminology,
cannot endure, for an event indicates the discrete and momentary. What
Lewis terms an enduring event is, in fact, a continuum of events, or Secondness as guided by Thirdness.

Lewis further holds, in the context of his metaphysical discussions,
that whatever is an object is a discrete individual, and that objects as
individuals answer to the law of the excluded middle,[59] a characterization that further seems to incorporate objects into the category of
Secondness. This is an example of Lewis's frequent switch, however, indicative of the pragmatic focus in general, between metaphysics and
epistemology. That this is meant as an epistemological assertion can be
seen from his statement that "it is not precluded to ask if objects, as we
distinguish them, are not abstracted by relation to something distinctive
of the human":[60]

> There are stars in the heavens, but constellations only for our seeing.
> Perhaps likewise there are molar masses only for our senses, directed
> upon the quanta or wavicles which inhabit the ocean of energy. But at
> least the potentiality of so appearing to us, instead of otherwise, and of
> being discriminable as just these molar masses, in just these relations to
> one another, is in the ocean itself, as constituted independently of us.[61]

An object as an individual, then, depends upon interaction with a
"minded organism," but the potentiality of thus appearing is in the independently existing reality itself, for an object as an experienced particular is an abstracted portion of some continuum of events. This poten-

---

57 / Ibid., p. 244.
58 / Lewis, "Realism or Phenomenalism?" p. 341.
59 / Ibid., p. 342.
60 / Ibid., p. 346.
61 / Ibid. This is an example from science; not a reification of scientific content.

tiality is not the potentiality of ideal archetypes or substantive features in any sense, but is rather the potentiality inherent in "modes of persistence" or "continuities."[62] Thus, what is inherent in processive concreteness is the potentiality for being grasped in terms of discrete objects or objective facts, which is possible only because the processive concreteness contains modes of persistence that our meanings can cut into in ways that allow us to anticipate future experience. The object as an experienced particular is dependent upon the Secondness of organism-environment interaction, but to call an object an event is to create categorial problems.

To avoid the categorial confusions that plague discussions of pragmatic metaphysics when processive continuity in its concreteness is confounded either with one of its analytically delineated activity modes or with its features that emerge in relation to the noetic activity of man, the following discussion will modify the category of Secondness. Though seemingly the most "sparse" of the activity modes, it in fact attempts to carry too heavy a load. The following development will exclude the concept of the individual a well as the concept of existence from this category. As has already been shown, the laws of noncontradiction and the excluded middle do not hold true of the independently real in its generality aspects of possibility and potentiality, but only in its aspect of the "particularity" or "individuality" of events. Neither do they hold true of the independently real in its aspect of Secondness as the event. To apply these laws to the bare interaction event is meaningless, and for two reasons. First, the interaction itself is brute, blind, privative. Any positive characteristics belong rather to that which interacts, portions of a processive continuity. Second, though Peirce characterizes the individual as the determinate in all respects, he notes, after delineating the category of Secondness in terms of the individual, that the absolute individual "cannot exist, properly speaking. For whatever lasts for any time, however short . . . will undergo some change in its relations."[63] Thus, in none of the activity modes are these laws of logic applicable. These logical laws apply to individuals, but individuals emerge in the context of world. The individual, to which the laws of the excluded middle and noncontradiction apply, is the individual that emerges as the independently real is grasped by the structures of pragmatic meaning. Indeed, the act, as a metaphysically discrete determinate individual is an ideal-

---

62 / Ibid., p. 341.

63 / Peirce, 3.93 n. Neither can the absolute individual, for Peirce, "be realized in sense or thought" (3.93). As was seen in chapters 4 and 2, there is a fundamental universalizing aspect to sense, as well as a fundamental indeterminateness to meaning.

ized abstraction similar to idealized anteception as a point of temporal discontinuity. What it would be at an instant, it cannot be, because of its radically temporal nature. An event does have a unique character, but only because, as Dewey indicates, one cannot "isolate an event from the history in which it belongs and in which it has its character."[64]

The characterization of existence will be excluded from the category of the event, not because existence excludes events, but because existence includes much more. Spatio-temporal reality exists, but spatio-temporal reality, as processive concreteness, includes possibilities and potentialities as well as events. The objection may be made that existence is the arena of natural resistance, what we encounter, that facticity that is there and that our knowledge must adequately incorporate. We encounter possibilities and potentialities as well as actualities, however, and these former, as well as the latter, have a brute facticity and natural resistance that our knowledge must incorporate if it is to be successful. Thus, what exists, what is spatio-temporally real, is processive concreteness in all of its ontological activity modes, in all of its ways or manners of behaving. Existence and spatio-temporal reality are coextensive.[65]

The ambiguities of the term *actuality* tend to parallel the ambiguities of existence. In converse fashion, *actuality* will be used, in modified form, to characterize the activity mode of Secondness, but will not be applicable to processive concreteness in general. To say that processive concreteness is real, it exists, yet cannot be characterized as actual may appear a bit strange. But if processive concreteness is characterized as actual, then we are faced with the confusing claim that actuality includes potentiality and possibility, when actuality, as a philosophic category, is intended precisely to distinguish an aspect of reality other than potentiality and possibility.

The objection may be raised that to refuse to call concrete existence actual is to fly in the face of common sense rather than to provide a metaphysics that accounts for our common-sense experience. Actuality, however, as a philosophic concept that contrasts with possibility or potentiality, and actuality as it is used in common sense, seem subtly at odds with each other, and may well be the source of categorial confusion. For example, common sense can well speak of actual potentialities, or say that something is actually possible, meaning by this that

64 / Dewey, *Experience and Nature*, p. 84.

65 / This is intended to deny neither that there emerges an increased richness of spatio-temporal reality as it relates to the human, nor that there are other kinds of reality which emerge within the human world.

these possibilities and potentialities are connected with real conditions, with spatio-temporal conditions, or with present conditions. To avoid such conceptual muddles, actuality will be used as an analytic categorial distinction, and cannot be applied to any "space-time slab" of reality in its concreteness. Processive concreteness is the arena of activity, but activity can be understood only in terms of all three ontological activity modes.

Further, the category of Secondness, as indicative of a distinct activity mode of events will be characterized not as actuality but as actualization. It is the category of events, of interactions or transactions that are actualizing activities. And it must be stressed again,[66] but now from the focal point of the interaction rather than that which interacts, that the interactional or transactional event cannot be understood in terms of two self-contained things that come together, but rather as an aspect of a contextual whole in which each ingredient, including the interactional event itself, is what it is because of the nature of the contextual whole. Peirce's use of the term *reaction event* may well be misleading in this respect. This category of "actualizing" or "actualization" leads to two diverse sets of potential problems.

First, by changing "the actual" to the activity of "actualizing," concreteness seems to have disappeared. What does actualizing activity actualize? It actualizes potentialities. How do potentialities emerge and develop? They emerge and develop from actualizing activities and a "substratum" of possibilities. The concretely rich matrix of possibilities, potentialities, and actualizing activities seems to have become an ephemeral matrix indeed. Here, however, two interrelated types of concreteness that are crucial in understanding ontological activity modes should be noted. First, as has already been indicated, process is concrete in the sense of being indefinitely rich. It is "malleable" to our interpretive directions, not because it is lacking in relations, but because it is abundantly rich in interacting events emerging from and giving rise to an indefinite richness of possibilities.[67] Second, and more relevant for the immediate problem at hand, it is concrete in the sense that it is, as James so well expresses, the "living, moving, active thickness of the real."[68] Processive concreteness is the ontologically dense universe that intrudes within experience. The ontological activity modes express the thick ontological density of "the causal dynamic relatedness of activity

66 / See chapter 1.
67 / See chapter 4.
68 / James, *Pluralistic Universe*, p. 116.

and history."[69] Further, when one gets at the center of such a thick activity, it can be seen why the laws of the excluded middle and noncontradiction do not hold, for, as James again so insightfully notes, place yourself in the interior thickness of the doing, and you see that in its concreteness it has the potential for breaking into the most contradictory characterizations.[70] Thus, processive concreteness in its various activity modes has what Peirce calls a generality that eludes the principles of noncontradiction and the excluded middle, or as Lewis notes, a generality that "overflows" such lines of demarcation,[71] not because it is either amorphous or ephemeral, but because it has the indefinite richness of a dense, opaque, thick, changing process. Indeed, the category of the potential can best be expressed in terms of concrete dynamic tendencies, dynamic tendencies toward actualizations of varying types under varying types of circumstances, operative within processive concreteness.[72] To substitute for the ontological density of activity modes a concretely rich but ephemeral matrix of abstract possibilities, potentialities, and actualizing events is to forget that the categories represent modes or ways in which an ontologically dense processive concreteness functions or acts.

The above discussion shows that concreteness cannot be equated with facts or objects, for facts and objects are discriminated from processive concreteness by the activity of conscious organisms.[73] Further, the concrete does not mean fully determinate. No slab of processive concreteness is fully determinate. Thus, again, in the sense that actuality indicates the determinate, the finished, the final, processive concreteness cannot be characterized as actual. The philosophic concept of actuality seems more and more to be one of those categories that emerged in the context of substance philosophy, but led to confusions within the context of a metaphysics of activity, for there is nothing that is fully determinate, finished, final, except the actualizing events, the events of actualization.

This statement immediately brings in a second potential problem, for pragmatism is at times accused of an over-futurism. In some sense, crit-

---

69 / Ibid., p. 122.

70 / Ibid., p. 117. This "breaking into" is of course not a breaking up into parts but an emergence into novel traits.

71 / Lewis, "A Pragmatic Conception of the A Priori," *Collected Papers*, p. 232.

72 / The concrete nature of possibilities as spatio-temporal will be seen in the following discussion. This does not preclude other senses of "possibilities" and potentialities which will emerge in the context of "world."

73 / This point will be developed in some detail in the following chapter.

ics suggest, reality, for the pragmatist, consists in the future. Such a charge stems from both epistemic and ontological directions. Peirce does claim that reality consists in the future.[74] This however, is not a metaphysical statement but an epistemological statement.[75] Successful prediction is the only way we can know that our meaningful claims fall within the range of alternatives presented by the tendencies in nature.

Yet pragmatic metaphysics, even when clearly distinguished from epistemological issues, is at times accused of over-futurism because the emphasis on the "would-be" of real potentialities apparently requires that the future actuality be real now in some sense. Here again, however, is evidence of categorial confusions. There is indeed a very great difference between "future actualizations," "future possibilities of actualizations," and "present possibilities of future actualizations," though these (and especially the latter two) are often used interchangeably. The difference between possibility and actuality is not the difference between future and present, but rather past, present, and future can be viewed in terms of possibility or actuality, or, in the present terminology, actualizations or interactional actualizing events. When these various facets are distinguished, it becomes clear that the pragmatic emphasis on the "would-be" does not put undue emphasis on the future, and does not require that future actualizations in some sense be real now, but rather it requires that present possibilities for future actualization be real. Future as well as past are drawn into the present for pragmatism, but they are drawn into the present in the form of potentialities and possibilities engaged in an ever-advancing process of actualization. This is possible only because the present contains actualizations, potentialities, and possibilities, all emergent from the past and projecting toward a novel future. Again, the concept of fixed actuality seems to muddy or, perhaps better, to stagnate the waters.

The above sketch indicates that the understanding of the functioning of ontological activity modes in the passing present cannot be separated from an understanding of the relation of this passing present to past and future. Before turning to this latter issue, however, the following discussion will deal more directly with the former one. As has been shown, events are that aspect of existence or processive concreteness that actualizes possibilities. In the process they enter into what will be called *cohesive* and *contextual matrixes*. A *cohesive matrix* is a network of potentialities in the process of actualization. Any cohesive matrix has

74 / Peirce, 8.284.
75 / Peirce's dual senses of reality were discussed in the previous chapter.

an integrative directional flow. Yet, any cohesive matrix is indefinitely rich, and in its concrete potentialities it is both functionally diffused and embedded in a matrix of possibilities. The network of potentialities that constitutes a cohesive matrix can best be understood as a conglomerate of potentialities. The term *conglomerate* is used to indicate that some of the potentialities constitutive of a cohesive matrix have a loosely knit independence from the others, and that all need not be actualized for the integrative flow to continue in its functional character. This conglomerate nature of a cohesive matrix is the result of its functional diffusion. Any cohesive matrix has an integrative functional character in terms of dynamic potentialities that give it an organic wholeness. Yet it has a functional diffusiveness such that the actualization of some of its potentialities does not always require—though sometimes it may—the actualization of specific potentialities throughout its functional diffusiveness, and not all of its potentialities need be, or in fact can be, actualized. Such potentialities are potentials for the realization of some among a range of alternative possibilities. Potentialities are always operative within a concrete matrix of possibilities. A cohesive matrix, constituted by an integrative directional flow manifesting functional diffusions, as embedded in a matrix of possibilities, will be called a *contextual matrix*. The functional diffusions of a cohesive matrix permeate other contextual matrixes. Conversely, any contextual matrix is permeated by the functional diffusions of other cohesive matrixes. Whether or not an integrative directional flow permeates another contextual matrix is dependent upon how, and which of, its functional diffusions permeate that matrix.

These interpenetrating functional diffusions shape the changing horizonal dimensions of a matrix. The horizonal dimensions of a cohesive matrix extend through any spatio-temporal field of its functional diffusions, while the horizonal dimensions of a contextual matrix are contoured, in addition, by any and all possibilities that are alternative possibilities for the temporal advancement of the cohesive matrix, that are possibilities for temporal selectivity by the conglomerate of potentialities constituting the cohesive matrix. As possibilities for temporal selectivity by potentialities are actualized, they enter into the horizonal dimensions of a cohesive matrix, either by giving rise to new potentialities, or by becoming ingredient in the further development of existing potentialities. As possibilities become incorporated into the conglomerate of potentialities constitutive of a cohesive matrix, its horizonal dimensions change. And the horizonal dimensions of the contextual matrix change as well, for the possibilities in which the cohesive matrix is embedded change. Thus, the conglomerate of potentialities constituting any cohesive matrix includes the potentiality for incorporating new potentialities and possibilities within its cohesive and contextual spatio-temporal horizons. The incorporation of potentialities into a cohesive matrix can be of such a nature as to alter either its integrative directional flow, or a functional diffusion in a manner nonessential to the integrative directional flow. In either case, the horizonal dimensions of the cohesive and contextual matrix change, but in the latter way, the change is not of such a nature as to give rise to a new integrative directional flow. The emergence of a new integrative directional flow is a result of which and how functional diffusions are affected. When a new integrative directional flow arises, the cohesive matrix, and hence its contextual matrix, has ceased to be as a discriminable matrix. New cohesive matrixes arise centered around new integrative directional flows.

The term *integrative* here is not intended to mean contractive as opposed to expansive. *Integrative* is equivalent to "determinative of its unified functional character." Such an integration can be seen as a spreading out, or as a drawing in. Indeed, in this instance, these two diverse directional expressions are opposite sides of the same coin. Any determination within a contextual matrix involves at once a restriction and an expansion. Any appropriation of a possibility by the actualizing of a potentiality is at once both restrictive and expansive. Any new actualization restricts in that it negates a range of potentialities and/or possibilities that "could have been actualized" but are no longer real for the contextual matrix as it is becoming, yet at the same time it opens new vistas of potentialities and/or possibilities that were not real for the contextual matrix that is now passing.

The phrase *diffused throughout* another matrix is used rather than the phrase *part of* another matrix to avoid any metaphor that might suggest a building-block model. A matrix of more encompassing scope is not composed of "parts." Rather, while any cohesive matrix can be understood in terms of its integrative directional flow or in terms of its functional diffusions, any functional diffusion within the context of an encompassing contextual matrix itself is a cohesive matrix having an integrative, but functionally diffused, directional flow embedded in a matrix of possibilities. Thus, it has a contextual matrix as intricate as, but partially different from, the contextual matrix of which it is itself a functional diffusion, although its continuance may be dependent upon its role as a functional diffusion. The distinction between a functional diffusion and an integrative flow is thus contextually relative. There are no ontological building blocks. Rather, there are various scopes or levels of interpenetrating contextual matrixes. As James points out, things are 'with' one another in many ways, but nothing includes everything, or dominates over everything. The pluralistic universe is more like "a federal republic than like an empire or a kingdom."[76] Also, the term *diffusion* is intended to avoid the concept of spatial containment. Any processive concreteness is diffused throughout that to which it temporally relates. Such temporal relationships involve pasts, presents, and futures.

What are possibilities or mere "may-be's" within the context of one contextual matrix are, within another contextual matrix, a part of the conglomerate of potentialities constitutive of its cohesive matrix. Conversely, what are potentialities within the context of one contextual matrix are, as functionally diffused throughout other contextual matrixes, part of a range of possibilities within which other conglomerates of potentialities constitutive of other cohesive matrixes operate. Thus, potentialities and possibilities are alike dynamic or dispositional tendencies,[77] but dynamic tendencies and the transactional events that actualize them occur in partially intermeshing matrixes, and the difference between the "would-be" of potentialities and the "may-be" of possibilities is a function of the role of dynamic tendencies in relation to a cohesive matrix. The potentialities constitutive of a cohesive matrix are at once functionally diffused throughout a multiplicity of possibilities, each of which is a potentiality within a cohesive matrix that it helps to constitute.

Among the other potentialities and possibilities included within any contextual matrix there is, at any time, the potentiality and/or the possibility either for its continued endurance, or for its closure, or for both. Though of course both endurance and closure cannot be actualized at the same time, the actualizing of a tendency to endure may at the same time be an actualizing of the tendency *toward* closure. Thus, any emerging interactional event is an instance of the actualization of the tendency to endurance or the tendency toward closure, or both. No closure is absolute, however, but rather, as Dewey notes, whenever something ends, something else begins, or, in other terms, the closure of one history is the beginning of another.[78] In the intermeshing of contextual matrixes, nature is, indeed, "a scene of incessant beginnings and endings."[79] Through the interactional events of the ever-emerging present, inter-

76 / James, *Pluralistic Universe*, pp. 144–145.
77 / Other types of possibility will emerge within the context of "world."
78 / Dewey, *Experience and Nature*, pp. 83–85.
79 / Ibid., p. 83.

acting dynamic tendencies give rise to changing contextual matrixes, to changing cohesive matrixes, and to changing integrative directional flows; in this latter case, the cohesive and contextual matrixes do not change their horizonal contours, but rather cease to be, giving rise to new cohesive and contextual matrixes.

Until now, the concept of quality, though mentioned in passing early in this chapter, has been deliberately omitted from discussion for three reasons. First, discussions of quality usually relate to ontological dimensions emerging from the context of organism-environment interaction. Second, because Peirce lumps together quality, novelty, and the "may-be" of possibilities within the category of Firstness, frequently Firstness is held to be the most elusive of Peirce's categories at best, and at worst, some sort of systematic dump heap for what will not fit into the category of Secondness or Thirdness. The premature entrance of quality into the present discussion could only lead to ambiguities of interpretation, some of which result in the above types of criticism. Third, while the earlier discussion focused on developing the parallels of categories among various pragmatists, any categorial delineation of quality would have pointed toward apparent conflict at that point. While Peirce places quality in the category of Firstness or the "may-be" of possibility, Lewis views quality, as an objective property, in terms of a potentiality or dispositional trait, and quality, as an emerging content within the immediacy of organism-environment interaction, in terms of the dispositional traits as they manifest themselves through the Secondness of interactive immediacy.[80] Such transactional emergents are, for Lewis, as metaphysically real as the dispositional traits, but their reality consists in their emergence through organism-environment interaction. As Lewis summarizes, the apprehended sense content and the objective reality known "belong to different categories."[81] Thus, while Peirce relegates quality to Firstness, Lewis views it alternatively from the perspectives of either Thirdness or Secondness.

With what has thus far been developed, however, these potential problems can be used to clarify further the position of speculative pragmatism. Within the context of organism-environment interaction, quality can be understood as a "mere may-be" or as a "would-be," for this distinction is functionally dependent upon the matrix in terms of which it is understood. Thus, quality may be understood as a dispositional trait of a cohesive matrix, or it can be seen as a possibility within the con-

---

80 / Lewis, "Realism or Phenomenalism?" p. 343.
81 / Ibid., p. 344.

textual matrix in which the vital, conscious organism as a cohesive matrix is embedded, a mere "may-be" for possible selective actualization by some among the conglomerate of potentialities of the cohesive matrix that constitutes the vital, conscious organism. As has been shown, not only are possibilities and potentialities real only as embedded in concrete contextual matrixes, but also the distinction between possibilities and potentialities is not absolute, but is a functional distinction based on the role of dynamic tendencies within a specific contextual matrix. In either case, qualitative experience requires the interactive immediacy of the actualizing event of organism-environment interaction.

Quality, however, is not limited to matrixes inclusive, in some way, of vital organisms. Though experienced qualities are emergent within the organism-environment interaction that actualizes possibilities or potentialities, the ontological status of quality is not dependent upon organisms. As Dewey notes, vital and conscious events exhibit qualities "not *fully* displayed"[82] in the simpler ontological relationships, and he specifically notes that concerning temporality there is a difference between temporal order and temporal quality, and "temporal quality is an immediate trait of every occurrence whether in or out of consciousness."[83] Emerging events are qualitative in other ways because of their fundamental temporal quality, for as has been seen, they carry with them their histories. Further, events are abstractions from processive continuity. Thus, the emerging processive continuity as a continuum of eventful interaction carries with it a continuum of changeable and changing qualities[84] in which any event "is both beginning of one course and close of another."[85] From this perspective, quality can be seen as belonging to the category of actualization or eventful interaction, but eventful interaction is the actualizing of potentialities and possibilities, and its character cannot be separated from this history it carries with it. Thus, Dewey can note that causal mechanisms and temporal finalities with their qualitative endings are phases of the same natural processes.[86]

82 / Dewey, *Experience and Nature*, p. 92 (italics added).

83 / Ibid.

84 / As can now be seen, the static spatial continuity of a qualitative continuum grasped by the organism in the moment of idealized anteception requires the temporality of the universe for its very possibility. In the idealized instant of "brute having" the temporally rooted interpretive function of meanings is "withheld," but the brute having of the static spread-outness of spatial continuity in that idealized moment devoid of the meanings embodied in man's dispositional tendencies of response presupposes the very temporality from which it is an idealized abstraction. (See chapter 4.)

85 / Dewey, *Experience and Nature*, p. 85.

86 / Ibid., p. 83.

Qualitative character, then, is both ontologically pervasive and a function of all three ontological activity modes; it cannot be identified with any one activity mode alone, though its various aspects can be understood from the perspective of the various activity modes. Thus, quality, far from being an ontological "simple," a possible "building block," is an emergent within the context of interacting ontological activity modes. Its being is a function of the complexities of intermeshing matrixes.

In qualitative experience the actualizing event is the interaction of potentialities, one of which is a function of a vital, conscious cohesive matrix. It carries with it the history of the organic cohesive matrix, as well as the history of an ontologically other cohesive matrix.[87] As was shown previously, the formation of the sensory core of schematic structure within the context of anteceptive experience involves the unity not of a discrete content of a separate sense, but the unity of a portion of a qualitative continuum. Now this situation, like all human situations, can be seen to be a function both of the temporality of the organism and the temporality of that universe with which it is in interaction. Further, in a fashion analogous to experience, the distinction must be made, within the context of intermeshing matrixes, between qualitative character emerging in a matrix and the qualitative character of a matrix. Changing qualitative character within a matrix need not change its qualitative character as a matrix.

Change of qualitative character of a matrix is not, however, equivalent to a change of integrative directional flow or integrative function. When there is a new cohesive matrix, and hence a new contextual matrix, there is a new qualitative pervasiveness, but there can be a new qualitative pervasiveness of any matrix without such a change. An integrative directional flow is such that the endurance of a continuity of actualizations can guide a diversity of more rapid changes in an orderly fashion that they would otherwise not have. Yet, as these changes occur—changes that do not alter the integrative directional flow, but rather are a function of it—a change in the pervasive quality of a matrix can occur as well. Indeed, if a new integrative function emerges, there is not a change of pervasive quality within a matrix, but rather a new matrix has arisen. Further, a cohesive matrix has a pervasive quality that cannot be understood as a function just of its integrative flow and functional diffusions,

---

87 / This analysis, as indicated above, may be made alternatively by speaking in terms of an organic cohesive matrix and the possibilities of its contextual matrix, or in terms of the potentialities within a cohesive matrix that includes the organism plus more.

as these two aspects are isolated from their contextual matrix. The entire concrete richness of a contextual matrix has its own pervasive quality, and in the interactional events of the ever-emerging present, interacting dynamic tendencies give rise to contextual matrixes permeated by a new qualitative character that enters into the qualitative tonality of the cohesive matrix. In a fashion analogous to what has been found in experience, the quality of any matrix, like the quality of any experienced context, is a result of a here-and-now concreteness that renders it both unique and unified. These features are again due to the nature of any contextual matrix as both functionally diffused throughout, and incorporating the functional diffusions of, other contextual matrixes.

This point, however, leads directly to the issue of novelty. And, like quality, it will be seen that novelty cannot be understood in terms of any one ontological activity mode, but rather must be understood as a function of all three, though its approach in terms of each can present it in different lights. The idea may be held that if all possibilities as independent of noetic activity are in fact potentialities or dynamic tendencies of processive concreteness, then the universe, apart from man, is in fact deterministic. Though possibilities bring novelty into any contextual matrix, such novelty holds only from within the perspective of a matrix and disappears in the light of the overview of intermeshing matrixes. This, however, misses the character both of the intermeshing of contextual matrixes and of true temporality. James's characterization of the universe well expresses the character of the intermeshings, when he observes that the universe is "many everywhere and always, nothing real escapes from having an environment . . . the sundry parts of reality may be externally related."[88] The nature of functional diffusions is such that any matrix incorporates an environment, part of which need not be internally related to it. Further, though every functional diffusion is itself a cohesive matrix of a nature more limited in scope, at least in some respect, than the matrix of which it is a functional diffusion, there is no one matrix that "contains" all the others as parts to a whole, for the nature of functional diffusions is such that intermeshings are always partial and incomplete.

Yet, a further objection may be that though there is no relation of whole to parts, there is an interwoven continuity of matrixical intermeshings. This is indeed true. True novelty, however, does not deny but

88 / James, *Pluralistic Universe*, p. 144.

rather requires such continuity. As James observes, in expressing his agreement with Peirce, to "an observer standing outside of its generating causes, novelty can appear only as so much 'chance,' while to one who stands inside it is the expression of 'free creative activity.' . . . The common objection to admitting novelties is that by jumping abruptly, ex nihilo, they shatter the world's rational continuity."[89] However, novelty "doesn't arrive by jumps and jolts, it leaks in insensibly, for adjacents in experience are always interfused, the smallest real datum being both a coming and a going."[90] James further notes, in this discussion of novelty, that the mathematical notion of an infinitesimal contains, "in truth, the whole paradox of the same and yet the nascent other, of an identity that won't *keep* except so far as it keeps failing, that won't transfer, any more than the serial relations in question transfer, when you apply them to reality instead of applying them to concepts alone."[91] Any cohesive or contextual matrix is at once one and many. In its integrative flow it has a unity, but through its functionally diffused dynamic tendencies it is also in a continual process of becoming "other," and its dynamic "loose play," its "selectivity" from a matrix of possibilities, both affects and is affected by the temporally emerging present as events that won't keep, because the isolated event is an abstraction from a history and future of becoming "other."

Novelty can be understood only as a function of all three activity modes. The event, as the idealized limiting point of the temporal present, is the idealized moment productive of interactive novelty. Possibility, as the "substratum" for alternative realizations of potentialities, is the "substratum" for novel emergents. Potentiality, as the creativity of dynamic tendency in its "loose play," in its indeterminateness for the selectivity of alternative possibilities of actualization yet to be realized, is at once the foundation of lawful endurance and the bearer of a novel future. As such, any contextual matrix is at once, to use Dewey's terms, the union of the "settled and the unsettled, the stable and the hazardous."[92]

Yet there is no discontinuity, for as Mead notes, in a passage that could well characterize any contextual matrix in any of its aspects, reality, in "belonging to a system, and having its nature determined by its relations to members of that system, when it passes into a new sys-

89 / Ibid., p. 153.
90 / Ibid.
91 / Ibid., p. 154.
92 / Dewey, *Quest for Certainty*, p. 194.

tematic order will carry over into its process of readjustment in the new system something of the nature of all members of the old."[93] Change itself requires this feature, for "change involves departure from a condition that must continue in some sense to fulfill the sense of change from that condition."[94] Mead tends to see change, in this sense, as opposed to the happening of events, in relation to intelligent organisms,[95] but in the intermeshing of matrixes such a cosmic situation is to be found. In its integrative flow any matrix has a stability of potentialities in the process of actualization, but as functionally diffused, it is in a constant process of becoming other that leads to its various degrees of possible change, from the almost irrelevant change of contextual possibilities to the transformation of an integrative flow. And change, from insignificant alteration of a minor functional diffusion to determination of a new matrix, is a function of interacting dynamic tendencies that continue to endure in the emerging contextual network in some sense, though they may have been greatly altered by the novel contextual matrix that they now permeate or to which they have given rise.

The matrixical context of novelty within continuity can best be clarified by the use of Mead's concept of sociality. Sociality for Mead is the capacity of being several things at once. It is a process of readjustment. The term *social* refers not to the new system, or new matrix, but to the *process of* readjustment.[96] The social nature of matrixes as intermeshing continuities accounts for the ontological character of novelty or emergence, for the social character of the universe is found "in the situation in which the novel event is both the old order and the new which its advent heralds."[97] And, this "phase of adjustment," which comes between the universe "before the emergent has arisen" and "after it has come to terms with the newcomer," must be a feature of reality, if emergence is to be possible."[98]

The social character of reality as relational and temporal, and understandable only in terms of all three ontological activity modes, constitutes at once its character of novelty. The eventful actualization of a potentiality in the selection of a possibility, an actualization to which

93 / Mead, *Philosophy of the Present*, p. 52.

94 / Mead, *Philosophy of the Act*, p. 331.

95 / Ibid.

96 / Ibid., pp. 47–49.

97 / Ibid., p. 49.

98 / Mead, *Philosophy of the Present*, p. 47. Mead of course holds that novelty is a feature of the universe independently of conscious organisms.

intermeshing matrixes must adjust, is the source of both novelty and the continuity that makes it possible. As Dewey so well states of the ontological status of the divergent characteristics of the universe, "They are mixed not mechanically but vitally like the wheat and tares of the parable. We may recognize them separately but we cannot divide them, for unlike the wheat and tares, they grow from the same root."[99] Thus, the unsettled, the unstable, the novel emergent, is not a characteristic that holds only in relation to man's noetic activity, but is there regardless of such a presence. The indeterminate situation is objectively indeterminate, independently of consciousness. Thus, it is potentially problematic for the conscious organic function whose horizonal dimensions it enters.

As has been shown, any contextual matrix, as a cohesive matrix embedded in a concrete multiplicity of possibilities, is both unique and uniquely unified, and thus "no mechanically exact science of an individual is possible. An individual is a history unique in character."[100] No scientific law is a description of the exact structure and behavior of any "slab" of processive concreteness. Yet, the integrative directional flow of the cohesive matrix grounds a basis for similarity of function with other concrete cohesive matrixes, and thus, in its concrete lawful mode of behavior, it grounds a basis for the worldly emergence of generalizing or universalizing laws. Laws express recurrent types of conditions under which integrative directional flows of particular types function, and in so doing, express the conditions for the emergence of actualizing qualitative events.

A contextual matrix has been seen to have, like an experiential context, a concreteness that both unifies it and renders it unique. It also has, like an experiential context, a system of interrelating dispositional tendencies. In human experience, the indeterminate richness of the concreteness of intermeshing matrixes is ordered by the dispositional generation of pragmatic schemata constitutive of the internal dynamics of pragmatic meaning. The ontological system of intermeshing dispositional tendencies, as indefinitely concrete, is revealable in various ways through various meaning structures, and is universalizable and "intelligible" through the network of such structures, though "in itself" it contains neither universals[101] nor inherently intelligible order. But this "does not mean that nature has lost intelligibility. It rather signifies that

99 / Dewey, *Experience and Nature*, p. 47.

100 / Dewey, *Quest for Certainty*, p. 199. The ambiguous uses of "individual," discussed earlier, can be ignored in this quotation for present purposes.

101 / See chapter 4, n. 59.

we are in position to realize that the term intellig*ible* is to be understood literally. . . . Nature is capable of being understood. . . . The devotion we show to the ideal of intelligence determines the extent" to which the universe "is congenial to mind."[102]

Nor does processive concreteness contain either determinate structure or permanence. Structure is the structure of processive endurance. Processive endurance, to become determinate structure, requires the activity of a discriminating mind. Processive endurance, because of its concrete richness of intermeshing matrixes, is that which is orderable or structurable relative to a consciousness that "cuts" into it in ways that will work. Further, process is the ontological foundation of "permanence" in experience. Permanence is man's name for the stability aspect, the cohesive matrix in its integrative directional flow, processive endurance. Some cohesive matrixes as enduring lend themselves to reversibility of temporally ordered perspectives, and thus to the label of "the unchanging" or the permanent. Others, which do not admit of such reversibility, are themselves seen as processes. Either may be characterized as constant to the degree that their cohesive matrixes manifest processive endurance. Thus, one can speak consistently of the constancy of change. "Gross" events within experience of course cannot be equated with the category of "event" as an ontological activity mode, but rather are functions of the intermeshing matrixes incorporating all three activity modes of processive concreteness. Gross events are distinguishable from the permanent and the constant in terms of the duration of the temporal episode in which the processive endurance of a discriminable matrix has its being.

The human organism finds its ontological status within the reality of intermeshing matrixes. Organism-environment interaction is a specialized instance of the intermeshing matrixes which constitute processive concreteness in general. The human organism, as a cohesive matrix becomes conscious, has the unity of an integrative directional flow, yet is in a constant process of "becoming other" due to the functional diffusions of other matrixes, both conscious and unconscious, that contour its horizonal dimensions, and due conversely, to its functional diffusions, which are spatio-temporally spread throughout any matrix that enters its horizonal field. Thus, it both is affected by and affects its environment. The organism and its environment are what they are in their respective characters because of their intermeshing matrixical contexts. Some of the matrixes that both affect and are affected by the character of

102 / Dewey, *Quest for Certainty*, p. 215.

the conscious organism are other conscious organisms. Like all matrixes, the human matrix is inherently social. In distinction from inanimate matrixes and less sophisticated organic matrixes, however, the human organism can consciously direct its creative appropriation of what enters its horizonal dimensions. The conscious and intelligent guidance of creative appropriation converts novelty into human freedom. Further, as has been seen, the human organism can experience the anteceptive sense of its creative functioning, and, through reflexive awareness, can come to understand the character of its own integrative directional flow within a matrix of potentialities and possibilities in constant process of actualization.[103]

What light does the above examination of ontological activity modes throw upon the relation of the present to the past and the future? If only past and future actualizings were involved, then the passing present would be merely a deterministic push from the past or pull from the future. Past and future are, however, conditions involved in the present, not in their aspect of actualizations, but in their aspect of continuity or possibility.[104]Neither the past nor the future, in their aspect of possibility, denote settled entities that have been or will be, for just as past and future enter into the total character of the passing present as present possibilities, so the hereness and nowness of present actualizings enters into the character of the past and the future, changing the possibilities inherent in them as real possibilities. Any interaction or transaction between possibilities occurs in a passing present that grows out of a past and emerges toward a future. The passing present carries both novelty and creativity in a way that reaches backward into the past and forward into the future.

Once again, Peirce's analogy of the chalk line may be helpful. The past actualizing of a first chalk line has an aspect of continuity that contains possibilities present now in a second chalk line, cut somewhere across the containing one. Yet, the second chalk line, as an actualizing event in the emerging present, has eliminated forever certain possibilities that before were real possibilities. They are no longer pasts for a next emerging chalk line. And the present chalk line is "rich with the future" because of the real present possibilities of future cuts that reflect upon its character; indeed, its character can be said to be consti-

103 / See chapter 4 for a discussion of the "I" and the "me" as functional aspects of the self.

104 / The term *possibility* in the discussion here is being used to cover both *potentiality* and *possibility*. This general use was anticipated in the discussion of terminology early in the chapter.

tuted by those present possibilities. Thus, the unique, emergent here-ness and nowness of the present changes the character of the past as it pushes into the future, but it can do this only because it is continuous with and partially determined by the past and the future in the sense indicated above. Clearly, then, pragmatism puts undue emphasis neither on the future nor on the past, but rather it draws the past and the future into the present in the form of present possibilities of actualizations that are real now.

In Mead's central doctrine of the nature of the past, he is concerned to show that it is not only our viewpoint or interpretation of the past that has altered, but rather the past itself has changed, for the past "in itself" is not a past at all. If we could recapture the past in its total concrete-ness, simply as it occurred, it would not be a past for any present, but would be simply a recaptured present, a present that once was. Its rela-tion to the present is the very ground of its pastness.[105] Yet, this once again turns out, within Mead's focus, to be explicitly directed not to-ward the relation between past and future in an independent ontological reality, but toward the objective reality of the perspective of the inter-preter that elicits the meaningful structure of the past in light of his in-terpretation of the present.[106] Mead's discussion of the past as it changes through interpretation has its correlate in the relation of the past to the present in the processive concreteness of intermeshing matrixes.

The present possibilities and potentialities of what is past relate to the present as the conditioning factor of its pastness. The poten-tialities and possibilities of a past present are gone, but the past, as the past to the emerging future, exists now as the potentialities and possi-bilities diffused within the present, and as any present to which it re-lates changes, so it changes, no matter how slight this change may be, for its potentialities and possibilities that make it what it is in its con-creteness change. Thus, the past, as contextual and cohesive matrixes whose horizonal contours intermesh within present matrixical con-texts, is not fixed and final, but in a constant process of change. Certain past actualizations have occurred. In this sense the past is obdurate, finished, final. Yet, in another sense the past is never finished, for the possibilities to which these actualizations give rise are functionally diffused throughout the processive concreteness of the present, and as these possibilities change, the past, in its matrixical richness, itself

---

105 / Mead, *Philosophy of the Present*, pp. 14–16.

106 / As occurs so frequently in Mead's discussions of ontological issues, these two types of focus are not clearly distinguished, and even when he begins with what seems to be the former type, an unacknowledged transformation to the latter is usually made.

changes. As long as there is a present actualizing possibilities, there is a changing past. Such changes are independent of our perspectives, though the changing past, as a past in relation to an emerging present, has, like all matrixical relationships, an indeterminateness born of an indefinite richness that the human mind, through the structures of pragmatic meaning, must render intelligible.

The above sketch of a metaphysics of pragmatism envisions a universe of interacting qualitative continuities guided by, but not determined by, the lawfulness or potentialities inherent in a continuum in its nature as a continuum; a universe in which the passing present brings with it temporally emerging activities and the novel directions of emergent "habit takings"; a universe in which we are at home and with which our activities are continuous; a universe in which our lived qualitative experience can grasp real emergent qualitative features of reality, and in which our creative concepts embodying abstract or logical potentialities and possibilities can grasp the real dynamic tendencies of reality to produce operations of a certain type under certain types of circumstances with a degree of regularity; in short, a universe that is both grasped by, and reflected within, the internal structure of pragmatic meaning. It is to an understanding of "world" as an emergent backdrop for the interplay of pragmatic meaning and the independently real that the following chapter can now turn.

Seven

Worldly Encounter, Perspectival Pluralism,

and Pragmatic Community

HOUGH THE CLASSICAL American pragmatists refer to "the world" quite frequently throughout their writings, they never explicitly clarify the concept. Such a lack can well go unremarked, for *the world* is a common-sense term which slides easily—indeed too easily—into a common-sense identification with "what is the case" or "what there is." This unquestioned common-sense identification provides the unquestioned basis for many of the criticisms hurled at, and misleading labels attached to, the position of classical American pragmatism. When such an identification is questioned, however, and various statements concerning the world are interrelated for a development of their systematic import, the holistic structure of the perceived world is seen to reflect throughout the three-directional openness which is at the very heart of the pragmatic understanding of experience.

The world, as foundational of meaningful encounter with the independently real, though not ontologically other than the independently real processive concreteness with which the organism interacts, is not independent of the character of the knowing process. Rather, as a product of both ingredients, it reflects characteristics of each, though it mirrors neither exactly. The human encounter with the processive concreteness of the independently real universe is worldly encounter, for through the contours of a world, the contours of the independently real manifest themselves within experience.

As has been seen, meaning is not constituted from on high by some transcendent intellect as the rationalist would have it, nor is it constituted as cause to effect by a union of impressions hitting against senses, as the traditional empiricist would have it. Rather, meaning comes to be in our behavioral rapport with that which gives itself in experience. Meaning is already there for conscious acts, because conscious acts emerge within a meaningful world. This does not mean, however, that we discover meanings already metaphysically embedded in the world in the spectator-realist sense. Rather, the world is the world of perception, the perceived world, the field of perception in which things emerge as meaningful within our experience. The individual lives in a world of things of which he is not conscious, an experienced world in which noncognitive, prereflective acts take place and within which reflection arises. Yet such a world is what it is only in relation to an organism. Such a world is the level at which sense emerges in experience, for meaning begins to emerge at a level prior to that of conscious acts. Such a world is the basic context of meaning for all perception, and therefore for all sensation. Its basic contours begin to take shape in anteceptive experience; as such, it is the spatio-temporal horizonal "schema" within which schematic types can emerge. At this foundational level it is both preobjective and prepersonal. By the time these features emerge through the stuctures of pragmatic meanings, the world is already there. Such a world is, to greater or lesser degree, implicitly operative throughout pragmatic vision, but it is best brought into explicit focus in terms of the concreteness of behavior as a corporeal or vital intentionality in Mead's development of "the world that is there."

The world that is there is indeed "there"; yet for Mead "there is no absolute world of things."[1] The world is "there" as a context of meaning within which reflective acts take place, but it is "there" with such meaning only in its relation to an organism. As Mead states, the reflective act:

> Takes place within a world of things not thus analyzed; for the objects about us are unitary objects, not simple sums of the parts into which analysis would resolve them. And they are what they are in relation to organisms whose environment they constitute. When we reduce a thing to parts we have destroyed the thing that was there. We refer to these differences as the meanings these things have in their relationship to the organism.[2]

1 / Mead, *Philosophy of the Act*, p. 331.
2 / Mead, *Philosophy of the Present*, pp. 116–117.

James expresses this relatedness of organism and world or, in his terms, self and world, in his claim that "the world experienced (otherwise called the 'field of consciousness') comes at all times with our body as its centre, centre of vision, centre of action, centre of interest. Where the body is is 'here'; when the body acts is 'now'; what the body touches is 'this'; all other things are 'there' and 'then' and 'that'."[3] The significance of these positional words is that they "imply a systematization of things with reference to a focus of action and interest which lies in the body; and the systematization is now so instinctive (was it ever not so?) that no developed or active experience exists for us at all except in that ordered form. . . ."[4] Or, as he elsewhere summarizes, "The world of living realities . . . is thus anchored in the ego considered as an active and emotional term."[5]

Indeed, this ego, as active and emotional, is the vehicle by which a pluralistic universe becomes a meaningfully organized world. Such a pluralistic universe is the precondition for the interactionally unified world of pragmatism, for with a pluralistic universe, "so far from defeating its rationality, as the absolutists so unanimously pretend, you leave it in possession of the maximum amount of rationality practically attainable by our minds. Your relations with it, intellectual, emotional, and active, remain fluent and congruous with your own nature's chief demands."[6] Creative selectivity, rooted in active interest or corporeal, vital intentionality within a pluralistic universe, thus yields the world as the meaningful perspective for, or context of, experience, for "'Ever not quite' has to be said of the best attempts made anywhere in the universe at attaining all inclusiveness."[7]

Prereflective lived experience in its behavioral rapport with the world, then, provides the meaningful context within which perception of objects takes place. Without such meaning, there would be no objects of perception, since objects of which we are conscious are experienced in terms of their meanings and the meaningful backdrop in which they are rooted. The world as the horizon of all our experience provides the meaningful constancy in which the constancy of the thing is grounded, and the thing in turn provides that meaningful constancy in which the constancy of qualities is grounded. Perception involves an act of adjust-

3 / James, *Essays in Radical Empiricism*, p. 86, n.
4 / Ibid.
5 / James, *Principles of Psychology*, 2, p. 926.
6 / James, *Pluralistic Universe*, p. 144.
7 / Ibid., p. 145.

ment between an individual and his world, and within such acts of
adjustment qualities function in experience. Thus, while experienced
qualities are always qualities of the "thing," the "thing" is always a
"thing in the world."

We see, then, that a meaningful world emerges through man's behavioral interaction with the independently real. Further, such experience
is first had in a world about which there is neither doubt nor conscious
belief.[8] Such a world is the precondition for the emergence of doubt and
conscious belief, for questioning cannot occur without the world as the
context within which the doubt and questioning make sense. Thus, the
resolution of any problem requires the world as the backdrop of all that
takes place in perception. Problematic contexts emerge within the context of the world, and within the problematic situation, data and verification instances gain their meaning and significance in terms of the
meaningful, interwoven net by which they are lifted out of the concrete
matrix of possibilities of experience there for discrimination. Thus, the
pragmatic understanding of the dynamics of experience as experimental
requires the world as the backdrop of all that takes place in perception.
Indeed, the world, in its most foundational sense, can be said to be the
"solution," provided by the dynamics of experience as experimental, to
the potentially problematic situation of the indefinite concreteness of
the ontologically real within which the organism is immersed, and with
which it must deal successfully.

The interrelation of the above account of our behavioral relation to
the world with the dynamics of perceptual experience can be seen in
Dewey's description of the disintegration of the perceptual situation because of the frustration of an ongoing act:

> Generalized, the sensation as stimulus is always that phase of activity
> requiring to be defined in order that a coordination may be com-
> pleted. . . . The search for the stimulus is the search for the exact condi-
> tions of action; that is, for the state of things which decides how a
> beginning coordination should be completed.
>
> Similarly, motion, as response, has only functional value. It is what-
> ever will serve to complete the disintegrating coordination.[9]

Such activity occurs always from the backdrop of the world that is
there, for it is from such a backdrop that meaning formation and meaning replacement can take place.

---

8 / Mead, *Philosophy of the Act*, p. 37.
9 / Dewey, "The Reflex Arc Concept in Psychology," pp. 107–8.

Thus, Mead emphasizes that "it is palpably illegitimate to resolve all reality into such terms of individual experience, after the fashion of the phenomenalist or positivist, since the very definition and distinctive character of the individual's experience are dependent upon its peculiar relation to a world which may not be stated in such terms, which is not analyzed, but is simply there."[10] And the world that is there, and that lends its character to the character of an individual experience, is what it is through its relatedness to the corporeal intentionality constitutive of preflective behavior.

This emergence of objects or facts from the backdrop of an intentional mind-world relationship, expressed above in terms of concrete human behavior, is developed by Peirce and Lewis as an examination of the way in which that meaningful projection that is the world provides the backdrop for the rigors of more sophisticated awareness rooted in sense experience. This difference in levels of focus reflects no difference in the relationship intended. Rather, the logic of world as an intentional unity can be expressed through a focus on the most concrete activity of organism-environment interaction, or through a focus on the level of functioning of more consciously grasped interrelationships rooted in such a foundational understanding of world. To this latter aspect the discussion will now turn.

The foundationally real world, for Peirce and Lewis, as for the other pragmatists, is the perceived world.[11] This real world is also characterized by both Peirce and Lewis as the world of perceptual facts.[12] The world is an interrelated system of facts, but facts are not independent of the intentional unity between knower and known. As Lewis observes, "'fact' is a crypto-relative term, like 'landscape'. A landscape is a terrain, but a terrain as seeable by an eye. And a fact is a state of affairs, but a state of affairs as knowable by a mind."[13] Or as Peirce notes, a fact "is so much of the real Universe as can be represented in a Proposition, and instead of being . . . a slice of the Universe, is rather to be compared to a

10 / Mead, *Philosophy of the Act*, p. 35.

11 / As Peirce states, "The real world is the world of sensible experience" (3.527), or, in other terms, the real world is the world of "insistent generalized percepts" (8.148) which are not representative of any underlying reality other than themselves (2.143). As Lewis emphasizes, "Let the connection between what is presented in sense and the idealized abstractions of the system be as remote as you please, this connection is of the essence" of any truth about nature (*Mind and the World Order*, Appendix A, p. 399).

12 / Lewis, "Facts, Systems, and the Unity of the World," *Collected Papers*, pp. 383–384; Peirce, 2.141.

13 / Lewis, "Replies to My Critics," *The Philosophy of C. I. Lewis*, ed. P. A. Schilpp, Library of Living Philosophers Series (La Salle, Ill.: Open Court, 1968), p. 660.

chemical principle extracted therefrom by the power of Thought."[14] Any fact is inseparably combined with an infinite swarm of circumstances, which make no part of the fact itself.[15] Such a world of facts rigorously obeys the laws of noncontradiction and the excluded middle, for dichotomy rules the realm of meanings, and "it is part of the process of sensible experience to locate its facts in the world of ideas."[16] As Lewis points out, "anything which could be appropriately called a world must be such that one or other of every pair of contradictory propositions would apply to or be true of it; and such that all the propositions holding of it will be mutually consistent."[17] This grasp of the sensible in terms of a consistent system of meanings is the very essence of the sensible world. As Peirce stresses, "This is what I mean by saying that the sensible world is but a fragment of the ideal world."[18]

Further, the system of meanings in some sense limits the facts that may occur "in the world," for, as Peirce notes, "we know in advance of experience that certain things are not true, because we see they are impossible. . . . I know it is not true, because I satisfy myself that there is no room for it even in that ideal world of which the real world is but a fragment."[19] Thus, what can occur "in the world" must conform to the possibilities allowed for by the world of ideas, or the system of meanings in terms of which we approach it or through which it is constituted. To better understand what can possibly occur in the world, it will be helpful at this point to turn to a closer examination of the various senses of *possible* as these relate to the issue of world.

Possible experience can mean possible in the sense of *consistently thinkable*, or it can mean possible in the sense of *metaphysically possible*. This latter type of possibility was the topic of the previous chapter. Possible in the sense of consistently thinkable is, however, open to some misunderstanding if not further clarified. In addition to the distinction between the consistently thinkable and the metaphysically possible, Peirce distinguishes between what he calls the *essentially* or *logically possible* and the *substantially possible*, while Lewis distinguishes, in parallel fashion, between *absolute possibility* and *relative*

---

14 / Microfilm Edition of the Peirce Papers, Sect. 647, p. 8.

15 / Ibid.

16 / Peirce, 3.527–3.529. See also Lewis, "Facts, Systems, and the Unity of the World," p. 387.

17 / Lewis, *Analysis of Knowledge and Valuation*, p. 56.

18 / Peirce, 3.527.

19 / Ibid. Any "ideal" world is founded ultimately in the interactional orientation of corporeal intentionality constitutive of prereflective experience.

possibility.[20] *Essential* or *absolute possibility* means logical conceivability, or the absence of self-contradiction. *Substantial* or *relative possibility*, however, refers to the relation which something considered has to present information. In this sense *possible* means consistent with everything known about the world. *Possible* in this second sense seems to indicate, as it relates to the sensible world, a type of *physical possibility*. The present position will refer to these distinctions in terms of the *formally possible* and the *situationally possible.*[21] The two types of possibility in the functional relation discussed below constitute what will be called epistemic possibility operative within the world.

The above discussion tends to indicate that while situational possibility must imply formal possibility, formal possibility need not imply situational possibility. Peirce well observes that of those possible combinations that "occur in the ideal world, some do and some do not occur in the real world; but all that occur in the real world occur also in the ideal world."[22]

Here, however, it must be noted that if a proposition that is formally possible but not situationally possible is combined with the larger body of given information, a formally impossible set results. As Peirce observes, "Two propositions contradictory of one another may both be severally possible, although their combination is not possible."[23] As Lewis well notes, there is a "plurality of equally cogent systems which may contain the same body of already verified propositions but differ in what else they include."[24] What else they include is not merely what facts will be, but also what facts conceivably may be. Thus, at any time, a range of what is possible to occur may be determined ideally or logically, though what specific possibility will in fact be actualized in the future cannot be determined in this manner. The worldly unity of this epistemic possibility with metaphysical possibility, neither of which can be understood at the expense of the other, is evinced in Peirce's claim that

20 / C. I. Lewis and C. H. Langford, *Symbolic Logic* (1932; reprint ed. New York: Dover Publications, 1959), pp. 160–161; Peirce, 4.67, 3.527. These passages also provide the characterizations of them which follow.

21 / *Situational possibility* as opposed to *physical possibility* can hold of any type of world, not just those worlds incorporating spatio-temporal reality. These differing types of world will be indicated below.

22 / Peirce, 3.527.

23 / Peirce, 3.527. As Peirce notes, "It is an anacoluthon to say that the occurrence of something is impossible because it is self-contradictory. It rather is thought so as to appear self-contradictory because the ideal induction has shown it to be impossible (3.531).

24 / C. I. Lewis, "The Structure of Logic and Its Relation to Other Systems," p. 372.

to conclude from the above type of discussion "that there is nothing analogous to possibility" in the independently real, but that this mode appertains "only to the particular limited information we possess, would be even less defensible than to draw precisely the opposite conclusion from the same premises. It is a style of reasoning most absurd."[25]

Thus, though what may occur "in the world" cannot be understood apart from the noetic structure that grasps, this does not lead to a conventionalism, for the real world is a special part of the "ideal world. Namely, that part which sufficient experience would tend ultimately (and therefore definitively) to compel Reason to acknowledge as having being independent of what he may arbitrarily, or willfully, create."[26] Conversely, though the hereness and nowness of spatio-temporal processive concreteness is independent of our meaning structures and the possibilities that they allow, what the hereness and nowness can consistently be held to be is partially determined by the range of meaningfully projected ideal possibilities within which facts can consistently emerge.

The world as the horizon for all knowledge cannot itself be exhaustively known both because of the nature of meaning projections and the concreteness of the independently real. Thus, though there is a "possible world for every self-consistent system," yet Lewis asserts that "no conceivable knowledge can ever be adequate to a world."[27] Why? Because "our knowledge fixates a whole system of facts but cannot exhaust it."[28] A fixated system of facts can never be exhaustively known because any meaning has its own implicated meanings that limit the range of possibilities of experience—though of course they do not determine which possibility will become actual. We can never know the precise range of possibilities or the complete implications of any meaningful delineation we make. Though the projection of a meaning system limits the alternatives possible within it, the richness of the possible alternatives thus fixed can never be fully grasped. What is implied here is the objectivity of intentionally grounded relationships. Though it is true that we can never know a slab of reality in its spatio-temporal completeness—whether we mean the space-time slab denoted by a single meaning or by a total set of propositions—it is also true that having only limited intellectual powers, we cannot know all the implications of fixed possibilities allowable in any systematic conceptualization of

---

25 / Peirce, 4.68.
26 / Peirce, 3.527.
27 / Lewis, "Facts, Systems, and the Unity of the World," p. 390.
28 / Ibid., p. 386.

experience. The world is determined by a system of facts, but facts are not independent of the selective knowledge process, and though our knowledge fixates a system of facts or delineations within the concretely real, it cannot exhaust them because of their infinite number. No knowledge can be adequate to a world because it would require precisely such a completed system of facts.[29] And just as knowledge cannot be adequate to a world, in that it cannot grasp the intentionally grounded richness of its content (and, mutatis mutandis, the space-time concreteness of its content), so it would seem that a world cannot be totally adequate to the independently real universe in that a different world, as the concrete content delineated by a different meaning projection, could delineate within the concreteness of nature from a different perspective, giving rise to different objectifications.

A system of facts that constitutes our orderly world of experience is that perspective of the indefinitely rich independently real matrix of possibilities for conceptual ordering that has been carved out by a system of meanings. Knowledge is abstractive and selective. Facts, though concrete, are nonetheless selective in the sense that a system of facts, as the concrete content denoted by a system of meanings, is one way in which processive concreteness can be delineated or ordered. Neither facts within the world, nor the world itself as an orderly system of facts, can be understood apart from the system of meanings that constitutes the organizing activities of mind.

Thus, underlying the very possibility of empirical knowledge is an intentional relation between man and his world; what facts our world reveals are partially dependent upon the interrelated structures of the meanings we bring. While the concrete richness of the matrix for possible discrimination of uniformities, a concrete matrix constituted by the continuity of an indefinitely rich processive universe which "swims in indeterminacy,"[30] is independent of our conceptualizations and the possibilities they allow, the manner in which uniformities are delineated is partially determined by the range of interrelationships within which perceived facts can emerge. From this concretely rich universe, through the perspective of a meaning system rooted in active interest and intent, meaningful uniformities emerge within our world, or, conversely, the world emerges as the backdrop for the discrimination of meaningful uniformities. Thus, it can be seen why schemata cannot be

---

29 / Thus, Lewis can say that "the relation of a system to a world which includes it is the relation of knowledge to reality" ("Facts, Systems, and the Unity of the World," p. 387).

30 / Peirce, 1.171–1.172.

understood just as a collection of uniformities linked together by habit in spectator fashion.[31] Without the intents embodied in dispositional modes of response, there are no meaningful uniformities, but the apparent chaos reflective of an overabundance of possibilities for discrimination, and without the emerging backdrop of a world, these intents cannot gain their directional focus. Facts and the world in which they are situated emerge neither from mind alone nor from the universe alone, but rather from the interaction of the two that constitutes experience.

The foundationally real world thus emerges through the interaction of noetically or epistemically projected possibilities with the indefinitely rich matrixical possibilities of processive concreteness. At its most rudimentary level, worldly contours begin to emerge through the rudimentary temporal pulsations of anteceptive experience, as this primordial inseparable unity of organism-environment interaction yields the beginnings of order from the seeming chaos of a processive concreteness abundantly rich in possible orderings. At the level of prereflective experience, the consistency of projected possibilities is established through the need for consistency of behavior and thus manifests itself through the action orientation of vital or corporeal intentionality. At a more reflective level, this meaningful network emerges as the "ideal world," as the realm of the consistently thinkable within which the facts of experience must be located. The world answers to the laws of excluded middle and noncontradiction because it is the regulative ideal of that which can be conceptually articulated and made precise to an ideal limit. Yet, the constitution of the world is prior to grasping any object as an object in the world. It is the inexpressible meaningful totality which is prior to and makes possible the separation of particular objects or facts or particular meanings from its backdrop, which is prior to and makes possible the interpretation or explication of its aspects. Concrete matrixes are discriminated according to intents, drives, aspirations, needs, pulsations of life—conscious or unconscious—operating within the horizonal contours of a world. Thus, the world is at once the basis for every experience and the ideal of a complete synthesis of possible experience.

The world of common-sense experience, as it emerges from the anteceptive field, is the spatio-temporal real world in the sense that it most incorporates the spatio-temporal richness of processive concreteness as foundational for the being of man in the world and the knowing by man

31 / See chapter 2.

of the world. Thus, its reality is foundational for other worlds. To say it is foundational for other worlds is not meant to indicate that it is a building block for other worlds, or a container for other worlds, but rather that in its foundational character it permeates all other worlds. As has been seen, it permeates not only the world of science, but also the world of logic, whose fundamental principles are rooted there. Further, derived spatio-temporal worlds, such as the world of science, are not reductions of the everyday world to something else, but when properly understood are enrichments of it, infusing it with new meanings.[32] Derived worldly realities can be real in various ways.[33] Thus, for instance, one may speak of Hamlet as real in the world of fiction, but the world of fiction is not a spatio-temporal real world; it does not exist. Yet, with its own type of reality it enriches the foundational world of perception, and its character is permeated to greater or lesser degree by the character of the foundational world.

As can be seen from the above discussion, the foundationally real world, the spatio-temporally real world, is ontologically one with the independently real processive concreteness of the natural universe. It is, metaphysically, that independently real. Yet, such a world is dependent upon the meaning system that grasps in a way in which reality as independent is not, for such a world is that perspective of the infinitely rich natural universe that has been delineated or "carved out" by a system of meanings.

Thus, the world as foundational is the context of meaning within which all other frameworks and objects may be articulated, in the sense that this world is the "outermost" content or encompassing frame of reference for the projection of a set of meaning structures within the independently real, and hence for the propositions that can delineate experience consistently within the context of these meanings. Such a world, then, opens in one direction toward the structures of the independently real and the possibilities it presents, and in the other direction toward the structures of our modes of grasping the independently real and the possibilities such modes of grasping allow. What can occur in the world must conform to the possibilities available within the world we have structured—though the world we have structured has arisen through

---

32 / This point is anticipated by the discussion in chapter 1 of the relation between science and common sense.

33 / James distinguishes seven derived worlds or in his terminology, "sub-universes," but views the world of sense experience as foundational for all others (*Principles of Psychology*, 2, pp. 920 ff.).

the successful interaction with the spatio-temporal possibilities offered by the independently real. Our worldly experience is throughout a function of the interaction of epistemic and metaphysical possibilities. Peirce summarizes this claim in his statement that "there is no *thing* which is in itself in the sense of not being relative to the mind, though things which are relative to the mind doubtless *are,* apart from that relation."[34] Or, in other terms, it can be said that what *occurs* must be ontologically possible, while *what* occurs must be epistemically possible as well.

It was seen in an earlier chapter that before one can make empirical generalizations about facts, one must have delineated facts through meanings that are prescriptive for the experiences that will constitute the experience of a particular kind of fact. Before one can make the empirical claim that a particular kind of fact is there, one must have the structure of the experiences that are to count as exemplifications of the presence of a particular kind of fact. In the matrixical richness of processive concreteness the foundation for natural classes, for natural definitions, is to be found. As Peirce notes, however, "Truly natural classes may, and undoubtedly often do merge into one another inextricably,"[35] and thus, boundary lines must be imposed, although the classes are natural.[36] The concrete matrixical richness of possibilities for discrimination is there; where the lines of demarcation are drawn is, in part, a human decision. Like the boundary lines of natural classes, the "boundary lines" that constitute the world in which we live as the backdrop for the facts that can emerge may be differently drawn, giving rise to different possibilities within the world.

From this backdrop of world the ambiguities of "nature" can be clarified. First, there is nature as the independently real, as the indefinitely rich processive concreteness of which we are a part. Though rich with generative activity, its concrete character cannot be stated in terms of specific causal connections, for such a statement requires the perspectival focus on "the significant" as opposed to the "irrelevant" within a discriminated context. Second, there is nature as our worldly environment, as that which we partially create through our interactive unity with processive concreteness. This worldly environment, as it emerges from anteceptive and everyday experience, is the level at which we discriminate, within the rich matrix, the causal relations of everyday experience.

34 / Peirce, 5.311 (italics not in text).
35 / Peirce, 1.209.
36 / The Microfilm Edition of the Peirce Papers, Section 427, pp. 40–41.

Nature, in this second sense, includes the reality of perspectives. Perspectives are emergents within the temporal structure of experience, but are revealed as characteristics of nature. As Peirce elucidates this understanding of nature in relation to his famous diamond example, "Remember that this diamond's condition is not an isolated fact. There is no such thing . . . it is an unsevered, though precise part, of the unitary fact of nature."[37] And, as Peirce observes of this "unitary fact of nature," "Nature, in connection with a picture, copy, or diagram does not necessarily denote an object not fashioned by man, but merely the object represented as something existing apart from the representation."[38]

Finally, there is nature as an object of science, which we reflectively abstract from our everyday worldly natural environment as a second-level understanding of this environment. The events of the nature of the world of science cannot be confounded with the events of processive concreteness. Nature as processive concreteness is the foundation for our everyday worldly natural environment; nature as a system of scientific events is reflective abstraction from it. The character of the indeterminate generative activities and the causal relations sustained within temporal passage in the first two senses of nature cannot be reduced to the character of the causal relations holding among the events in the world of science.

The above discussion shows that the objects within our natural world do not copy the independently real, but rather emerge through our modes of grasping the independently real natural universe. Nor do the modes of grasping via which emerge the objectivities within our world copy the independently real, but rather they serve as tools for "cutting the edges" of the indeterminate richness of the independently real natural universe. Finally, the world within which specific meanings and beliefs arise, and within which objects or facts emerge for conscious awareness, is not a copy of an independent reality, nor is it identical with an independent reality in its character as independent. Rather, such a world is the encompassing frame of reference or field of interest of organism-environment interaction; the ultimate backdrop of intentionality within which emerging facts are situated; the "outermost" horizon of meaningful rapport by which human beings interact with the independently real. Thus, our world, from the most limited grasp of some one thing, to the most all inclusive comprehension of what facts con-

---

37 / Peirce, 5.457. Precisely his failure to recognize the mind relatedness of worldly nature, according to Peirce, leads Mill astray in his analysis of the "uniformity of nature" (6.67).

38 / Peirce, 3.420.

ceivably may be, is a function of the pragmatic interplay of meaning structures and the independently real and, as a function of both, mirrors neither exactly, though it reflects characteristics of each.

Only within the context of world can the nature of pragmatic truth be fully understood.[39] Just as pragmatic meaning could not be understood in terms of traditional alternatives, so pragmatic truth cannot be reduced to the traditional alternative of coherence or correspondence.[40] Further, just as pragmatic meaning could not be understood as one type of meaning contrasted with a more fundamental sense of meaning, so pragmatic truth cannot be understood as one type of truth contrasted with a more fundamental sense of truth.[41]

Because the hereness and nowness of the universe and the real interconnections it displays is independent of, yet enters directly into interaction with, our meanings and the possibilities they allow, coherence is not a sufficient criterion for the truth of empirical assertions. Rather, there must be a pragmatic interplay between these two factors. There is an ontological dimension to what appears within experience which limits our meaning projections in terms of workability. But, true knowledge, even ideally true knowledge, could not be correspondence, for the nature of our intentional link with the independently real through meaning structures, and the nature of this independently real as the indefinite richness of processive concreteness, makes the relation of correspondence senseless, indeed, literally so. The ideally true belief would be that belief that would perfectly work in anticipating possibilities of experience, but would work not because it adequately copied, but because it adequately "cut into" the independently real as a function of the world that makes it possible. The independently real answers our questions and determines the workability of our meaning structures, but what answers it gives are partially dependent on what questions we ask, and what meaning structures work are partially dependent upon the structures we bring.

Truth is agreement of belief with reality, but it is agreement with worldly reality, a reality that we have partially made. True beliefs con-

---

39 / In the earlier discussion of verification, the issue of the nature of truth was deliberately postponed. See chapter 3.

40 / Some type of coherence theory of truth operates within the framework of both idealism and ontological phenomenalism, while truth as correspondence fits within the framework of realism.

41 / Pragmatic truth is at times contrasted with some type of more fundamental "cognitive" truth.

form but they conform to the manner in which we have transformed processive concreteness into worldly encounter. Some beliefs are true and some are false, and which are true and which are false is independent of us; we cannot make them so. Without the making, without the creative noetic activity that structures a world, however, there can be no beliefs, true or false.[42] True beliefs are true before they are actually verified, but the very possibility of verification emerges from the backdrop of the transformation of processive concreteness into worldly encounter. Or, in terms used earlier, without the prescriptive truths of a priori meaning networks there can be no descriptive truth or falsity. Truth is truth relative to a context of interpretation, not because truth is relative, but because without an interpretive context the concept of truth is meaningless. Truth changes in the sense that contexts, without which

42 / The view that for James pragmatic truth is "made" in a radically subjectivist sense that must be distinguished from another kind of truth stems mainly from the implications of "The Will to Believe." Chapter 4, however, notes that the perception of oneself can affect and redirect the developing potentialities of oneself as an ontologically concrete being. A belief concerning oneself can lead to the emergence of new potentialities or actualize or reintegrate one's present potentialities which then become incorporated into the context of interacting potentialities within a unified situation. In some limited types of cases, the changing potentialities of the concrete organism which emerge in the situation can be contributing factors in the context which verifies the belief.

Thus, for example, the belief that I am capable of jumping a particular hurdle may develop and or actualize a potentiality, which, as incorporated into the situation, makes the belief true.

Or, believing that I can sustain a relationship with God may bring about a unification or a more meaningful reintegration of the potentialities of this concrete center of activity, both among themselves and as directed toward the rest of the universe. Thus, the belief in God may produce God as a living force in one's life, verified, in the only way any claim is verified, by the workability of the belief as an organizing and unifying perspective in the ongoing course of experience. Indeed, James's distinction in relation to science between creativity as the cause of production and verification as the cause of preservation (see chapter 1) is relevant here. If such verification does not occur, the belief will not be sustained because it will not function in a workable way. Implicitly operative here is an absolute distinction between scientific method and scientific content. What differs in the cases of scientific and religious experience is not the dynamics of creative constitution, directed activity, and verification in the ongoing course of experience, but rather, the nature of the data to be integrated, and hence the nature of the experiences that verify. In brief, the types of data whose integration serves as verification of the belief in God, are precisely those that science, as a focus on a particular kind of content, rules out of court.

Even in these special cases in which the changing potentialities of the believer enter into the context that verifies or falsifies the belief, given the contextual conditions, including the effects of the belief on the believer's own concrete potentialities, the belief is either true or false relative to these verificatory conditions and we cannot make it otherwise than it is.

we cannot talk about empirical truth, change. What was true relative to a particular context does not change relative to that context; rather, contexts within which empirical truth functions change. We discover truths about our world only because we have first prescribed contours for our world.

The truths about our world, as empirical claims, are verified or falsified in the ongoing course of experience by hard evidence. Such verification is always incomplete, for there is always more experience to come that could lead to the recognition that what we claim as true is, in fact, false. Empirical claims are true or false because they work in yielding the anticipated consequences within the ongoing course of experience, and these consequences extend into an indefinite future. Truth *claims* relative to an interpretive context are always subject to change, because empirical verification is always incomplete, but the *truth of* the claim relative to a context does not change. A belief shown false was never true, though the claim to truth may have been based on justifiable evidence when made.

The prescriptive contexts within which such empirical truth operates, however, cannot be verified or falsified by experience, for they set the structures for what is to count for experience of a particular type. They are accepted or rejected according to criteria of workability in letting us deal meaningfully with experience, but workability in this case is not a question of simple empirical verification by the "hard evidence" of facts, even of facts subject to diverse interpretations. These meaningful contexts are prescriptive of the worldly contours that make possible the facts that serve as the verification of empirical claims, and hence cannot themselves be empirically verified or falsified, though their usefulness as prescriptive tools for the delineation of empirical truths may be called into question on other grounds according to accepted pragmatic criteria of workability.

Truth as pragmatic is thus both made and found. The so-called tensions within pragmatic thought between truth as made and truth as found, between truth as changing and truth as fixed, result from focusing on diverse aspects operative within the dynamics of pragmatic truth. We create the interpretative frameworks within which beliefs can emerge and be found true or false, and within which investigation can tend toward an ideal limit.

When a community of interpreters have a common network of meanings via which the "facts of experience" as relevant to a particular topic or issue can emerge, then investigation will indeed converge toward a common limit.[43] But neither truth nor facts occur atomistically. And when a segment of interpreters experience different facts because of a different interpretative meaning-network for cutting into the rich continuity of experience, then such convergence cannot occur. The criterion for adequately cutting into the indefinitely rich matrix of possibilities of experience is workability, but workability can be established only relative to some meaningful network by which experience is caught. Thus, there can be a plurality of interpretations among varying groups of interpreters on various topics. For, each group, identifiable by varying nets or perspectives for the catching of experience, is variously structuring some contours of a world. But, as has been seen, even the lines of demarcation of distinct groups of interpreters can be difficult to discern, for such differing networks are embodied in differing attitudes of response and may be present when disagreeing interpreters think their differences can be resolved "by merely collecting the facts." Thus, worldly pluralism is often hidden from view in the misplaced drive toward a common conclusion based on "the evidence."

In one sense, there is not only a pluralism within the world, but an absolute pluralism of worlds, for in one sense the world within which conscious belief, questioning, and discussion emerge becomes many different worlds because of new meanings, shaping new worldly contours, that emerge from varying attitudes of response to problematic contexts. In another sense, pluralism within the world emerges from the backdrop of a common world, for in its deepest sense, the questioning and doubting that changed the world could only occur within a context that did not change, but lent the prereflective constancy and communality of its meaning to the meaningfulness of both the problem and its resolution. Thus, in a sense, we restructure the world. Yet, in another sense, we restructure only within the world.

Worldly reality is, then, inherently perspectival. Not only are perspectives real within our world, but without them there is no world. Further, our world incorporates a perspectival pluralism, for differing ways of cutting into processive concreteness or prescribing contours of a world constitute differing perspectives within the world. Such pluralism, when properly understood, however, should not lead to the view that varying groups are enclosed within self-contained, myopic, limiting frameworks or points of view, cutting off the possibility of rational dialogue, for two reasons which will be discussed in turn. First, varying perspectives open

43 / This convergence is emphasized by Peirce.

onto a more fundamental perspective. Second, without perspectival pluralism true pragmatic community cannot be.

Because any perspectival pluralism is rooted in the rudimentary contours of anteceptive experience, and because the character of anteceptive experience is temporally rooted in the structure of human behavior as anticipatory and the nature of experience as experimental, the rudimentary contours of world, as it emerges from the anteceptive field, reveal a common human perspectival structuring, in which these features are manifest, and from which a plurality of perspectives can emerge. Thus, any particular perspective opens outward onto a commonly structured anteceptive field, though the articulation and development of this field through the structures of emerging perspectives may take various forms. Such an anteceptive openness prevents the closure of perspectives, for all perspectives are temporally rooted in the common conditions of their very possibility. The possibility of the "sociality" of worldly perspectives, like the "sociality" of intermeshing matrixes, is rooted in the fundamental features of temporality.

Any derived worlds are rooted ultimately in the spatio-temporal world of everyday experience, and the perspectival pluralism within this world is rooted, ultimately, in an inarticulate, vague, rudimentary world whose contours are set by the structure of perspective required by the temporal stretch of human behavior as anticipatory or experimental. Though "the world that is there," which lends its constancy to questioning and to new resolutions of problematic situations, is itself a meaningful organization of the independently real, and could conceivably have been structured differently, yet this conceivably different world could not be one that belied the fundamental features of anteceptive experience.

From this backdrop of worldly features the pragmatic understanding of community can be brought into focus, for pragmatic community, as it will be developed, is one that does not negate, but requires, individuality, freedom, and perspectival pluralism. Pragmatic community is inherently pluralistically perspectival, not in the sense that various perspectives blend to form or to tend toward a unified whole, but in the sense that community is constituted by the ongoing socializing adjustment of diverse perspectives that may frequently be "incommensurable"[44] in the sense that adjudication among them cannot occur in terms of an unchanging, prestructured, already articulated framework or

44 / This concept is of course taken from Thomas Kuhn's *The Structure of Scientific Revolutions*, 2nd ed., enl. (Chicago: University of Chicago Press, 1970).

set of criteria for determining their truth or falsity. This claim may seem to imply that Peirce's pragmatic community of interpreters tending toward "a final ultimate opinion" is not a pragmatic community on these terms because of its "monistic" nature. But, as will be seen, even such a seemingly monistic community involves the socializing adjustment of diverse perspectives at some level. Indeed, as Peirce well notes, there is not a straight development, but rather a self-corrective diversity of interpretations, abductive inferences, and arguments in constant process of adjustment as they interweave to form a fiber of understanding. The ensuing discussion will attempt to elucidate such a process.

To ask if a new perspective, as ingredient within the world, is a product of an individual or a community, or to ask which is prior, the individual or the community perspective, leads directly to the understanding of the relation of the individual and the community. Such sets of alternatives, like so many that have been found wanting throughout the development of speculative pragmatism, are false sets. The best place to begin a closer examination of this aspect of worldly existence is with the issue of our worldly past. The previous chapter showed that a past is a past only in relation to a present characterized by novelty, and as any novel present emerges, the matrixical complexes of processive concreteness, as a past to an emerging present, change also, no matter how insignificant this change may or may not be. To understand our worldly past, however, the issue must be placed in the context of the reality of perspectives. The worldly past changes with the emerging worldly present because, in addition to the above change, new perspectives emerge to incorporate it as an explanation of how the emergent present came to be. The past as an explanation of our present is now a different past because it must explain the emergence of something that before was not there to be explained. The worldly past thus changes as it explains how a novel worldly present came to be. Yet, the novel present itself gains its significance, is incorporated into a new perspective, because of its relation to a past that can now explain it. There is no worldly present without the past as its explanation, yet there is no worldly past without the worldly present for which it is an explanation. Each changes, is incorporated into a new worldly perspective, because of its relation to the other.

The following discussion will proceed by analogy with this understanding of worldly pasts and presents. The last chapter showed that freedom emerges when intelligence can consciously guide the selection of alternative possibilities, when there is conscious choice guided by meaningful anticipation. In addition, the possibilities that enter the horizonal dimensions of man are worldly possibilities, or, in other terms, possibilities that emerge through the interaction of noetic and ontological possibilities. Mead refers to the community or society that partially constitutes the possibilities for developing selfhood as the "generalized other."[45] The following discussion will break with the conflation of community, society, and generalized other and will instead make a distinction between the generalized other, the social nature of experience as it grows out of the matrixical sociality as developed in the previous chapter, and pragmatic community. In accordance with the present distinctions, the individual can be contrasted with the generalized other but not with the community, for community is constituted by the dynamics of socializing adjustment between the individual and the generalized other. True community requires not just myself and the generalized other, or just myself as partially constituted by the generalized other, but myself as both partially constituted by and partially constitutive of the generalized other. Further, it requires this in the dynamic and changing manner of socializing adjustment.[46]

A generalized other that delineates and typifies not only facts but attitudes and institutional practices as well is, in a sense, a past that enters into the present choices of the "I" as it creatively structures its emerging present. Yet, the selective novelty of the I is true freedom, choice guided by anticipatory intelligence, only because this I is a functional aspect of a self that is continuous ontologically and noetically— hence is worldly continuous—with a generalized other that enters into its range of possibilities, in part because this generalized other enters into its perception of what these possibilities are.

As an object to myself, I am partially what the generalized other, of which I am a part, takes me to be. But the unique I both reflects and reacts to the generalized other in its own peculiar manner, and when the I selects a novel perspective, this novelty in turns enters into the generalized other that is now there as incorporating this novel perspective. This novel perspective is an emergent because of its relation to a generalized other that conditioned its novel emergence, and it gains its significance in light of the new generalized other to which it gives rise. In the

45 / See, for example, *Mind, Self, and Society* (Chicago: University of Chicago Press, 1934), pp. 152–163.

46 / These changes are not meant to indicate that Mead utilizes any of these terms in a simplistic way, but rather that his identification of the generalized other with the society or the community fails to integrate the ontological significance of socializing adjustment into his discussion, and hence does not lead to the complexities of community as developed below. The following discussion is not in any way a contradiction of Mead, but rather a development of something that lies implicit within his position as brought to bear on the present topic.

act of *adjustment between*[47] the novel perspective and the perspective of the generalized other, the social aspect of community is to be found. The social dynamic of pragmatic community lies in this continual interplay of adjustment of attitudes, aspirations, and factual perceptions between the generalized other, as the condition for the novel emergent perspective, and the novel emergent, as it conditions the generalized other. Thus, a pragmatic community of any kind is a community of socializing adjustment between the free activity constitutive of the novel individual perspective and the common perspective of the generalized other, and each gains its meaning, significance, and enrichment from this process of adjustment.

Just as the social nature of any matrix within processive concreteness is the key to understanding that novelty does not negate but rather requires continuity, so the reality of human creativity or human freedom or novel perspective does not negate but rather requires the continuity or tradition of human attitudes and activities. These are continuous with, and enter into, the system of creative possibilities that constitutes the dynamic developing human organism as a center of activity, and they each accommodate the other through the process of socializing adjustment. Apart from the perspective of the generalized other, there can be no individual perspective. Yet, apart from individual perspectives there is no generalized perspective. Pragmatic community is not just a community of activity, but is constituted in its very nature by the activity of socializing adjustment. The community is not something set over against the individual, nor is the community just a collection of individuals. Rather, pragmatic community requires the dynamic of socializing adjustment between individuals and the generalized other. Thus, in Dewey's terms, "no amount of aggregated collective action of itself constitutes a community. . . . To learn to be human is to develop through the give-and-take of communication an effective sense of being an *individually distinctive* member of a community; one who understands and appreciates its beliefs, desires, and methods, and who contributes to a further conversion of organic powers into human resources and values. But this transition is never finished."[48]

James expresses this process of socializing adjustment in his observation that the influence of a great man modifies a community in an entirely original and peculiar way, while the community in turn remodels

---

47 / This adjustment is not assimilation, but can best be understood as "accommodation."

48 / Dewey, *The Public and Its Problems*, vol. 2 (1984) in *The Later Works*, pp. 330, 332 (italics added).

him. This is because at any given moment both offer ambiguous potentialities of development.[49] Such a process is necessary for selfhood and
for the very being of individuality, for both are derivative from the sense of
"being with" in the process of socializing adjustment. As James stresses,
the self is always stretched outward toward others. Its integrity can only
be understood in terms of the social, for this center of creativity is never
felt in isolation, but always as extending outward toward others. Indeed,
for James, as for all the classical pragmatists, the individual exists in his
social relations.[50]

As can be seen, the generalized other changes as it incorporates or
adjusts to its own creativity, emerging as novel individual perspectives.
That which both founds and is founded upon this activity of socializing
adjustment is a community, and in its historical rootedness it develops
its own particular organs for the process of socializing adjustment. The
ability to provide the organs of adjudication within the ongoing dynamics of socializing adjustment constitutes a community of any type as a
community. The foundational world, in its deepest sense, can be understood as a community of communities. The very sense of being in the
world, as it emerges from anteceptive experience, is a sense of "being
with" in the activity of socializing adjustment, with the organs of adjudication immediately grounded in the fundamental features of temporally rooted behavior.

The process of socializing adjustment that constitutes the dynamics
of community can occur several ways, revealing diverse levels of adjustment. When a community is operating within a common system of
meanings on any one issue, then investigation can tend toward an ideal
limit of convergence. The manner of adjustment between a new perspective, as a novel interpretation of the facts, and the perspective of the generalized other, as the previously accepted interpretation within the

49 / James, "Great Men and Their Environment," *The Will to Believe and Other Essays*
(1979), *The Works of William James*, pp. 170, 170n, 171. The whole thrust of this essay
revolves around James's support of Darwin over Spencer, and his rejection of Spencer's
understanding of "the fatal way in which the mind, supposed passive, is molded by its experiences of 'outer relations'." This essay is not a defense of rugged individualism, but of human creativity.

50 / James, *Principles of Psychology*, i, pp. 279–283. Because of their diverse interests,
Dewey emphasized the community while James emphasized the individual, though their
respective understandings of each both require and are necessarily ingredient in the dynamics of socializing adjustment. "Community" here is not being used in the technical sense
developed within speculative pragmatism. Within this latter context, the individual and the
generalized other are the two poles, each requiring the other, for which community provides the organs of adjudication in the process of socializing adjustment.

community, is resolved by verification in the ongoing course of experience based on factual evidence, however elusive such evidence may be.

When a novel perspective brings a novel set of meanings by which to delineate facts, then the method yielding a process of adjustment that constitutes the dynamics of sociality within a community is not so easily resolved, for there is no longer a question of testing varying interpretations of the facts. Rather, there are now different perceptions of what facts exist. There are not just different interpretations to account for the facts, but there are different facts. Discussions enacted for the sake of bringing about an adjustment must stem from a generalized stance of agreement concerning the standards to be applied in making decisions among "incommensurable" frameworks for delineating facts that exist. Such standards may be difficult to elucidate, but as implicitly operative in the process of socializing adjustment by which conflicting meaning systems are adjudicated, they can be elicited for clarification through reflective focus on what is operative in the process of adjudication within the community.

Yet novel perspectives may at times emerge that are incommensurable not only with another a priori net for the catching of experience through the determination of what kind of facts exist in the world, but that also incorporate standards and criteria and solution goals, or kinds of problems important to resolve, that are incommensurable with those of another perspective. Thus, there are not only different facts, but different methods, standards, and criteria for determining which system of facts should be accepted. In a sense, these divergent perspectives have carved out divergent worlds[51]—be they divergent scientific worlds, or divergent ways of life, encompassing not just differing facts but differing goals, differing problems of importance, differing criteria for resolving differences, and hence differing organs for bringing about a process of socialization. This deepest level of incommensurability, which has been shown so clearly to lie embedded in the "structure of scientific revolutions"[52] is not different from the dynamics operative in lived experience, though in science, as the structure of experience writ large and made explicit, it is easier to dissect. Again, the methodology of science reflects the methodology of all experience, but each is more complex than first glance might indicate.

Yet such incommensurable perspectives, whether within the com-

---

51 / This is the most fundamental sense of incommensurability in Thomas Kuhn's *Structure of Scientific Revolutions*.

52 / Ibid.

mon-sense or scientific world, though in a sense structuring differing worlds, cannot, by the very nature of perspective as an open horizon, be closed to rational discussion for possibilities of socializing adjustment within one community. As has been seen, the interpretation of facts must work in anticipating the ongoing course of experience through empirical verification based on the evidence. Diverse perspectives for delineating facts must work, better or worse, in measuring up to the standards and criteria by which the community judges them, and in solving the problems which the community takes as important. And diverse perspectives that incorporate diverse standards and criteria and significant problems can be discussed in terms of their ability to resolve the potentially problematic situation that the foundational world, as it emerges from primordial experience, must resolve. Such a workability is articulated in various ways, is reflectively incorporated in differing evaluational criteria,[53] and in its ultimate ineffability, is reflected in differing traditions, differing rituals, and the emergence of differing goals as points of urgent resolution. Yet such diverse articulations stem from a vague, elusive, but real anteceptive sense of the temporal anticipatory stretch of human behavior, and the need for its anticipatory pulsations to mesh with the pulsations of that processive concreteness from which it has emerged, and with which it must successfully interact.

In any community, new organs for socializing adjustment in cases of incommensurability cannot be imposed from on high by eliciting the articulations of a past that does not contain the organs of resolution. New community organs must be created by calling on a sense of a more fundamental level of activity, based on a history of socializing adjustment that is in the process of formulating and developing itself and that will yield the new community organs of adjudication in the very process of emerging as a novel present that interprets its past as the condition of its meaningful emergence. If such new organs of adjudication do not emerge, then community has broken down.

In the ongoing process of socializing adjustment and the significance of the emerging present, some arguments or reasons gain vitality, while others fall by the wayside. Though neither are proved right or wrong, we "get over" some, but yield to the force of others. Such "getting over" or reinforcement is based on rational discussion, guided by a vague, anteceptive sense of the inescapable criteria of workability. Though the abstract articulations of workability take diverse, at times incommensu-

53 / Indeed, even incommensurable criteria for determining truth must be judged by their ability to work within the framework within which they emerge as criteria.

rable forms, the anteceptive sense of workability serves, ultimately, as the ineffable but inescapable and inexhaustible well-spring of vitality from which a community surges forth through rational discussion, leaving behind reasons and arguments that have become lifeless. In this way, over time, incommensurable perspectives, though not proved right or wrong, are resolved by the weight of argument as reasons and practices are worked out in the ongoing course of inquiry.

As has been shown, the relation of the individual and the generalized other in the process of socializing adjustment within community requires open horizons. No community is constricted by closed horizons, either in terms of possibilities of penetrating to more fundamental levels of community, or to wider breadth of community. Indeed such an either-or is itself a false dichotomy, for expansion in breadth is at once expansion in depth, since all derived communities are rooted in and open onto the foundational world, or community of communities, as it emerges from anteceptive experience. Within any derived community, the socializing adjustment of incommensurable perspectives at any level requires not an articulated imposition from on high, but a deepening to a more fundamental level of community. As two communities recognize their openness of horizons in coming to understand the perspective of the other, they make a socializing adjustment founded on a deeper or broader community. Such a socializing adjustment involves neither assimilation of perspectives, one to the other, nor fusion of each into an indistinguishable oneness, but an accommodation in which each creatively affects, and is affected by, the other through accepted organs of adjudication of some sort. The primordial world, then, as it emerges from anteceptive experience, is a community of communities not in the sense that it contains many self-enclosed communities, but in the sense that it is that foundational community upon which the horizonal dimensions of all other communities ultimately open.

To understand one's own stance on any issue is to understand its inherently perspectival approach in transforming the rich matrix of experiential possibilities into an orderly system of facts, and the illumination that other perspectives can rightfully cast upon such richness. In coming to understand the perspectival pluralism and the dynamic of socializing adjustment constitutive of pragmatic community, one can, at the same time, come to recognize the enrichment to be gained by understanding the perspective of the other and—as important—to recognize the enrichment to be gained by understanding what is implicitly operative in one's own perspectival approach. The foundation for such a perspectival pluralism, rather than for the drive toward unanimity in final knowledge, is to be found in the emergence of a world from anteceptive experience as the true pragmatic community of communities. The understanding of a radically diverse way of life, or way of making sense of things, is not to be derived by imposing one's own reflective perspective upon such diversity. Rather it comes by penetrating through differences to the sense of various ways of making sense of the world, as it emerges from the anteceptive field as a primordial world of "being with" in the process of socializing adjustment, deriving its essential characteristics from beings fundamentally alike, confronting a common reality of processive concreteness.

At this point the novelty and diversity of perspectival pluralism may be thought to lead to the view that true progress in knowledge is impossible, that there is no progress, only difference. This type of criticism again presupposes false dichotomies. Perspectival pluralism, incorporating, at its deepest level, the endless activity of socializing adjustment rather than convergence toward final completed truth, does not involve the stultifying self-enclosement of a relativism in terms of arbitrary conceptual schemes, or a historicism in terms of present happenstance. Rather it involves a temporalism in which the ontological rootedness of perspective emerges within the context of a past that presents itself in the richness of the present, and that is oriented toward an indefinite future in a process of socializing adjustment. Historical rootedness is at once ontological rootedness, and the temporal dimensions of both enter into the perspectival awareness that constitutes present knowledge as conditioned by, but also as a conditioning factor of, processive concreteness,[54] worldly encounter, and a tradition that articulates and develops its characteristic features in particular ways.

Knowledge as cumulative and knowledge as changing do not lie in opposition. Rather knowledge as changing is also knowledge as cumulative, for any novel perspective emerges from a cumulative process or history of socializing adjustment that yields enrichment of intelligibility, both of the old and of the new. To demand of such a cumulative process that it tend toward a final unchanging truth is to misunderstand the nature of processive concreteness, the nature of noetic activity, and the dynamic of worldly encounter within which both are unified. Further,

---

54 / The self-directed organism incorporates being within processive concreteness as well as encounter with it through the intentionally grounded mediation of world. Its activities not only change worldly contours, but enter into and change the matrixes of processive concreteness. Worldly possibilities include both noetically based possibilities and possibilities of processive concreteness. Human activity enters into the changes of both types of possibilities, for it belongs to both.

to the extent that any perspective is reflective of its own conditions of possibility in its ontological and historical rootedness, it advances, for in such reflection it becomes conscious of the openness of its own horizon onto a primordial community of communities, and hence becomes open to the adjudicating dialogue of socializing adjustment within which it finds its own intelligibility and enrichment.

These last statements lead to the final two chapters of this essay. The concept of enrichment involves not just enrichment of intelligibility, but enrichment of life itself. The anteceptive pulsations of life, as they emerge into worldly experience, must not only be consonant with the pulsations of processive concreteness in an ongoing process of socializing adjustment for the sake of intelligent life, but for the sake of harmonious life.[55] The ontological foundations of value as a dimension of worldly encounter will be the focal point of the next chapter. Finally, speculative pragmatism, as a philosophical perspective, must reflect upon its own situatedness in the socializing adjustment of a philosophical community that has articulated itself through a tradition of systems in conflict.

55 / In refining this latter aspect in the next chapter, the very distinction itself will tend to dissolve.

Eight

The Value Dimension

UNTIL NOW the issue of value within pragmatic vision has been ignored, not because it is unimportant, or because it is isolated from other issues discussed throughout this essay, but because it is so interwoven with every issue that its import can best be developed in light of these other issues. The following discussion will speak of the value dimension of experience, for the experiencing of value is a dimension of the experiencing of the universe, as it emerges through organism-environment interaction from anteceptive experience toward the unity of self and world. The experience of value can best be set in its context by its inability to be caught within the dichotomies of past philosophies of value.

First, value is not something subjective, housed either as a content of mind or in any other sense within the organism, but neither is it something "there" in an independently ordered universe. As has been shown, objects and situations, as they emerge in human experience, possess qualities that are as ontologically real in their emergence as the processes within which they emerge. These objects and situations possess qualities not just of colors, sounds, resistance, and so forth, but qualities of being alluring or repugnant, fulfilling or stultifying, appealing or unappealing, and so forth. These latter qualities, like all qualities, are there in nature;[1] they are ontologically real emergents in the context of organism-environment interaction. Further, they are not reducible in any way to other qualities. Rather, value, as a quality of events within nature, is immediately experienced and irreducible. Value and valuings,

1 / This statement holds for the first two senses of nature as discussed in the previous chapter, nature as processive concreteness, and nature as worldly encounter. In the abstractions of nature as an object of physical science, value is left behind.

or valuing experiences, are traits of nature; novel emergents in the context of organism-environment interaction. They are real additive features within processive concreteness.

Second, values or valuings are not something that the individual experiences in isolation from a community, nor are individual values something to be put in conflict with, or in opposition to, community value. Further, the community value is not merely the sum of individual values, nor are individual values merely a reflection of community values. Rather, value and valuings, in their emergence within everyday experience, are dimensions of worldly encounter, experiential features within the context of the socializing adjustments of pragmatic community that have their roots in anteceptive experience.[2] In the satisfactions of the immediate pulsations of anteceptive experience with its emergent valuings, the experience of value begins to enter the process of socializing adjustment in the context of the ontological presence of other organisms. In the emergence of worldly contours, the experience of value emerges as both shared and unique, as all worldly experience is both shared and unique. The socializing adjustment between these two aspects gives rise to the novel and creative aspects within moral community as that which, like any community, provides the organs for adjudication, not only of diverse, but also of conflicting claims at various levels.[3]

Finally, this understanding of value leads neither to a relativism of arbitrary choice, nor to an absolutism of no true choice in shaping the value-ladenness of the universe; it involves neither nihilistic despair nor utopian optimism. Rather, it is a meliorism that holds that "the specific conditions which exist at one moment, be they comparatively bad or comparatively good, in any event may be bettered . . . it arouses confidence and reasonable hopefulness as [wholesale] optimism does not."[4]

Before proceeding, the use of terms must be clarified, for the term *value* is used within pragmatism to cover experiential emergents within a variety of circumstances yielding distinct aspects of the value situation. The term *value* is at times used to indicate immediately appealing qualities, problematic values, or direct valuings; to indicate experiences that are the outcome of intelligently organized activity, or a quality emerging from the unification of a context through intelligent activity;

2 / These relationships parallel, in the area of value, the relationships developed in the previous chapter.

3 / These various levels were discussed in the previous chapter.

4 / Dewey, *Reconstruction in Philosophy*, vol. 12 (1982) in *The Middle Works*, pp. 181–182 (bracketed word is not in specific quote but in surrounding text).

and, finally, to indicate objects, situations, or acts—in brief, objectivities of some sort—that are capable of yielding valuings in some sense. Though Dewey's use of the terms *de facto value* and *de jure value* has been criticized because they are held either to implicate him, or to appear to implicate him, in the naturalistic fallacy, this set of distinctions will be helpful in delineating the framework of value within the context of speculative pragmatism for two reasons. First, precisely because they, more than any other terminology within pragmatic discussions of value, tend to lead to the misplaced accusations of involvement in the naturalistic fallacy, this distinction can be used to attack the problem head on. Second, Dewey's own use of the terms involves an ambiguity that leads directly to the function of further distinctions, derivative from these, that will be made in the present context.

De facto value, according to Dewey, indicates the immediacy of the "satisfying," while *de jure value* indicates that which is the outcome of the resolution of a problematic or potentially problematic situation, that which is "satisfactory":

> To say that something satisfies is to report something as an isolated finality. To assert that it is satis*factory* is to define it in its connections and interactions. The fact that it pleases or is immediately congenial poses a problem to judgment. How shall the satisfaction be rated? Is it a value or is it not? Is it something to be prized and cherished, *to be* enjoyed? The latter "involves a prediction; it contemplates a future in which the thing will continue to serve; it will do."[5]

This distinction between de facto and de jure value is not an attempt to derive an ought from an is, a value from a fact. There is no problem of committing a naturalistic fallacy within the pragmatic understanding of value, for there is no fact-value distinction. The occurrence of the immediate experience characterized by value[6] is an ontological emergent within nature, on an equal footing with the experience of other qualitative endings as ontological emergents within nature. Values are as real as all other emergents within processive concreteness; the presence of value is an ontological condition within the context of intermeshing matrixes characterized by organic activity. Further, any experienced fact within the world can have a value dimension, for the value dimension emerges as an aspect of the context within which the fact functions as

---

5 / Dewey, *Quest for Certainty*, p. 208.

6 / Value may of course be positive or negative, or, in other terms, experiences are characterized by value or disvalue.

value relevant. Indeed, the experience of value is itself a discriminatable fact within our world.[7]

The distinction between de facto and de jure value, as expressed in the above quotation, is the distinction between experiencings that make no future claim and those judgments that make future claims by linking present experience to other experiences in terms of interacting potentialities or causal connections. In brief, de facto value is turned into de jure value by the organizing activity of mind in the ongoing course of experience as experimental. De jure claims emerge from the context of conflicting de facto claims, and are dependent for their validity upon these latter. As James summarizes, there is no "de jure relation, which antedates and overarches" de facto claims.[8]

Dewey holds that whether we reserve the term *value* for what has above been called *de jure value* is a minor matter, though it seems more proper.[9] What is important, rather, is "that the distinction be acknowledged as the key to understanding the relation of values to the direction of conduct."[10] Claims concerning de jure value have a normative function because they make a claim in terms of consequences of conduct as yielding that which is valuable. The following discussion will explore this relation between conduct and the normative aspect in light of further distinctions relating to de facto and de jure value. Once again, the present work does not hold that these further distinctions are not elusively operative within the framework of the pragmatic understanding of value, but rather that, because of ambiguous uses of terminology, their significance is at times lost to view and hence not fully utilized.

There seems to be an ambiguity in Dewey's use of *de jure value*, for at times it indicates that objectivity that is valuable because of its potential to yield valuing experiences, and at times valuing experiences themselves that meet certain conditions. Indeed, both of these uses of *de jure value* are to be found in his above delineation of de facto and de jure value, for it indicates distinctions in rating both the objectivity and the satisfaction.

Lewis makes a clear distinction between two senses of value: first, "as applying to passages of experience and signifying their immediately gratifying or grievous quality"; second, "as applying to objective enti-

---

7 / The experience of value within the world, like all worldly emergents, involves both noetic and ontological dimensions.

8 / James, "The Moral Philosopher and the Moral Life," *The Will to Believe and Other Essays,* p. 148.

9 / Dewey, *Quest for Certainty,* p. 209. Dewey tends not to follow his own advice.

10 / Ibid.

ties—objects, events, or properties of objects or events—and signifying potentialities of these for leading to the experiences" having immediately gratifying or grievous qualities.[11] Here, the distinction is explicitly between value immediately experienced and value as an objective claim concerning the potentiality for objectivities of some sort to yield valuing experiences. This clear distinction loses, however, an important distinction housed within Dewey's ambiguous use of *de jure value*. This can be brought to light by focusing on Dewey's position from a slightly different direction. Dewey holds that a natural end that occurs without intervention of human art is a terminus, a de facto boundary; however, such ends are not "fulfillments, conclusions, completions, or perfections" because they are not the consequences of prior reflection.[12] As long as we do not engage in experimental inquiry, "enjoyments (values if we choose to apply that term) are casual; they are given by 'nature,' not constructed by art."[13] In the latter sense, ends may be called consummations rather than termini, for "values are naturalistically interpreted as intrinsic qualities of events in their consummatory reference."[14]

Dewey thus makes the distinction between valuing experiences resulting from ends occurring casually or the valuings of qualitative termini, and the valuing experiences resulting from ends that are fulfillments of anticipated resolutions of a problematic context, fulfillments that result from the intervention of human art.[15] Whether Dewey intends a correlation of terminus and consummation with de facto and de jure value, as he seems to indicate, is ambiguous because of his ambiguous use of *de jure value*. In the following discussion, however, the difference between de facto value and de jure value cannot be correlated with the distinction between casual valuings and valuings as a quality of experiencing that results from intelligent inquiry. First, in the present context, both of these are de facto valuings. They are the immediate value experiences as they are had in their immediacy, value experiences that as a matter of fact, "are," regardless of how they come to be. These will be called, respectively, *de facto terminus value* and *de facto fulfillment value*.[16] Further, valuings that set a problematic context may themselves

11 / Lewis, "Values and Facts," *Values and Imperatives*, ed. John Lange (Stanford: Stanford University Press, 1969), p. 89.

12 / Dewey, *Experience and Nature*, p. 86.

13 / Dewey, *Quest for Certainty*, p. 212.

14 / Dewey, *Experience and Nature*, p. 9.

15 / This point will be reintroduced at the end of this chapter.

16 / This is not an attempt to provide an exegesis of what Dewey "really" intends in his usage, but rather is a developmental use of his distinctions as they can function to clarify speculative pragmatism. Though the specific use of Dewey's terms may at times contra-

be de facto fulfillment values, not de facto terminus values. As has been seen, any ending is at once a new beginning, and what serves as problematic, the de facto valuings, within any context may itself be either de facto termini valuings or de facto fulfillment valuings, though the resolution of any problematic context can be understood only in terms of possible de facto fulfillment valuings as a conclusion of the organizing activity. De facto valuings of any kind, as they conflict and hence initiate inquiry, are problematic valuings.[17]

Dewey's use of *de jure value*, not as it refers to what is here called *de facto fulfillment valuings*, but to objectivities capable of yielding such experiences, will be called *objective value*. The term *de jure value* will be retained to indicate a pervasive quality of the reciprocal relation between possible de facto fulfillment value and objective value, a relation that can be adequately captured neither by one of the latter distinctions alone, nor by using one term ambiguously to cover both.

Here it becomes important not to fall, within the understanding of value, into a parallel of the rudiments of a spectator theory of knowledge, or the confusion of meaning and verification. Earlier chapters showed that a three-fold distinction and interrelation must be made among the immediacy of anteceptive experience, experience of a world of objectivities, and the functionally "immediate" character of experience within this world.[18] These distinctions become relevant here, beginning, in the ensuing discussion, with the latter two. The very distinction between de facto fulfillment valuings and de facto terminus valuings is contextually relative, for the causal valuings within any context are the products of some previously organized habitual modes of response to types of situations having, originally, their own problematic character, at least in some minimal sense. There are no brute de facto terminus valuings within everyday experience. Though objective values are what they are only because they have the potential for producing value experiences, value experiences are what they are in part because of the objective value meanings through which they emerge. Just as there was seen to be a functional relation between intended object and the character of perceptual experience, so there is a functional relationship between intended objective value and the quality of value experience. De jure quality permeates experience because of meanings that interpret

---

dict his own intended use, the position developed does not deviate from the basic thrust of his general position.

17 / The actual experiencing of fulfillment value may be a problematic value in the broader context of conflicting values in process of resolution.

18 / See chapters 2–4.

objects in terms of possible de facto valuings. In the functional relation between the objective claim and the possible de facto experiences within the internal structure of meaning, de jure value emerges as a pervasive character or quality of the meaning, and hence as pervading the unified field of its application within the ongoing course of experience.

Just as any objectivity emerges from the creative fixation and organization of experiences by habit as a rule of generation of pragmatic schemata as the relational generality of varying possible acts under varying circumstances yielding varying results as perspectives of an object, so problematic values are creatively organized and unified through objective value meanings that indicate varying types of activity, under varying circumstances, yielding varying resultant experiences of the value possibilities of the intended objectivity.

Thus, any immediate valuing experience is structured by its fusion with the richness of the objective value belief in its integrative function, with the fullness of its meaning in terms of other possible value experiencings, both at other times and in other situations, because the objective value meaning, like all meaning, is irreducible in principle to actual experiences, and because the meaning incorporates an indefinite number of schematic forms of possible experiences under varying conditions.

The immediate experiencings, the valuings within everyday experience, reflect, in their immediacy, the objective value claims emerging through the structures of pragmatic meaning. In everyday experiencing, valuings reflect valuations. Emergent values, as dimensions of passages of experience, emerge within the backdrop of moral community, and reflect in their very emergence the structures of such community.

Immediate fulfillment value is thus de facto value in that, as a matter of fact, it is. It has a "pragmatic certainty"[19] because it is experienced whether or not related anticipated experiences occur. In its very unquestionable immediacy, however, it is fused with precisely that objectivity about which mistake is always possible. Thinking an objective value has been attained infuses the de facto fulfillment valuing with the richness of the objectivity, but objective belief may turn out to be cognitively wrong. Thus, a de jure value claim can always be mistaken, though the experience of de facto fulfillment value is neither true nor false, but rather just is. There is no such thing as a false de facto fulfillment value experience, but there can be a false sense of the validity of the experience as indicative of an objectivity capable of yielding further

19 / See chapter 3.

value experiences. Thus, there can be a false experience of de jure value, or rather a false sense of the presence of de jure value.

Further, just as any meaning is irreducible to any indefinite number of experiences, actual or possible, but rather sets the structure of verifying instances, so the meanings that yield value objectivities set the conditions for verification instances, actual or possible. De facto fulfillment valuings or consummations are precisely such actual verification instances of the objective belief, and their character is permeated by the conditions of possible verification instances contained in the internal structure of meaning. The worth of any objective claim, its truth, lies in its workability, its verification in actual instances, but its meaning is the condition for the possibility of such verification and it fuses its structure into the verifying instances. Similarly, the truth of an objective value claim lies in its verification instances, and the structure of the objectivity intended is fused into the verifying instances, funding them with the richness of the processes which led to their occurrences. Just as successful actions in light of any objective beliefs are instigated as a result of the belief, but not usually in order to explicitly verify the belief, so successful integrations of values in de facto fulfillment valuings are instigated as a result of objective value belief, or of emerging objective value belief, not in order to verify the belief. Yet, in both cases, the successfully integrated experience serves as implicit verification. The verification is a by-product, so to speak, of successfully ongoing experience, and as the sole function of the meant perceptual objectivity is the successful ongoing experience, so the sole function of the objective value claim is the successful ongoing integration of experience in yielding de facto valuings. Only when belief is called into question are actions instigated for the purpose of verifying the belief. A valid claim concerning the de jure quality of a value experience lies in the correct awareness of the workable relationship between the objectivity as valuable and the de facto fulfillment valuing experience. Further, and analogously with the earlier development of meaning and verification, as objective belief breaks down, the de facto valuing changes in its quality. Any attempt to get at a brute de facto valuing apart from a network of objective beliefs is impossible, for data, abstracted in a problematic context, are abstracted from, and gain their structure within the significance of, a backdrop of objective beliefs. The relation between data and objective meaning is always functional in all areas of human experience.

Thus, de facto fulfillment value, even in its unquestionable immediacy, reflects the structures of moral objectivities within which it emerges. In brief, just as "immediate experience" is never the experience of pure immediacy, but is shot through with the structurings of objectivities as these emerge within pragmatic meanings, so the "immediate experience" of valuing is shot through with the structurings of "moral objectivities" as these emerge within pragmatic meanings. The immediate experience of de facto fulfillment value is permeated by the pragmatic meanings in terms of which the experience is the experience of that which resolves a potentially problematic situation, and which has the potentialities for the production of other valuing experiences. As Dewey notes, "Even in the midst of direct enjoyment, there is a sense of validity, of authorization, which intensifies the enjoyment."[20]

The extent of one's awareness of this functional relation, or, in other terms, the extent of one's awareness of the meanings that enrich experience, determines the extent of the fulfillment versus terminus value to be found in de facto experiencings. The difference between a de facto terminus and de facto fulfillment valuing lies in the utilization of objective value meanings within which value experiences emerge, in the difference in the richness of, and the conscious awareness of, the meanings within which they function. If there is no de facto fulfillment value, if there is no conscious awareness of the relation between the value experience and objective value meaning, then no de jure quality emerges, for if de jure quality is a character rooted in the internal structure of meaning, then it can only emerge in experience through awareness of the meanings that permeate and organize experience. New ideals, new de jure values, are new moral meanings that emerge in the organization of conflicting de facto claims, and their organizational structure, as a relation between possible de facto value experience and objective claim, is permeated by de jure value quality. Thus, moral awareness enhances value experience, for the level or intensity of the richness of de facto fulfillment valuing is a function of the meanings that infuse it. Thus, for all the pragmatists, moral action is planned rational action rooted in the awareness of meanings.

Indeed, part of the development of the harmonious life is to make valuings as reflective of valuations as possible. Only when one gets de facto valuings from that which reason sees as valuable, can one develop a truly integrated self. Such cultivation can proceed only when one is aware of the relation, within value meanings, between the de facto experiences and the network of processes which can culminate in their occurrence. Thus, taste, as Dewey notes, far from being that about

20 / Dewey, *Quest for Certainty*, p. 213.

which one cannot argue, is one of the most important things to argue about.[21] The cultivation of taste is the cultivation of the correct infusion of de facto valuing with objective meaning. Only when immediate valuings are valuings that reason sees are, or can be, organized into the objectively valuable, can there be a life of harmony. Reason thus performs its proper moral function by enriching the immediacy of value experience in a way that reflects awareness of moral meaning and validity of application in concrete situations.

A problem may seem to emerge here. The above discussion may seem to indicate a tendency toward the stagnation of values, in that objective value claims bring valuings in line with them. The situation, however, is no different from the general situation in which the character of experience that is structured by meanings serves as verifications of the correct application of the meanings. Just as the appearance breaks down as the objectivity breaks down or the meaning fails to work adequately, so as moral objectivities break down, there is an accompanying change of value quality in the immediate experience. In neither case is this a vicious circle, but a cumulative interplay. When habitual modes of organizing behavior do not work in organizing potentially problematic situations of conflicting valuings, new moral objectivities emerge that in turn give a different funded quality to the immediacy of de facto valuings. This reciprocal structuring, as grounded in the workability of the functional relation between the two incorporated within pragmatic meaning, and as bestowing a de jure quality to the experienced relationship, must work as an *organic unity* in the ongoing course of experience in increasing its value-ladenness. Such a workable relationship, to remain workable, requires not stagnation but constant openness to change. The ensuing discussion will turn to this point, and in doing so, must return to the anteceptive field, though this route to the openness to change may at first appear to lead in precisely the opposite direction.

Immediate value experiencings, as these emerge as dimensions of the pulsations of anteceptive experience, are prior to the development of the valuable emerging through the structures of pragmatic meaning. As has been seen, however, anteceptive experience reflects, in its very nature, the rudimentary pulsations of a vital intentionality, and the mode of focusing on, or abstracting from, or delimiting within the stream of anteceptive experience reflects the character of the meaningful objectivities that we interpret the experience to be an instance of. What reveals itself as the stuff of the stream of anteceptive experience is not just a

21 / Ibid., p. 209.

content revealed, but rather the product of a "taking" which can fulfill the anticipatory structure of human experience as experimental. Purposive organic response infuses the features of its creative, vital intentionality into the very fabric of the anteceptive field, and its anticipatory character demands the function of verification as the fulfillment of expectation. Because of this, even within anteceptive experience, no de facto terminus value is a mere terminus, but rather it emerges as a product of vital pulsations temporally stretching toward anticipatory fulfillment, no matter how rudimentary such expectation may be; the temporal stretch of human behavior carries the felt continuity of anticipation and fulfillment into the very texture of the valuing experience even at its most rudimentary level. Thus, "pure" de facto terminus valuings are not to be found even in rudimentary anteceptive experience because of its temporal, anticipatory, experimental character. The temporal stretch of human behavior, not just as anticipatory but also as consummatory, is experienced within the durational flow of felt temporality.

Though anteceptive valuings have an aspect of de facto fulfillment value, there is no de jure quality, for they are not organized around enduring objectivities; they have not been taken up into the network of pragmatic meanings by which they are organized in terms of a structural network of other possibilities of experiencing. As such anteceptive valuings become incorporated into the structure of objective value meanings, and as they are experienced within the context of these meanings, and promoted because of these meanings, they become the experiencing of the valuable within the context of worldly encounter, just as any anteceptive experience, as incorporated within the structures of pragmatic meaning, becomes the experience of worldly objectivities. Neither at any time, nor at any level of awareness, is there a brute de facto terminus valuing that does not partake of the features, however rudimentary, of de facto fulfillment valuings. Nor are there, within worldly encounter, de facto valuings that do not reflect the funded character of objective valuations, as incorporated in the structures of pragmatic meanings.

Further, even the valuings of anteceptive experience are a product of the rudimentary beginnings of socializing adjustment, for the valuings of pulsations satisfied are valuings emerging from the satisfaction of that which has been partially shaped by the ontological presence of the activity of the other. The anteceptive sense of ontological presence is at once the anteceptive sense of other active organisms whose ontologically rooted pulsations intrude within experience. Thus, even the valuings emerging in most casual fashion in the pulsations of anteceptive experience are the satisfactions of that which has been partially molded by the ontological presence of others that enter the organisms' horizonal dimensions. As anteceptive experience emerges within the worldly contours of everyday experience, de facto valuings are partially shaped by the institutional practices and doctrines of the generalized other in the context of the socializing adjustments of pragmatic community. Immediate valuings, as they emerge in experience, are in part products of socializing adjustment, and reflect in part the norms and standards of the community.

Thus, not only do moral norms and moral standards originate within the socializing adjustment of community, since prior to such activity there can be no moral situation, no moral rules or standards, but also the very immediacies of valuings emerge within the context of such activity, for the pulsations of an isolated individual are artificial abstractions; they are not to be found even at the level of anteceptive experience. The ontological presence of the other active organism, as much as the ontological presence of processive concreteness in general, shapes the direction of vital pulsations and the consummations that yield valuing experiencings. Even at this rudimentary level, the temporal stretch of anticipatory fulfillment is intertwined with the anticipatory fulfillment of the other with resulting adjustments of each. Thus, the anteceptive sense of value emerges as intertwined with the anteceptive sense of being with, and emerges, within the context of worldly encounter, as the awareness of moral community as that context within which socializing adjustment occurs.

Just as pragmatic meanings must organize the welter of anteceptive experience by enriching it with meanings to the highest degree possible, must make sense of all experience, not relegating any to the unreal, so the moral norms of a society must incorporate and integrate the valuings of all to the highest degree possible, not relegating any out of court, for the emergence of conflicting claims from the pulsations of anteceptive experience yields a democracy of valuings of which none can make initial claim to superiority. De facto valuings do not become valuable in terms of some prestructured hierarchy of values, but rather every de facto valuing asserts a claim and demands consideration precisely because it emerges from the anteceptive domain as a tendency satisfied. The moral democracy of conflicting claims emerges from the anteceptive field. Thus, James holds that "claim and obligation are, in fact, coextensive terms; they cover each other exactly," for "every de facto claim creates in so far forth an obligation."[22] In order to incorporate conflicting values it becomes necessary to restructure part of our moral community. Here, in the area of value experience, the dynamics of socializing adjustment operative within any type of community are to be found.

To develop the dynamics of socializing adjustment in the area of value experience, some further distinctions within the concreteness of experience as it emerges from the anteceptive field must be made. Until now, the term *pulsation* has been used to indicate the anticipatory, vital intentionality or creative drive of the organism as intertwined with an ontological presence. In such rudimentary pulsations, impulses, emerging habits, and the creative center from which both spring are indistinguishable. These distinctions, though unrecognized in anteceptive experience, become important as anteceptive experience develops into worldly encounter. An initial diversity or "semi-chaos"[23] of impulses is transformed into habitual ways of acting by interaction with an environment in ways that promote or frustrate initial tendencies. Thus, diversity and flexibility become lessened as habitual ways of acting take over, become institutionalized, and in turn are reinforced by institutions that promote or frustrate initial tendencies. What has been omitted in the above statement, however, is the role of the vital intentionality or creative drive of the individual in its entirety. And, here the appropriation of the term *impulsion* as used by Dewey will be useful, though again this is an appropriation within the context of speculative pragmatism, and is not intended as an exegesis of his concept. While an impulse is specialized and particular, *impulsion* for Dewey "designates a movement outward and forward of the whole organism to which special impulses are auxiliary."[24]

Impulsion, within the context of speculative pragmatism, is the ongoing advancement of the processive concreteness that constitutes an organic matrix. In its concreteness, it is inexhaustible by any number of actualizations of dynamic tendencies that, beginning as the diversity of impulses, settle into habits of response, as some emerging dynamic tendencies intermesh adequately with the possibilities presented by the surrounding environment, while others do not. Like any slab of concreteness, impulsion is not a collection of dynamic tendencies, but rather is that ongoing advance of an ontological density that manifests itself in

22 / James, "The Moral Philosopher and the Moral Life," p. 148.

23 / See chapter 4.

24 / Dewey, *Art as Experience* (New York: Capricorn Books, G. P. Putnam's Sons, 1958), p. 58.

the actualizations of tendencies. Impulsion is that wellspring of human creative activity that prevents the repetition of habitual modes of behavior and the formalized institutions they involve from settling into sterile rigidity, and rather keeps the moral situation, when rationally directed, flexible, vital, and changing. Impulsion is that concreteness of human existence that incorporates a vital intentionality, that manifests itself in emerging impulses and in habits of response as embodied in dispositionally generated meanings, but whose creativity and ongoing development cannot be understood as a collection of such impulses and habits, but as the concrete foundation for their emergence. Indeed, similar habits stem from unique impulsions, and thus are embedded in a unique concrete matrix of creativity that enters into the course of novel direction takings, for impulsion, in its concreteness, overflows any impulses that, in their workability, become habits of response giving rise to, and in turn being reinforced by, institutionalized practices.

The anteceptive sense of impulsion, as the concrete advance of the human matrix, is in fact the anteceptive sense of the I functioning: an anteceptive sense of advancing creativity directed outward toward the ever-emerging possibilities within its contextual matrix. Or, in other terms, the anteceptive sense of the I functioning is a sense of the ontological density of one's creative interaction with a surrounding environment. Like anteceptive experience in general, the anteceptive sense of the I functioning underlies and overflows any grasp by intelligent reflection, and thus cannot be exhausted by any number of pragmatic meanings that are brought to bear on itself. And, like any anteceptive overflow, it provides both uniqueness and unity to the experiential grasp in terms of pragmatic meanings, and renders this center of creativity, as grasped, unique and uniquely unified. As such anteceptive overflow enters into the context of moral awareness as fused anteception, it provides a vague "moral sense" of fittingness that, far from being the result of inculcated principles, is the primordial foundation for their acceptance or eventual overthrow. Though the creative advance of impulsion, like any "slab" of processive concreteness, is never totally grasped by the pragmatic meanings by which it becomes intelligible, yet, intelligent reflection on this concrete center of creativity via pragmatic meanings, fused with the anteceptive overflow of the sense of the I functioning, yields an awareness of impulsion as that which demands fulfillment in the ongoing course of experience, and as that which governs the adequacy of particular impulses and habits in the context of emerging value.

Because emerging, changing energies of impulsion immersed in emerging, changing situations cannot be captured in the confines of institutionalized or habitual ways of acting, the moral order of socializing adjustment must be in a continual process of self-created re-creation, and thus, in Dewey's words, "Man is under just as much obligation to develop his most advanced standards and ideals as to use conscientiously those which he already possesses."[25] As new standards and ideals emerge, the rational order that underlies a moral community and that provides the adjudication process in the ongoing dynamics of socializing adjustment is at times re-created as well. Though the slow evolution of such a re-creation may at times be difficult to discern, it may sometimes seem to manifest itself with startling energy and immediacy.

The previous chapter showed that the temporal rootedness of knowledge, properly understood, involves not mere change but real development. Similarly, the temporal rootedness of the self, properly directed, leads to a moral situation not of mere change, but rather of real growth. Because of the concrete richness of impulsion, integration and harmonizing cannot be achieved by the stifling of emerging energies that overflow the rigidity of habits and institutions, but rather by their incorporation into new workable patterns of behavior. As Dewey so eloquently proclaims, more "passions, not fewer, is the answer. . . . Rationality, once more, is not a force to evoke against impulse and habit. It is the attainment of a working harmony among diverse desires."[26] Thus, change, rationally directed, leads to growth.

In the breakdown of the workable value situation, in the reconstruction and reintegration of values, the anteceptive sense of the I functioning comes to the fore. Thus, there is the opportunity for a new integration that more adequately fulfills the demands of impulsion, for awareness of this center of creativity, though momentarily lost through the objectivities of moral meanings, is yet more available in its concrete immediacy to the anteceptive sense of its functioning.[27] The acceptance of inculcated habits and the formalized rigidities to which they lead, the focus on unchanging moral objectivities, prevents the reconstruction and reintegration of values. At the same time, it prevents the heightened anteceptive experience of impulsion, as that which demands fulfillment and which provides the elusive sense of moral "fittingness" to the particularities of the habits to which it gives rise. Indeed, when the valuings resulting from particular habits or specialized interests are not at the same time satisfactions of the demands of impulsion, of the outward

25 / Dewey, *Reconstruction in Philosophy*, p. 180.

26 / Dewey, *Human Nature and Conduct*, vol. 14 (1983) in *The Middle Works*, pp. 136–137.

27 / See chapter 4.

movement of the organism in its entirety, then there is conflict and stultification, rather than harmonizing growth. The rigid stifling of diversity can lead to stultification through fanaticism of various sorts and degrees, but undisciplined diversity not guided by a sense of the unity
from which it stems, can also lead to stultification.

Further, growth cannot be understood only in terms of the organizations of one's own interests. The growth of the self is a process by which
it achieves fuller, richer, more inclusive, and more complex interactions
with its environment. The self, not as a substance, but as processive creativity becomes conscious and reflexive, emerges in the context of "being
with" as part of its very nature. Thus, workable solutions cannot be
understood just in terms of the artificiality of oneself in isolation, but
rather they must be workable for all those whose interests are there to
be adjudicated. Because the very sense of self is a sense of being with
through creative adjustment, Mead can hold that the process of recognizing the interests of others does not require that one become a sacri-
ficed self, but rather that one become a larger self.[28] Growth incorporates an encompassing sympathetic understanding of varied and diverse
interests, thus leading to tolerance, not as a sacrifice but as an enlargement of self, not as something totally other but as something sympa-
thetically incorporated as an expansion of one's self.

The ability to recognize perspectival limitation and to appropriate its
openness onto other perspectives is growth of the self. Indeed, our selves
are partially constituted by our social relations, and the conflict of self
and other can only be resolved by a more encompassing self stemming
from the growth of self fulfillment. Such growth involves a greater ability both to create, and to respond constructively to the creation of, the
novel valuing experience, the novel value meaning, the novel perspective. Such growth is at once an enlargement of the self and an integration of the self, for indeed, impulsion is the advance of an organic matrix
in its concreteness, and in this advance expansion and integration are
two sides of the same coin.

Because the human matrix is "free," has self-directed creativity,[29]
such integrative expansion can be more perfectly attained, but also can
be more fully disrupted and set in conflict. The human organism, then,
has the capabilities for both the best and the worst that the universe is
capable of producing in its ongoing activity of socializing adjustment.
However, even the production of the worst contains an incipient spring-

---

28 / See Mead, *Mind, Self and Society*, p. 386.
29 / See chapters 6 and 7.

board toward the best. When distorted values lead finally to a moral crisis and the breakdown of unreflectively accepted moral order, there is a unique opportunity for the revitalization of moral experience in the heightened anteceptive sense of impulsion, as it emerges in the breakdown of the moral situation, and for a surge of moral growth. Thus, in the light of the present, one can interpret the darkest episodes of the past precisely as episodes of moral distortion that gave rise to renewed moral growth. Here again, however, the human matrix, as self-directed creativity, has the potential for ignoring such opportunities. Moral crisis provides the *opportunity* for a surge of revitalized growth; the free, creative, self-directed organism must take advantage of such an opportunity through anteceptive sensitivity and intelligent reorganization of moral objectivities. Dewey, then, can hold that growth itself is the only moral "end," that the moral meaning of democracy lies in its contribution to the growth of every member of society,[30] and that growth involves the rational resolution of conflict—conflict between duty and desire, between what is already accomplished and what is possible.[31] Similarly, Peirce can "bless God for the law of growth with all the fighting it imposes."[32]

Thus, though the process of socializing adjustment itself affects the vital drives; though neither the emergence of moral norms and practices nor the emergence of brute valuings occurs apart from the socializing adjustments of concrete organisms; though the very experiences of the individual are derivative from the anteceptive sense of being with as it emerges into the relation of self and world, yet the impulsion of the I in its uniqueness brings unique tendencies and potentialities into the shaping processes of socializing adjustment; brings creative solutions to the resolution of the conflicting and changing claims of de facto valuings; and restructures the very moral behavior or moral practices and the institutionalized ways of behaving that helped shape its own developing potentialities. Though moral deliberation involves "social intelligence," the reaction of the individual against an existing scheme becomes the means of the transformation and restructuring of habits and institutional practices.[33] Again it can be seen that the concept of individualism, when removed from its atomistic setting, gains its import in indicating neither an isolatable element in, nor an atomic building block of, a community, but rather in indicating the instigation of creative adjustments

30 / Dewey, *Reconstruction in Philosophy*, pp. 181, 186.
31 / Dewey, *Ethics*, vol. 5 (1978) in *The Middle Works*, p. 327.
32 / Peirce, 6.479.
33 / Dewey, *Ethics*, p. 173.

within a community, adjustments that creatively change both poles that operate within the adjustment process.

The drive toward betterment through creative growth in the dynamics of socializing adjustment is a natural offspring of the anteceptive sense of creativity, of ontological density, and of being with. The anteceptive sense of creativity, of efficacy, is the motivating force for meliorism: one *can* make things better; one *can* increase the value-ladenness of the universe. The anteceptive sense of the pulsations of the ontological concreteness of this center of creativity, which is inexhaustible by any number of emerging drives, impulses, or habits, along with the anteceptive sense of the ontological presence of other creative centers with which it is inextricably intermeshed, embeds melioristic motivation within the context of a sense of open horizons and of a demand toward ever more encompassing growth. Though Dewey refers to growth as an "end," he does not intend this in a technical sense of "end," and indeed, growth can best be understood not as an end to be attained, but as a dynamic embedded in the ongoing process of life, just as experimental method is not an end to be achieved, but a dynamic embedded in the ongoing course of experience. Experimental method, as applied in the moral context, is in fact the melioristic attempt to increase the value-ladenness of a situation through a creative growth of perspective that can incorporate and harmonize conflicting or potentially conflicting values. But the expansion of a moral perspective, though not independent of intelligent inquiry, is not merely a change in an intellectual perspective, but rather is a change that affects and is affected by the impulsion of the organism in its total ontological concreteness. Growth of moral perspective is growth of the self as an organic whole, and such growth is rooted in the sense of impulsion. This foundation of the melioristic drive manifested in rationally directed growth, which lies in the features of the anteceptive field, is a foundation the sense of which, like the sense of temporality, is dubitable in principle, and is often doubted at the levels of reflection. In the area of moral value, such doubting leads frequently to the false assumptions of perspectival closure or perspectival absence, with the respective resulting positions of moral relativism on the one hand, and moral absolutism on the other. If one is to avoid the resulting extremes of irresponsible tolerance or dogmatic imposition, the issues of moral diversity and moral conflict can best be grasped in terms of the structure of open horizons within the context of socializing adjustment and community.

Though moral diversity can flourish within a community, when such diversity becomes irreconcilable conflict, the activity of socializing adjustment must lead to the development of new organs of adjudication, if community is to be maintained. When such organs of resolution cannot evolve as a common ground of adjudication in the process of socializing adjustment, then moral community has broken down. And, because any community opens outward onto ever deepening and broadening horizons, the resolution of conflicting moral communities cannot be resolved by appeal to abstract principles, but by a deepening and expanding of horizons to a level of community within which the organs of resolution can be found through a deepening sense of primordial world. Such a deepening may change conflict into community diversity, or it may lead to an emerging consensus of the wrongness of one of the conflicting positions. Of course such a deepening does not negate the use of intelligent inquiry, but rather opens it up, frees it from the products of its past in terms of rigidities and abstractions, and focuses it on the dynamics of concrete human existence and the direct sense of value as it emerges from the features of anteceptive experience into the contours of a common world. The vital, growing sense of moral rightness comes not from the inculcation of abstract principles, but from attunement to the way in which moral beliefs and practices must be rooted naturally in the very conditions of human existence.

Lewis's distinction, unique among the classical pragmatists, between value and ethical theory attempts to find the compulsion to adhere to the moral imperative as unconditioned by impulses, inclinations, or desires, though the ground of the validity of imperatives must lie in human nature.[34] The ultimate grounding of the "categorical principle of morals"[35] lies, for Lewis, in the principle of consistency, but such a principle has been shown to be a pragmatic principle rooted in the temporal stretch of human behavior as anticipatory, and operates not from above the level of impulses, inclinations, or desires, but precisely through their temporal rootedness in the structure of human behavior at the very heart of experience as experimental. Further, the principle of consistency can ground the demands of universality and impersonality in value judgments only if one already recognizes that such a denial would involve a pragmatic inconsistency because no claims are of privileged status. The final justification for universality and impersonality is rooted, like the principle of consistency itself, in the features of the anteceptive field. Again it can be seen, this time from the perspective of its value dimension, that the world, as it emerges from the anteceptive

---

34 / Lewis, *The Ground and Nature of the Right* (New York: Columbia University Press, 1955), pp. 85–86.

35 / Lewis, *Our Social Inheritance*, pp. 98–99.

field, is at once the basis for every experience and the ideal of a complete synthesis of possible experience, and the ideal itself has its roots in the anteceptive field. The vitality of the increasing inclusiveness of abstract moral ideals stems from a correlative deepening of the moral sense toward its foundations in anteceptive experience.

That the resolution of conflicting claims requires a deepening of the sense of the foundational world as it emerges from anteceptive experience is to be found in Dewey's understanding of religious experience as a relationship of one's self with the universe as the totality of conditions with which the self is connected. This unity can be neither apprehended in knowledge nor realized in reflection,[36] for it involves such a totality not as a literal content of the intellect, but as an imaginative extension of the self.[37] Such an experience brings about not a change in will, but rather a "change *of* will as the organic plentitude of our being."[38] This imaginative ideal, which allows one to "rise above" the divisiveness of illusory closures, comes in fact by a "delving beneath" to the anteceptive sense of the possibilities of a deep-seated harmonizing of the self with the universe,[39] rooted ultimately in the features of the pulsations of the anteceptive field. Such an ideal is the limiting ideal of fully attained growth.

Throughout the above discussion of value, the creation of moral meanings has been shown to go beyond what is directly experienced. Without such meaning structures there is no moral world and no moral objectivities or norms. Further, the significance attaching to moral norms in terms of anticipated consequences gains its fullness of meaning from, and in turn fuses its own meaning into, the matrix of valuings.

Habit creatively organizes concrete experience in terms of moral objectivities, while these objectivities in turn give significance to the immediacies of more concrete experience. Thus, the immediacies of value apprehensions are funded with enriched meaning. These latter emerge for conscious awareness within the context of a meaningful world of perceived moral objectivities. True to the model supplied by scientific method of the relation between the more concrete and the more reflective, qualitative immediacy conditions all the constituents of a given objective experience, but in turn the constituents of a given objective experience enrich the qualitative immediacy with the meaningfulness of the transactional context within which it emerges. The very experi-

36 / Dewey, *A Common Faith* (New Haven: Yale University Press, 1934), p. 19.
37 / Ibid., p. 18.
38 / Ibid., p. 17.
39 / Ibid., p. 16.

ence of immediate valuings is funded with a meaningful backdrop of accepted or rejected objective values. Such a creative structuring of experience brings moral objectivities into an organizational focus from the backdrop of an indeterminate situation, and as constitutive of dispositional modes of response, yields directed, teleological, or goal-oriented activity. Truth can only be claimed if the experiences anticipated by the possibilities of experience contained within the meaning structures are progressively fulfilled. These, of course, are precisely the features of scientific method as set forth earlier.[40] Thus, experience as art,[41] which for Dewey is essential in the development of value, is precisely the artful functioning of scientific method within the ongoing course of experience. Or, conversely, the model of scientific method, as abstracted from the ongoing activity of the scientist, is the art of experience writ large[42]—in the sense that in science these ongoing dynamics are more explicitly developed and hence the ingredients easier to distinguish.

Until now the present work has been concerned with developing the various features of speculative pragmatism as a systematic philosophical vision emerging from its focus on the model of scientific method. The concluding chapter will attempt to reflect on the nature of philosophic system itself, as viewed from the perspective of speculative pragmatism.

40 / See chapter 1. The dynamics operative within the area of value has been seen to reflect, also, the added complexities of scientific method developed in the previous chapter.

41 / See n. 15.

42 / Dewey does not equate art and fine art. If the art of experience is the artful application of scientific method, then in the reflections of science one can find this method "writ large" in the sense that its various facets are more explicit and hence easier to distinguish. However, in aesthetic experience one can find this method "writ large" in a different sense, for in aesthetic experience, the method should be found in its most intensified concrete unification or fusion. This is precisely what is to be found in Dewey's understanding of fine art and aesthetic experience.

Nine

The Nature of Speculative Pragmatism:

Toward a New Understanding of

Philosophic System

THE CONTEMPORARY unease with the traditional notion of systematic philosophy is embedded in the structure of speculative pragmatism as a philosophic system. The history of metaphysical speculation, as embodied in philosophic system, is a history evincing positions that have systematically denied or rejected the sense of temporality, creativity, novelty, fallibilism, pluralism, perspectivalism, and openendedness—in short, the key dimensions of speculative pragmatism—in favor of the eternal, the fixed, the final, the certain, the absolute spectator grasp, the ultimate completion, the perfected whole.

The traditional paradigms for philosophizing within which "normal philosophy" proceeded as the working out of accepted problems within the confines of accepted types of frameworks,[1] though differing in many and varied ways, contained certain common features found in every paradigm that set the parameters of what kinds of questions could be asked, what alternative answers were possible, what kinds of facts there could possibly be. Perhaps the single feature most common to the structure of all paradigms in the philosophical tradition of systems in conflict is the assumption of the spectator theory of knowledge and the ultimate reification of the abstractions of reflective philosophical think-

---

1 / This of course parallels Kuhn's understanding of "normal sciences."

ing, be they the eternal Platonic forms or the eternal Newtonian particles. Such content, illicitly projected as the ultimately real, produced a reality composed of atomic units themselves immune to the changes and continuities for which they must account. The pervasive textures at the heart of lived experience were ignored in favor of the various second-level reflective problems of spectator philosophy, and, especially since the time of Descartes, the particular problem of how a subject can bridge the gap to know an object. Using the isolated elements of second-level philosophic reflection, philosophy attempted to put back together that which it had unknowingly already pulled asunder, and since the isolated elements could not recover the interwoven textures of the pre-philosophical experience from which they emerged, these abstractions were then read back into common-sense experience as an explanation of how common-sense experience "really" operates, uncritical common-sense experience to the contrary notwithstanding. It was the reflective theory, not common-sense experience, that dictated, and if the theory must ignore the textures of primordial experience, there was no problem, for the way to reality was not via primordial experience, but by the reified content of philosophic abstractions. Either the objects of second-level reflection replaced the flux of sensible experience, or the relation between the two was stood on its head.

Much of contemporary philosophy, operating within the seemingly novel paradigm of language, or within other seemingly novel paradigms radically restrictive of the nature and limits of philosophical pursuits, and thus avoiding philosophic system, has yet not succeeded in breaking with the alternatives offered by, and hence the possible solutions allowable by, traditional paradigms. Though the alternatives and possible solutions may take distinctively new turns, and though seemingly new alternatives and new limitations emerge, too often they can be seen as new paradigmatic twists to old paradigmatic offerings. The alternatives, whether expressed in newer or older fashion, of realism-antirealism, objectivism-relativism, subjectivism-objectivism, foundationalism-antifoundationalism, correspondence-coherence, realism-idealism, empiricism-rationalism, are all alternatives that grow out of reflective frameworks that ignore the fundamental, creative, interactive unity at the heart of lived experience.

The biggest hindrance to capturing the tenor of the pragmatic vision is that it elucidates a radically new paradigm, one in which long-accepted types of alternatives do not apply, and in which the tradition of possible facts, as possible answers to the allowable alternatives, no longer exists, for these facts and alternatives are no longer meaningful in terms of the paradigmatic structure. As long as pragmatic doctrines are understood within, or developed in terms of, one of the family-related sets of alternatives of the very paradigms it has rejected, then though specific aspects of its position may be further developed for specialized purposes, the significance and uniqueness of its systematic vision is lost.[2] Part of the difficulty the classical pragmatists have had in presenting their position is that they were working within the contours of an elusively new paradigm for which a philosophic tradition strewn with incommensurable paradigms yet had no adequate language, no adequate alternatives, and no adequate range of possible philosophic "facts." Within the contours of this elusive novel paradigm, speculative pragmatism has developed as a further articulation of its structure.

The paradigmatic novelty of classical American pragmatism must apply not only to its understanding of the world, but to its understanding of itself. To understand speculative pragmatism as philosophic system from within its own perspective is to view it not just as one more system in a tradition of systems in conflict, but rather as a system that recognizes that to understand itself, it must view itself as an emergent perspective that is an outgrowth of that tradition, and which in turn accounts for, or makes meaningful, that tradition through a reinterpretation of it as a past that yields, and is explained by, this novel emergent perspective. Thus, it must offer not just a system based on the evidence it sees, but it must account for the fact that different philosophies differ as to what constitutes the nature of evidence. It must offer not just a theory of truth, but it must account for the fact that different philosophies differ as to what constitutes the nature of truth. It must offer not just foundations, but it must account for the fact that different philosophies differ concerning the very foundations of philosophy. It must be not just another system in conflict, but it must account for the fact that there can be systems in conflict.

Speculative pragmatism must also account for the fact that systems in conflict can develop within a philosophical community that can recognize a loss of vitality of certain issues and answers, even though there is a formal incommensurability within that community concerning criteria of truth, evidence, and foundations. Working within the various sets of alternatives, according to the various models that give rise to them, arguments are continually presented that are rigorous and forceful, if one has already accepted the paradigmatic structure of allowable alternatives

---

2 / For example, the pragmatic analysis of Willard Van Orman Quine and the recent pragmatic concerns of Richard Rorty.

and lines of questioning. Many of the possible answers, however, though emerging with continued logical vigor, are beginning to emerge as peculiarly devoid of vitality. Thus, in spite of the array of conflicting paradigms, there is indeed a philosophic community that, according to some extra formal sense, does come to a loose consensus concerning the loss of vitality of certain issues and alternatives, and does recognize the need to grope toward new possibilities. And thus it does, in some vague sense, provide the organs for adjudication within a commonly held historical process. The answer here, like the answer for the understanding of the broadening of any adjudication process, is to be found not by appeal to some higher abstract principles, but by a deepening to foundational roots. This is the topic to which the ensuing discussion will turn.

A philosophy, like any knowledge structure, does not conform to a pregiven world that is "there" and that one philosophy will "find" in spectator fashion. Rather it is a perspective on a common-sense world infused with the meanings of various derived worlds. This world is constantly in the process of remaking, and as it changes, the philosophic reflection upon it changes. Such reflection in turn infuses with new meanings the world from which it emerged. Second-level reflections, including the reflections of philosophy, not only emerge from pre-philosophical worlds,[3] but enrich them with new meanings that in turn partially change these worlds. Indeed, "the world is ceaselessly becoming what it means." The role of philosophy is to enable us "to capture the meaning which it has for us."[4]

Thus, for example, Plato's understanding of philosophy as an escape from the temporality of the sensible world to a world of absolute truth and unchanging forms was a view of the nature of the philosophic enterprise that developed and lasted in various forms because it *worked* in taking account of the Greek world, a world not fused with the meanings gained both from various second-level reflections properly understood, and from the very fact of a history of changing and conflicting second-level interpretations. The world of Plato was indeed a different world than we have today, and Plato's philosophy in turn gave impetus to maintaining the perceptions of the day. Though various philosophies emerge that claim to attain that which is beyond the temporally rooted sensible world, or to reinterpret it through categories that break the temporally

---

3 / The reference to prephilosophical worlds in the following discussion is a reference to the common-sense world enriched with the meanings of second-level reflections of various types. This is the world that philosophy attempts to understand.

4 / Mead, *Philosophy of the Act*, p. 515.

rooted sensible world apart, and make its "real" features conform to a structure imposed from above, yet the adequacy of any philosophic system lies in its ability to make sense of the prephilosophical world in which the philosopher is rooted, or, in other terms, its ability to work in interpreting that world.

Earlier it was shown that in one sense we restructure the world, yet in another sense we restructure only within the world. In one sense different philosophies structure different worlds, both because they may arise from different prephilosophical worlds, and because there may be different philosophical worlds emerging from a single prephilosophical world, but in turn enriching it with different reflective meanings. Yet in another sense, different philosophies can structure different worlds only because they are rooted in the conditions that make possible the emergence of any world, and because the philosopher is rooted in these conditions. Though common-sense worlds, which include the enrichments of their meanings gained from the second-level reflections of their times, change, yet the anteceptive sense of the features within which any world must emerge do not change. Such an anteceptive sense has been shown not only to underlie but to overflow that which is expressible through the structures of pragmatic meanings, and to provide a vague sense of "fittingness." Not only must any world, whether of common sense, science, or philosophy, be rooted in the features of temporality, but it must conform to the elusive, but real, anteceptive sense of workability, as the criterion for the development of any system of meanings. Such a criterion of workability for any system of meanings in relation to the world within which it functions is the prephilosophical evaluative sense of the adequacy of formal philosophical conceptions, including formal theories of truth.[5] To come to grips with a tradition that articulates itself through a history of systems in conflict, yet has an ability to recognize loss of vitality of the most soundly developed systems through a vague sense of lifelessness, a system must uncover and elucidate the common conditions for the possibility of diverse philosophic worlds, and the prephilosophical, primordial, elusively vague, but persistent sense of workability that is rooted in these conditions.

The characterization by speculative pragmatism of processive concreteness as independent of noetic activity is itself a noetic enterprise that draws into its constituted world an articulation of that which it

---

5 / Thus, for example, an understanding of truth in terms of coherence or correspondence is accepted because it *works* in rendering intelligible the truth situation within a certain philosophic network of meanings.

constitutes, within its system, to be the unconstituted.[6] However, it draws it into its world, not in an attempt to escape or restructure or eternalize the temporally located prephilosophic world within which it functions, but rather in an attempt to bring within a unifying perspective the conditions for the possibility of the emergence of any world. And though this perspective itself necessarily enters into the attempt to grasp the prephilosophical textures of experience, there is a difference. It does not attempt to ignore, change, or distort the reality of these prephilosophical textures of experience in order to make experience fit within the structures of a closed system imposed from above, but rather, in reverse fashion, roots its system in them.

Thus, it develops an open philosophic system or explanatory structure, giving rise to a view of explanation rooted in, rather than distortive of, the pervasive features of primordial experience, and to a view of systematic structure rooted in, rather than opposed to, a history of evolving change. Any philosophic system is inadequate if not grounded in the level of the full richness of lived experience. The second-level philosophic reflections must be grounded in lived experience, and be constantly fed by such experience. Such an open system is explanation rooted in and verified by lived experience, not direct grasp of "being in itself." Though rooted in the lived level, it is never completely adequate to the lived level. It is open to change and development, just as all second-level interpretations are open to change and development. Because of its openness, and the conditions within which it emerges, such a system must be recognized as tentative, not certain, and thus Peirce received "the pleasure of praise" from what "was meant for blame," when "a critic said of me that I did not seem to be absolutely sure of my own conclusions."[7]

The renewal of vitality in any reflective attempt to do justice to the richness of the foundational level requires a return to that foundational level. Speculative hypotheses, to maintain philosophic vitality, must not only be firmly rooted in and fed by lived experience, but must be verified by lived experience. Further, the very model of scientific method, which gives rise to the characterization of experience as experimental in the return to lived experience, is itself always in need of verification by that lived experience which, if pragmatism is correct, reveals such dynamics in its ongoing process. In brief, the model is an adequate model

6 / Thus, in a sense, the categories of metaphysics, as a characterization of that which is independent of worlds, enters into the world as a meaningful enrichment of it. (See chapter 5, n. 13.)

7 / Peirce, 1.10.

only if a description of lived experience does in fact display such dynamics in its most fundamental aspects. A description of lived experience, however, must emerge from the ground up, so to speak. This does not mean that such description claims to root itself in brute uninterpreted prephilosophical data, but rather that it turns to prephilosophic experience with a "cultivated naivete."[8] Once again, the more reflective both arises from and permeates the more concrete—not as a vicious circle, but as a cumulative process of progressive insight—and the interrelation of the two must work as an organic unity that gains its vitality within the ongoing course of experience. One can philosophically ignore the anteceptive sense that underlies and overflows the formalizations of philosophy, but one cannot really escape its persistent wellspring of vitality.

These anteceptive features are not postulated from the structure of a theory, but vaguely sensed as the experiential roots for any theory. Their articulation is a development growing from within the features of prephilosophical lived experience, not an imposition from without. The claim that speculative pragmatism emerges "from beneath," rather than "from above" does not involve the popular claim to be a presuppositionless philosophy. Any philosophical stance includes presuppositions. The foundations of speculative pragmatism, however, are held to be prior to the level of presuppositions, in the sense that its presuppositions do not yield supposed philosophical foundations, but rather the articulation of its prephilosophical foundations leads to the incorporation of its presuppositions. Speculative pragmatism is not claiming to be a presuppositionless philosophy; it is claiming that its presuppositions are not imposed upon, but rather arise in the context of articulating the features of, the anteceptive experiential sense.

This does not mean that this prephilosophical "data" from which it begins is brute uninterpreted data. Brute data is not possible. It is brought into the focus of awareness for philosophical reflection by presuppositions as vague anticipations and assumptions that regulate the manner in which anything can be brought into focus within experience. Anticipations and assumptions, however, are not at the start the reflective presuppositions contained in an articulated philosophical stance, but rather are themselves prephilosophical anticipations and assumptions that are inarticulately fused within an emerging, delving, focal activity yielding anteceptive sensitivity, and all must be rendered intelligible through the emerging presuppositions of the second-level reflec-

---

8 / Dewey, *Experience and Nature*, p. 40. See chapter 1.

tions of philosophy. The formalized reflections of philosophy can in turn render the prephilosophical starting points more intelligible by locating them within the structure of a systematic stance. Thus, for example, speculative pragmatism attempts neither to create freely nor to free itself from ontological commitments, but rather to reveal the way in which there is an ontological commitment at the very heart of the experience that grounds such attempts. The foundations of speculative pragmatism can thus be said to be prior to the level of presuppositions that develop in the process of elucidating these prephilosophical foundations.

The articulations of speculative pragmatism, as second-level reflections emerging from a primordial sense of the textures of experience, must be open to change and development as all second-level articulations are open to change and development. Thus, its development of the structure of pragmatic meaning, its categorial delineation of the features of processive concreteness, may be replaced by other second-level developments and characterizations. The temporal rootedness of meanings, however, is foundational for the very possibility of the replacement of its own meanings with others. To deny the temporal rootedness of meanings would seem to deny the very possibility of the history of changing reflective articulations.

Our categories cannot escape from their temporal rootedness and from constant openness to change; because change is constant,[9] attempts to grasp it are not. Because perspectival horizons open ever outward, no system can claim the finality of closure. But the features of thinking that are rooted in the constancy of change and that allow for the grasp of change through changing concepts or categories must be constant. To say that the structure of meaning is temporally rooted is not to say that meaning may change its structure and become nontemporal. Rather, it is to say that temporal rootedness grounds the structure of meaning, and that the anticipatory character of vital intentionality is part and parcel of the temporal flow. Temporality itself, and the generation of meaning in time, is an ahistorical constancy. The temporal rootedness of meaning is the constant characteristic that allows for changing contexts. It provides the constancy of manner in which humans respond to changing conditions. From *within* the context of speculative pragmatism, it can be said that without assuming these conditions no argument for their lack can be developed. To deny these claims is to elucidate a novel perspective through changing categories emerging from a

9 / See chapter 6.

temporal past. No such dialectical "proof" for speculative pragmatism can be claimed, however, for such a maneuver of "reaffirmation through denial" holds only for those already operating within a mutually accepted framework. Thus, Lewis points out that philosophy "can be nothing more at bottom than persuasion."[10] The following discussion will turn to the understanding of persuasion.

Rigorous argument in philosophy has its role within a philosophic system, but any philosophic system emerges from basic intuitions, and can be persuasive for another only in terms of intuitions that are not justified by rigorous argument. *Intuition* as here used can be roughly equated with *anteceptive sense* as it underlies, overflows, and is incorporated within the perceptions of common sense. The term *intuition* will be used, however, because it makes a point here in the way in which *anteceptive sense*, perhaps, cannot.[11] Because of the initial understanding of the model of mathematics, and a desire for the supposed certitudes of philosophic foundations that were, in fact, reflective creations grounded in foundations ignored by philosophic thinking, *intuition* served a function in philosophy that again stood it on its head. When such supposed intuitions didn't work, they were dismissed as merely psychological, and the way was paved for the tendency for philosophic arguments to be viewed as psychological persuasions. In philosophy, as elsewhere, however, the threat of irrationality to overcome rationality requires a deepening to the roots of rationality, and the evolution, within a historically grounded community, of new organs of adjudication.

Intuition, as the starting point of philosophical system as here intended, is neither an indubitable starting point from which to argue logically, nor is it merely a psychological occurrence with no rational claim to be heard. Intuition, as here used, is not something clear and distinct, but something vague and inarticulate; intuitions well up from anteceptive experience, not from reflective rationality. Such intuitions, as made articulate and precise through the structure of a philosophic system, will only hold persuasion if others, through such a system, find that it throws into focus intuitions that were before vaguely inexpressible or submerged through the weight of distortive structures. Thus, the switch from proof to persuasion is not the switch from rationality to psychologism, or from absolutism to arbitrary relativism, but rather it is a recognition that rationality as articulated second-level reflection

10 / Lewis, *Mind and the World Order*, pp. 207, 23.

11 / The term *intuition* as here being developed is of course not the type of intuition against which all the pragmatists were reacting. Rather, it is intended to help express the basis from which their attacks on traditional notions of intuition stem.

emerges in philosophy as an attempt to render intelligible imprecise, tentative, often initially inarticulate intuitions. Such intuitions are embedded in a cultural context and influenced by it, but they are further and more deeply rooted in that which yields the very possibility of influence by cultural contexts and by historical situatedness. The uncovering of such intuitions requires a deepening to a primordial level that grounds the alternative possibilities for their formal articulation.

The persuasiveness of a system, then, does not lie in a strictly logical force, or in a strictly empirical force in the sense of pointing out transystematic worldly facts that other philosophical positions must accept, but rather in its forcefulness in arousing basic intuitions of the textures of experience that "ring true to life," infusing its structure with vitality, even as another takes on the lifelessness of artificiality. Thus, James characterizes the process by which one accepts a philosophical view as "life exceeding logic . . . the theoretic reason finds arguments after the conclusion is once there."[12]

The final evaluation of speculative pragmatism lies ultimately in the only kind of evaluation that can really keep any system alive, no matter how solid its arguments or how numerous its "facts." Do the intuitions from which it grows, and its articulation and development of these intuitions through a unifying perspective, help highlight a basic sense of the pulse of human existence and the conditions in which it is emmeshed? The elusive philosophic spirit that permeates the writings of the classical American pragmatists grows precisely from common intuitions of such a pulse of existence, common intuitions that shape the pragmatic character of the several paths via which they enter and articulate the various dimensions of a common vision. Within the context of such common intuitions speculative pragmatism has attempted to capture, in its own way, the common philosophic spirit that they nurture.

12 / James, *Pluralistic Universe*, p. 148.

Works Cited

JOHN DEWEY

The writings of John Dewey have been collected in a definitive edition, edited by Jo Ann Boydston and published by Southern Illinois University Press, Carbondale and Edwardsville. The volumes containing *The Early Works* (1969–1972) and *The Middle Works* (1976–1983) have been completed, and *The Later Works* (1981–) is well under way. The following writings by Dewey are all contained in this series, with the exception of some of his later works which are not yet available there. These latter are listed in the manner in which they are presently available.

Art as Experience. New York: Capricorn Books, G. P. Putnam's Sons, 1958.

A Common Faith. New Haven: Yale University Press, 1934.

"Does Reality Possess Practical Character?" *The Middle Works*, Vol. 4, 1977.

Ethics, The Middle Works, Vol. 5, 1978.

"The Existence of the World as a Logical Problem," *The Middle Works*, Vol. 8, 1979.

Experience and Nature, The Later Works, Vol. 1, 1981.

"Experience and Objective Idealism," *The Middle Works*, Vol. 3, 1977.

"The Experimental Theory of Knowledge," *The Middle Works*, Vol. 3, 1977.

"How Do Concepts Arise from Percepts?" *The Early Works*, Vol. 3, 1969.

Human Nature and Conduct, The Middle Works, Vol. 14, 1983.

Logic: The Theory of Inquiry. New York: Henry Holt and Co., 1938.

"Peirce's Theory of Quality," *On Experience, Nature and Freedom.* Edited by Richard Bernstein. New York: Bobbs-Merrill, 1960.

"Perception and Organic Action," *The Middle Works*, Vol. 7, 1979.

The Public and Its Problems, The Later Works, Vol. 2, 1984.

"Qualitative Thought," *The Later Works*, Vol. 5, 1984.

The Quest for Certainty, The Later Works, Vol. 4, 1984.

Reconstruction in Philosophy, The Middle Works, Vol. 12, 1982.

"The Reflex Arc Concept in Psychology," *The Early Works*, Vol. 5, 1972.

WILLIAM JAMES

The writings of William James are being collected in a definitive edition, *The Works of William James*, edited by Frederick Burkhardt and published by Harvard University Press, Cambridge, 1975–. All the works cited are volumes contained in this series.

Essays in Radical Empiricism, 1976.
The Meaning of Truth, 1975.
A Pluralistic Universe, 1977.
Pragmatism, 1975.
The Principles of Psychology, 2 vols., 1981.
Some Problems of Philosophy, 1979.

THOMAS KUHN

The Structure of Scientific Revolutions, 2nd ed. Chicago: University of Chicago Press, 1970.

C. I. LEWIS

An Analysis of Knowledge and Valuation. La Salle, Illinois: Open Court, 1962.
The following essays are contained in *The Collected Papers of Clarence Irving Lewis*. Edited by John D. Goheen and John L. Mothershead, Jr. Stanford: Stanford University Press, 1970:
    "A Comment on the Verification Theory of Meaning."
    "Experience and Meaning."
    "Facts, Systems and the Unity of the World."
    "Logic and Pragmatism."
    "A Pragmatic Conception of the A Priori."
    "Pragmatism and Current Thought."
    "Realism or Phenomenalism?"
    "The Structure of Logic and Its Relation to Other Systems."
The Ground and Nature of the Right. New York: Columbia University Press, 1955.
Mind and the World Order. New York: Dover Publications, 1929.
Our Social Inheritance. Bloomington: Indiana University Press, 1957.
"Replies to My Critics," *The Philosophy of C. I. Lewis*. The Library of Living Philosophers Series. Edited by P. A. Schilpp. La Salle, Illinois: Open Court, 1968.
Symbolic Logic (with C. H. Langford). New York: Dover Publications, 1959.
"Values and Facts," *Values and Imperatives*. Edited by John Lange. Stanford: Stanford University Press, 1969.

George Herbert Mead

"The Definition of the Psychical," *Mead, Selected Writings*. Edited by A. J. Reck. New York: Bobbs-Merrill Co., 1964.
"Image or Sensation," *Journal of the History of Philosophy*, 1, Part 2, 1904, pp. 604–607.
"The Mechanism of Social Consciousness," *Mead, Selected Writings*.
Mind, Self, and Society. Chicago: University of Chicago Press, 1934.
The Philosophy of the Act. Chicago: University of Chicago Press, 1938.
Philosophy of the Present. La Salle, Illinois: Open Court, 1934.
"The Social Self," *Mead, Selected Writings*.

Charles Sanders Peirce

Collected Papers. Vols. 1–6, edited by Charles Hartshorne and Paul Weiss. Cambridge: Belknap Press of Harvard University, 1931–1935. Vols. 7 and 8, edited by Arthur Burks. Cambridge: Harvard University Press, 1958.
The Microfilm Edition of the Peirce Papers. Harvard University.
The New Elements of Mathematics. Edited by Carolyn Eisele. The Hague: Mouton Press, 1976.

Index